Fodor's EXPLORING
CHINA

FODOR'S TRAVEL PUBLICATIONS

NEW YORK • TORONTO • LONDON • SYDNEY • AUCKLAND

WWW.FODORS.COM

© Automobile Association Developments Limited 2007
Maps © Automobile Association Developments Limited 2007 (registered office : Fanum House, Basing View, Basingstoke, RG21 4EA, UK. Registered number 187883).

Published in the United States by Fodor's Travel, a division of Random House, Inc., and simultaneously in Canada by Random House of Canada Limited, Toronto. Published in the United Kingdom by AA Publishing.

Fodor's and Fodor's Exploring are registered trademarks of Random House, Inc.

ISBN: 978-1-4000-1768-3

Sixth Edition

Fodor's Exploring China

Author: **Christopher Knowles**
Revision Verifier: **Peter Ellegard**
Revision Editor: **Stephanie Smith**
Cartography: **The Automobile Association**
Cover Design: **Tigist Getachew, Fabrizio La Rocca**
Front Cover Silhouette: **Gina Corrigan/Robert Harding World Imagery/Getty Images**
Front Cover Top Photograph: **AA Photo Library**

Special Sales
This book is available for special discounts for bulk purchases for sales promotions or premiums. Special editions, including personalized covers, excerpts of existing books, and corporate imprints, can be created in large quantities for special needs. For more information, write to Special Markets/Premium Sales, 1745 Broadway, MD 6-2, New York, NY 10019 or e-mail specialmarkets@randomhouse.com

Printed and bound in Italy by Printer Trento srl.
10 9 8 7 6 5 4 3 2 1

A02985

How to use this book

ORGANIZATION

China Is, China Was
Discusses aspects of life and culture in contemporary China and explores significant periods in its history.

A–Z
Breaks down the country into regional chapters, and covers places to visit, including walks and drives. Within this section fall the Focus On articles, which consider a variety of subjects in greater detail.

Travel Facts
Contains the strictly practical information that is vital for a successful trip.

Hotels and Restaurants
Lists recommended establishments in China, giving a brief description of their attractions.

ADMISSION CHARGES
An indication of an establishment's admission charge is given by categorizing the standard, adult rate as:
Expensive (over 50 RMB)
Moderate (21–50 RMB)
Inexpensive (up to 20 RMB).

ABOUT THE RATINGS
Most places described in this book have been given a separate rating:

▶▶▶   **Do not miss**

▶▶   **Highly recommended**

▶   **Worth seeing**

Note on spellings
The official romanization system, *pinyin* (see page 271), has been used in this book. However, a few exceptions have been made where alternative, more familiar names have been adopted. In such cases both forms are given in the Index. The geographic legend on page 271 gives the English translations for terms used on the maps.

MAP REFERENCES
To make each particular location easier to find, every main entry in this book has a map reference to the right of its name. This comprises a number, followed by a letter, followed by another number, such as 176B3. The first number (176) refers to the page on which the map can be found, the letter (B) and the second number (3) pinpoint the square in which the main entry is located. The maps on the inside front cover and inside back cover are referred to as IFC and IBC respectively.

Contents

6

My China

Christopher Knowles has led dozens of tours in China since his first visit in 1981. He has also written guidebooks to Shanghai, Moscow & St. Petersburg, Japan, Southeast Asia, Tuscany and The Cotswolds.

No place has changed quite like China. Shanghai, which has become an almost exclusively modern city, would be practically unrecognizable to someone who visited even 10 years ago. Shenzhen, until the 1980s a small frontier settlement, has become a hub of international trade. Elsewhere, tangible signs of wealth, from limousines to high-rise buildings, abound.

When, in 1981, I arrived in Beijing, there was little sign that anything much had changed in the few years since the end of the Cultural Revolution. Foreign visitors were still a rarity, even in Beijing; a taxi could not be hailed on the streets, and you could not eat out after seven in the evening. The towns had been bled of vibrancy, and life in the countryside went on as it had done for centuries.

Economic miracles, however, are largely confined to the great cities. In the countryside, the problems of modernization are acute. At a time when China desperately needs enough rice to feed its massive population, its farmers are more interested in growing cash crops or leaving the farms altogether. There are other less tangible problems. China remains, appearances notwithstanding, a one-party autocracy. The Cultural Revolution produced an amoral generation which struggles to reconcile the freedom to become rich with ethical restraints. And there are the unresolved problems of the future of Tibet and indeed an indifference to the question of human rights in general.

My China is not merely a country of change, it is also a country of great beauty. Ancient villages nestle among hills whose slopes, after centuries of cultivation, have become staircases of scalloped terraces. Junks have become a rarer sight, but are still to be seen fishing on Lake Tai or struggling among the great liners and tankers in the port of Shanghai. Political upheavals have severed the Chinese from a natural sense of harmony, but they have failed to eradicate the habits of countless generations.

So, the China I love is a conundrum. Frequently comfortless, often profoundly frustrating, it is breathtaking not merely for its antiquity, or for its beauty, but, despite its years of calamity, for its self-confidence.

Christopher Knowles

Top: the Daning River

China Is

Nowhere in the world is the past more woven into the present than in China, and no other country can boast the sense of continuity that has been bred into the Chinese people over at least 3,000 years of continuous civilization.

PRESSURE OF HISTORY Chinese history has been a source of great strength and resilience in difficult times. Perhaps no other country could have survived such a cataclysmic event as the Cultural Revolution, only to become one of the world's fastest-growing economies a mere 20 years later. In few other countries, on the other hand, would the Cultural Revolution have occurred in the first place. The pressure to do as your forefathers have done and conform to ancient (and frequently outmoded) ideas is very great indeed in China.

Occasionally, it becomes too much for some parts of society to bear. The stranglehold exerted by the past so frustrated the young people of China in the 1960s that they were easily mobilized by Mao, assisting in his radical but ultimately futile attempt, to sweep away all reminders of the past and start over again. Ironically, the communism that Mao espoused has proved to be little more than the former imperial system under a new name.

CONSERVATISM So automatic, so widespread are the age-old habits of the Chinese that they may sometimes be confused with intransigence. One example of this is always giving the answer that the listener wants to hear. For more worldly Chinese this is frustrating, because these habits seem almost impossible to break.

At its best, Chinese conservatism— a determination not to change merely for change's sake, combined with a belief in the overriding power of precedent—is admirable; at other times it is tiresome, as when agreement is reached to do something in one way, only to find that ultimately the old way prevails.

OUTSIDE INFLUENCE Notwithstanding the damage wrought by time, revolution, and political upheaval, the tangible remains of China's ancient civilization are widespread; and even in the case of contemporary art and architecture the tendency is always to evoke the past. But the material residue from Chinese history is less important than the impact that the past has had on the Chinese mind. Chinese history is remarkable for the fact that outside influences have had almost no effect on the national psyche. Without an appreciation of this fundamental fact, it is impossible for the visitor to understand modern China.

10

> ❑ 'Our nation has a great responsibility...to enrich our culture with Western culture, and to enrich Western culture with our culture, so that they may fuse into a new culture.'—Liang Qichao, *Impressions From My European Journey*, 1919 ❑

Of the many issues facing the Chinese today, the most contentious is the battle between old and new: progress, in the modern Western understanding of the word, is seen in some quarters as an admission of defeat. The encroachment of Western values, for so long resisted, is considered a worrying phenomenon: for old communists, veterans of the Long March (a few of whom are still involved in the running of the country), it must sometimes seem that the values they fought for are being replaced by the free-for-all, capitalist values that they had sought so hard to suppress.

The ancient city of Beijing is now dominated by modern skyscrapers

THE TIGER AWAKES On occasion during the 20th century, when it seemed China was about to alter course, it was in fact merely retrimming its sails. Now, in the 21st century, change seems more certain; the challenge is to recover the best of the past and marry it to the realities of the modern world.

Opposite (top) and below: villagers in Yunnan display their effigies of local gods at Chinese New Year

11

The Chinese way of life is distinctive in many subtle ways. Western notions of the centrality of the self are alien to many Chinese, who see themselves in relation to family, community and the past, rather than as entirely free agents.

FAMILY The most important element in Chinese society is the family, an institution whose strength was sorely tested by events during the 1960s and 1970s, when, under Mao, children were encouraged to report the 'misdemeanours' of their parents and close relatives. But it was not long ago that most marriages were arranged by parents or by a professional matchmaker, and in more remote areas these practices have continued unchecked; even in major cities the matchmaker has recently made an unexpected comeback. Weddings are big affairs, and huge sums, out of all proportion to income, are often spent on the celebrations. Once married, the bride customarily moves in with her in-laws, at least until the new couple can secure their own apartment.

The idea of bachelorhood is virtually unknown among the Chinese

A member of the matriarchal Naxi people sits holding his grandson

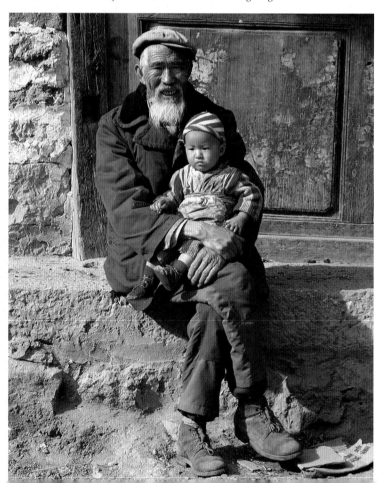

because children are considered essential to continuing the family line and for providing a means of support in old age. In this respect, the Cultural Revolution's emphasis on the enforced denunciation of relatives has only led to a subsequent resurgence of family loyalty, as well as to the pain of collective guilt.

❏ The Chinese have traditionally deferred to the elderly because, it is thought, old age brings wisdom. For this reason, the government, until recently, has consisted largely of older politicians. This is another frustration for many Chinese, for youth is admired, but only in the most patronizing way. ❏

The government's failed policy of one child per family (designed to alleviate the population problem) has led to the rise of a generation of 'little emperors', to whom the absence of siblings has meant unbridled adulation. It has also brought a certain lack of confidence because a large family meant security and influence. Nothing is more important than *guanxi*, that is, obtaining help, jobs, contracts or gifts from your relatives—an essential feature of Chinese life that Westerners might call 'nepotism'.

LOSING FACE Romantic love is not a Chinese notion. Pragmatism is the order of the day, though the younger, more independent-minded Chinese are demanding the right to make their own decisions. As a result, divorce, traditionally unutterably shameful, is becoming more widespread.

Indeed, the idea of shame, usually expressed as 'losing face' (*diulian*), is integral to the Chinese attitude regarding life. Losing face is more than just shame, however, for shame implies a subjective feeling of guilt whereas loss of face is something more—it is a slight, a missed opportunity, family shame, regional shame, a failure to perform a duty according to the expectation and judgement of one's peers, particularly in front of foreigners. It can be just one of these things, or a little of all of them.

PRIVACY The concern with 'face' creates all sorts of social tensions, especially in a highly controlled society. For this reason the Chinese tend to avoid situations where face may be lost, preferring anonymity to exposure. Contact with the outside world is making this more difficult— Western business investors in China often express frustration with Chinese lack of initiative, not recognizing that to many Chinese, being a faceless member of a crowd is the norm.

Lack of privacy also means lack of space. City apartments are generally small, and everyone has to be able to tolerate the activities of everyone else, which explains the Chinese ability to concentrate amid cacophony and to sleep at will. What seems intolerable to Westerners is in fact the essence of the Chinese way of life.

For newly-weds today, Western dress and a video or DVD recording are common for those who can afford it

13

China continues to be ruled by the Communist Party, though since the early 1980s and the beginning of the 'open door' policy, the country has demonstrated a willingness to adopt foreign trade investment and new ideas.

SELEC

MAC

COMMUNISM? In 1993, Ferrari made the first delivery of one of its luxury cars to a Chinese entrepreneur in China (despite the fact that there were few roads where such a car could be used). Shanghai now has a thriving stock exchange. In these, and in countless other ways, the traditional picture of Chinese life under communism is rapidly changing. Even so, all the

Top: Mao memorabilia
Below: McDonald's in Beijing exemplifies China's appetite for modern ideas

Party maxims and slogans are still trotted out by the government whenever the occasion arises. Despite a history of obstinate intolerance to democratic movements, not to mention the continuing suppression of Tibet and the detention without trial of numerous dissidents, there is reason to hope that the government has finally shed most vestiges of the Stalinist approach that once prevailed. By comparison with the years of the Cultural Revolution, life in China today is peaceful. But persecution continues and the average Chinese person has no legal means of avoiding the heavy hand of the state.

The Party still wields enormous authority; real freedom remains an elusive goal. If physical persecution is more of a rarity, deviation from accepted social norms incurs the wrath of local committees, who, in rural areas at least, have the power to take away jobs, homes and personal rights. However, the emergence of a market economy and a new middle class with money to spend is undoubtedly undermining communist ideals and the Party's influence on everyday life, certainly in cities.

And while outspoken criticism of government can still lead to arrest and imprisonment, the widespread use of the internet and mobile phones—China's 110 million-plus internet users put it second only to America and it has more mobile phones than any other country, at nearly 400 million—has given people more freedom to air their views via websites, blogs, email and text. An estimated 30,000-strong online police force monitors cyberspace in an effort to exert control. Many sites with anti-government content are actively blocked, while others, such as search engine Google, have resorted to self-censorship to be allowed in.

UNDERSTANDING If one considers Chinese history, the size of the population, and the vastness of the country with its variety of geopgraphy and peoples, then the current system of autocratic government is at least comprehensible. It is all that most Chinese have ever known; the history of intrusive government is almost as old as Chinese history itself. For many, the years since the end of the Cultural Revolution in 1976 have been a great improvement: farmers are allowed to keep and sell the surplus produce they grow, and married couples are no longer sent to work in different parts of the country, although many do live thousands of miles apart so they can each have good jobs.

FUTURE If Chinese communism has achieved anything, it has been to instil the Chinese with a sense of nationhood. It has, arguably, done much to eradicate the chronic poverty that cursed old China, although those affected by the disasters of the Great Leap Forward and the Cultural Revolution may disagree, and some areas of China, notably the arid northwest, remain as backward as ever. What the party has not really addressed is the issue of democracy. Yet prosperity has brought confidence and in some provinces (and not only Tibet and Xinjiang), there has been talk of secession. Independence for Guangdong or Sichuan is unrealistic, but that it is even considered indicates a yearning for greater autonomy and one that the central government may not be able to ignore, especially following the 1966 free elections in Taiwan, the first democratic transfer of power in Chinese history.

Posters asking for respect for authority are a common sight

Although China remains a communist country in formal political terms, informally ideological rectitude is the furthest thing from most people's minds. To make money has become the overriding ambition of a large number of people for whom the strictures of Marx, Lenin and Mao are mostly irrelevant.

COMPETITION The Chinese have always enjoyed a reputation for business acumen, and it is certainly possible to become rich in modern China. A visit to any of the major cities will quickly confirm this— wealthy citizens driving Mercedes and frequenting luxury hotels, happily spend in a day what the average Chinese person could not earn in a lifetime. The competition is as fierce as in any established capitalist society, package what they have to offer in an attractive and winning way.

IN THE BLOOD Making money, like the love of gambling, seems to be a compulsion in China. The appeal seems to be that money brings power, and it is power, more than wealth, that is seductive. Perhaps power is particularly attractive in China because it is almost the only significant way of rising above the common herd. Until

Rolls Royce Phantom outside the Pudong Shangri-La Hotel in Shanghai

and although a lack of sophistication in business matters still shows through from time to time (in the form of overbearing salesmanship, or a disregard for the ethical implications of contracts), the Chinese have learned remarkably quickly how to

recently, individuals achieved power by rising through the ranks of the Communist Party; although that remains the case to a certain extent, there is an alternative route to power and influence outside politics through money. Capitalism, albeit in diluted form, is now an accepted part of Chinese life, and although this system has its theoretical limits, the general feeling is that this strange mixture of Communist ideology and hard-faced business attitudes is here to stay.

SALARIES Only a few years ago it was impossible even to think of earning anything other than a pitiful state salary. Private enterprise was not just frowned upon, it was simply out of the question. The state would provide everything that the Chinese citizen could or, more correctly, should, desire. Everybody was on a salary scale that corresponded precisely to their social rank, and although the salary of officials tended to be higher than most, it had a defined limit. Even the Chairman of the Party, the top man in China, received a salary that was in line with this. Corruption was the more or less inevitable result of this policy, as officials extracted what price they could in compensation for low salaries.

❏ The colloquial Chinese euphemism for leaping into the rising tide of private business is *xiahai* or 'going down to the sea'. Many Chinese are willing to try. In an interview with a Western journalist, a young entrepreneur said, 'We just feel very happy when we see the company succeed.' ❏

has changed, and in major cities most have a finger in some enterprise, or work in a thriving factory or high-rise office. This transitional period is bringing great social change, especially for the coastal Special Economic Zones—one-time clones of Hong Kong, now outstripping it.

These zones have contributed to China's record-breaking economic growth, attracting a steady stream of

17

A newly purchased portrait of Sophia Loren is carried home on another status symbol, the motorcycle

SOCIAL CHANGE When economic reforms were introduced in the 1980s, ambitious city-dwellers were enraged to see peasants making a good living while they slogged in government bureaucracies for a pittance. This, too,

country people looking for work. Exploitation, low wages and poor working conditions ensued, but conditions are improving. The lot of those in traditional industries such as coal mining, where thousands die in accidents each year, remains bleak, however. But many students now study overseas, intent on ensuring a better future when they return.

More than 1.3 billion people, about one-fifth of the world's population, live in China, geographically the third-largest country in the world, and the forecasts are that this figure will soon reach 2 billion. The number of cities bearing unfamiliar names, yet with populations as great as those of New York, London or Tokyo, is astonishing.

HUMANKIND In China there are people everywhere—you are never alone, and every street is crowded. The roads between them, previously the preserve of a few trolley-buses, trucks, donkeys and bicycles, are rapidly becoming filled with cars. Even the landscape has been shaped by humankind, for every patch of fertile land, no matter how small, is under cultivation. Wilderness is rare, and magnificent works of nature, such as the Stone Forest near Kunming, are not left to stand for themselves but are 'enhanced' by the addition of human art.

SIMILARITIES Considering the size of the country, there are remarkably few regional differences north to south or east to west. A Chinese, it is true, is more likely to tell you the name of his town or province before his country, since for him the differences are great.

*Top: market day, northern Sichuan
Below: a Tibetan woman and child*

But for the outsider the homogeneity of Chinese culture is astonishing. There is even in existence a government committee whose task is to establish that the Chinese constitute a separate species. This is largely due to China's history, for despite the presence of 56 different nationalities within its borders, 92 per cent of the population is Han Chinese—that is, people with the physical characteristics of slim build, black hair and almond-shaped eyes, whose first language is Chinese, or a variant of it, and who loyally regard Beijing as the national seat of power. Traditional Han China is everywhere except Xinjiang, parts of Yunnan, Tibet, Qinghai, Inner Mongolia and parts of Manchuria, and has been so for some 2,000 years.

❑ Although most members of the minority peoples of China speak and write Chinese, there are in fact more than 30 scripts still in use throughout the country, about 20 of which, including Mongolian, Tibetan, Dai, Yi, Uyghur, Korean, Russian and Manchurian, have been in use for many hundreds of years. Others, for example that of the Zhuang who had no script of their own, were created in the 1950s on the basis of the Latin alphabet. ❑

NATIONALITIES The other 55 nationalities who make up the remaining population, comprise an element of Chinese life that cannot be ignored. Three nationalities, the Tibetans, the Mongolians and the Uyghurs, although comparatively few in number, occupy homelands that make up a large geographical proportion of the country: Tibet and Qinghai, Inner Mongolia and Xinjiang. In at least two of the cases, Tibet and to a lesser extent Xinjiang, local opposition to Han rule has manifested itself in violently rebellious outbursts that have occasionally caught the attention of the outside world. The Chinese government, which finds it hard to conceal its disgust with 'troublesome' minorities, deals with the problem by filling minority areas with Han Chinese, who are sent either under duress or through financial inducement. The result is that indigenous peoples then become minorities in their own lands.

DIVERSITY In Han China itself there is considerable cultural and linguistic diversity. There are the Hakka, for example, who were driven south

The Hani minority people of Yunnan hold on to their ancient ways

during the Song dynasty and can be identified by their distinctive fringed hats. There are the dark-skinned Tujias scattered among the mountains of Hunan, Hubei and Sichuan. Even the Cantonese, who are not a minority, differ physically from northerners and speak a dialect that is distinct from the dialects of Shanghai or Beijing.

The largest minority is the Zhuang, at over 15 million according to the 1990 census, most of whom live peacefully in the Guangxi Zhuang Autonomous Region of southern China. Almost indistinguishable from the Han, they may be related to the Vietnamese.

Most of the minorities have become absorbed into mainstream Chinese life, although the Chinese government continues to sponsor research into proving that the Chinese people constitute an individual species, distinct from *Homo sapiens*, that had its origins in China and not in Africa as the rest of the world's scientists believe.

In China, nobody wants to be a peasant farmer, and yet that is the fate of three out of four people. City-dwellers have traditionally looked down upon their country cousins, yet recent economic reforms have radically improved the farmers' lot (at least in the fertile areas of the country), and farmers are now among the richer members of Chinese society.

RURAL CHARACTER China remains predominantly rural despite attempts since 1949 to industrialize the country. Even in the major cities, open markets—and bicycles, lorries and beasts of burden loaded down with fresh produce to sell there—are still part of urban life. The fact that China is almost self-sufficient in food is remarkable when you consider the size of the population and that, with most of the country either mountain or desert, only a small percentage of land is suitable for cultivation.

The ingenuity and perseverance of the Chinese peasant are legendary, hence Mao Zedong's dictum, in his misguided attempts to reform China, to 'learn from the peasant'. This did not stop him, unfortunately, from trying to impose ideologies on these same farmers that led to the death by starvation of millions during the Great Leap Forward of 1958–59.

Harvesting in northern China's loess area, in the Hengshan Mountains

LAND SCULPTURE Such is the long-standing relationship between the Chinese farmer and the land that the very landscape is often defined by human activity. The most obvious example of this is terracing, a technique developed to make the most of undulating or hilly country-side. Taking the train from Changsha

❏ 'You glorify Nature and meditate on her;
Why not domesticate and regulate her?
You follow Nature and sing her praise:
Why not control her course and use it?'
—Xunzi, philosopher, third century BC ❏

to Guangzhou in midsummer, skirting the curving contours of tiers of densely planted land, or driving from Chongqing to Dazu when the rice is still under water, you cannot

Despite fast food reaching China, it's still the fresher the better on market day, Yunnan province

but admire the industry, creativity and regard for nature that has gone into the working of Chinese farmland.

LAND MANAGEMENT The fact that there are so few roads in China is because every piece of land is precious. Water is precious, too, and a single canal will provide irrigation for a succession of fields, while mud from its bed will be used, along with animal dung and human waste (still collected from cities), as manure.

Fuel, too, must be managed with care. Thus in the north, houses are traditionally built facing the south and the sun, away from the harsh desert winds from the northwest. In poorer areas, a large portion of the interior of the house is given over to the *kang*, a raised brick platform heated by the stove or by straw fires from outside and which may serve as a bed. Such arrangements are becoming rarer as farmers prosper.

Yet the same prosperity is bringing a new set of dilemmas, not just for farmers but for the whole of China—how to modernize without throwing half a billion people out of work and how to feed the population as the expansion of cash crops eats into land traditionally used for staple crops. Since the demise of the commune system in the 1980s, farmers have been responsible for providing quotas of staple crops to the government, in return for which they are theoretically allowed to rent a limited amount of land from the government for up to 30 years, and earn what they can from it. So long as farming remains largely manual, the rural population remains employed. But as entrepreneurial farmers, earning a private income from their leased plots, increasingly turn to mechanization encouraged by Western agronomists, the stability of the countryside looks unlikely to last, especially as in some areas the rural economy has stagnated, bringing social unrest, largely due to corrupt government officials who levy unrealistic taxes on local farmers.

China might be an essentially rural country, but it also has some of the largest cities in the world. In parts of those cities people still carry on their lives on the streets much as they have done for centuries.

PUBLIC FACE The reasons why the street is used as an extension to the home are not hard to fathom—poverty and a large population have meant simple and confined living space. In some parts of China, therefore, the street becomes a kitchen, a sitting-room, even a bedroom in the summer. The street is where everyone meets throughout the day so that tasks are accompanied by opportunities for

constant conversation. Shelling prawns, doing the washing, pumping up a bicycle tyre or playing cards may all take place simultaneously within a relatively short space, accompanied by exchanges of views and a general commentary on life. Although nobody appears to be taking much notice of traffic or passers-by, everybody is aware of what's going on around them.

THE STREETS In the wider world (just beyond the front door) lies the

The street, the open-air office of the self-employed businessman

Free-style disco dancing in the public park area of Tiantan, Beijing

commercial hub of the average small town. The open-air market is the liveliest area, but elsewhere on the streets there are barbers busy with their scissors and dentists advertising their skills with lurid paintings of a set of dentures. Noodles and bean curd are made on the spot, and dough sticks sizzle in blackened woks filled with hot oil. Tables and chairs are set up, and customers are served with simple fare; at night the tables may be illuminated with festoons of electric lights. In summer, people gather under street lamps to play cards or chess.

MOVEMENT Most striking is the restless movement that accompanies all of this. Despite the surface equanimity that appears like a glaze on Chinese daily life, there is a burning energy beneath. Watch some people eating or talking—even if the upper body is at rest, the leg pounds a beat on the floor and the eyes are constantly darting. Sometimes this latent energy can be disconcerting for visitors. Considering the crowded conditions, street brawls are a comparative rarity, but when they do occur it is with a ferocity blind to all plea or blandishment.

From the street it is but a short step to the public parks where, because of lack of space and privacy, local people gather to do those things impossible at home or that are preferred as group activities. The commonest of these activities is *taiji*, the slow, graceful exercise routines performed by squads of (usually elderly) people. In recent years some older residents have taken up open-air disco dancing in preference to traditional *taiji*.

Nearby, groups of equally elderly residents are likely to be enacting popular scenes from Chinese opera.

ENTERTAINMENT The streets of the newly prosperous cities have changed considerably and, superficially at least, are becoming similar to modern streets all over the world. However, in front of the karaoke bars and skyscrapers, and among well-dressed business-people, farmers from the countryside and members of ethnic minorities plod by in bewildered fascination, while peddlers and street performers are making a welcome return. Less welcome is the increasing number of beggars in the cities, but this seems to be an unavoidable part of the construction of a new China.

Chi fan le ma? *(Have you eaten yet?) is a form of greeting as unconscious (though not quite as flippant) as 'How are you?' in English. It demonstrates where traditional Chinese priorities lie.*

VARIETY The variety of styles and ingredients involved in Chinese cooking is a marvel. There are three principal regional cuisines—hot and spicy dishes made with chilli from Sichuan; northern-style cuisine using steamed bread and pancakes instead of rice, and preserved vegetables, such as salted and pickled cabbage, because of the freezing winters when nothing grows; and southern-style, involving light stir-fried dishes made from a vast array of ingredients, such as seafood, chicken and pork.

Top: candied haw berries, a winter treat
Below: Sichuan delicacies in traditional steamer baskets

FRESHNESS It is essential for all styles that when fresh food is used, it is as fresh as possible. It is a testimony to Chinese genius that they have developed a style of cooking that makes refrigeration unnecessary, despite the climate. Blessed with an abundance of good ingredients in the

❑ Soy sauce, the principal accompaniment to Chinese cooking, is perhaps the oldest known condiment. Made from the soya bean, its origins go back to sauces made from fish and game. When soya, or meat or fish, are mixed with salt and water or rice wine, the protein is broken down into amino acids which stimulate taste. ❑

most fertile areas of the country, the Chinese have become expert at extracting the essence of taste and aroma.

HISTORY A gourmet appreciation of food can be traced back to several centuries BC, as poetry of the period, listing dishes to tempt the departing soul back to the body, testifies. By the time of the Han dynasty a scientific approach had been formulated for cooking, and a basic rule was that the 'five sensations of taste' (sweetness, sourness, hotness, bitterness and saltiness) should be combined in a meal to achieve balance and harmony. Mincing and the thin slicing of meat and fish were also considered essential for releasing the full taste and aroma. Later, as China expanded its frontiers south and west, discovering new ingredients in the process, true Chinese cooking developed, although the basic tenets still held. The ancient cooking vocabulary is still used, even if it is quite inadequate to describe the full kaleidoscope of Chinese cuisine— as anyone who has experienced the true 'sweet and sour' pork will readily acknowledge.

METHODS Cooking methods are vital to the craft of the Chinese master chef. The best results depend on the precise control of heat, and this skill is considered crucial.

Although all methods of cooking are used, from braising and baking to boiling, steaming and roasting over a spit, there is one that is native to China. *Chao*, or stir-frying, involves cutting the ingredients finely and rapidly cooking them in a small amount of oil in a preheated wok, so they are quickly and evenly cooked. Such dishes must be eaten immediately to benefit from their *huoqi* (vital essence).

As the 14th-century imperial dietitian Hu Sihui put it, 'after a full meal do not wash your hair, avoid sex like an arrow, avoid wine like an enemy'. If the letter of this dictum is no longer heeded, the spirit certainly is.

WESTERN TASTE Westerners are sometimes surprised to discover that Chinese food in China tastes different from the food served in restaurants back home. Chinese cooking is regional, reflecting the country's many climates and peoples, and is often more earthy than the version served in Western restaurants. Stronger tastes can take some getting used to, but with a little perseverance, usually turn out to be highly satisfying to the palate.

Western-style fast food seems to have become popular among young urban Chinese. This has led to a rise in obesity among the young and a decline in the consumption of traditional snacks.

25

The proprietor of an outdoor restaurant hands out the food

Chinese music is unique, beautiful and instantly recognizable. Like many things in China it is based on theories conceived at least 2,000 years ago, theories that also influenced the music of Japan, Vietnam, Mongolia and Korea. Its distinctive qualities are dependent on two things—the instruments used and a chromatic scale that differs from that of the West.

26

HARMONY From earliest times music in China was held in the highest esteem and was an integral part of three important aspects of Chinese life: the festivals of the agricultural year, ceremonies linked to the imperial court, and religious rites. It was believed that the function of music was to enhance the harmony between heaven and earth (the earth being the fruit of the male principle of

Above: a performance in Tang costume; the instrument is the yueqin
Top: façade of a Beijing music store

yang and the female principle of *yin*). The music was based on a dozen notes from which were selected the basic notes of a series of five-note scales (corresponding to the five elements of earth, water, fire, metal and wood). The 12 notes arose from calculations based on the interval of the fourth and fifth, starting from a foundation note known as the 'yellow bell' (*huang zhong*), which was thought to be imbued with a mystical power, considered one of the eternal principles of the universe and the foundation of the well-being of the state. Each dynasty, in fact, had its foundation note, arrived at after only the most careful calculations. Absolute pitch, therefore, was a vital ingredient of

❏ A man was going to play a Chinese lute in the street, and many people gathered around to listen. But when the musician began to play, the crowd thought the music too insipid and soon dispersed, except for one man who appeared to remain standing in rapt attention. The musician exclaimed: 'There is still one who can appreciate fine music!' But the man replied: 'If I hadn't lent you that table to use as a stand for your instrument, I'd have gone as well!' ❏

Chinese music, so vital that as early as the first century BC, during the Han dynasty, an imperial office had been established, and one of its duties was standardizing pitch.

MELODY Despite these potentially inhibiting rules, traditional Chinese music is far from dull. Its two principal elements are melody and timbre. Traditional Chinese orchestras are extremely large, their component parts collectively producing a sound that is euphonious and rich; some of the orchestras employed to play at imperial temples in Beijing consisted of 150 musicians.

INSTRUMENTS Traditional music is still widely played and remains quite distinctive because of the instruments, which both look and sound substantially different from their Western counterparts, even when they share some broad similarities. The most typical instrument is the *zheng*, a long, narrow stringed instrument plucked

as it rests across the player's lap. This was the instrument of philosophers. Its main rival, an instrument that belongs more to the realm of traditional popular song, is the *pipa*, something like a lute, which became fashionable in the seventh century to accompany the songs of the Tang dynasty. Both these instruments simply sound solemn to Western ears. The Chinese originally classified their instruments according to the materials they were made of,

Flute player, Iron Pagoda, Kaifeng

which fell into eight categories: instruments with the qualities of stone, metal, silk, bamboo, wood, skin, gourd and clay. Music remains a ubiquitous feature of Chinese life. Although there are great differences between Chinese and European musical traditions, a little practice can allow anyone to acquire the Chinese taste.

In China, the principal spoken language is Modern Standard Chinese, based on the dialect of north China, especially Mandarin (from Portuguese 'mandar', to rule). It (and all China's many other dialects) is distinctive by virtue of its tones. The Chinese script goes back to 4000 or 5000 BC, is among the world's oldest written languages, and has a staggering 50,000 characters.

28

PICTOGRAPHS Chinese script has evolved from comparatively straightforward, miniature representations of the object in question, to highly stylized designs that need to be interpreted in order to be understood. It is thought that the original pictographs became more sophisticated as attempts were made to convey a meaning that could not be drawn. So, for example, the character for 'to arrive at' (*zhi*) derives from a picture of an arrow hitting a target. The next stage was to convey abstract concepts by combining two (or more) characters: thus the characters for sun and moon placed together became the character *ming*, meaning 'bright' or 'brightness'.

PRONUNCIATION By the time of the Han dynasty the written language had evolved to the point that a modern Chinese person would be able to read it aloud, although the meaning might be obscure. Chinese characters do not convey their pronunciation precisely, so the advantage of the script is that it is the same throughout the country and thus permits written communication between speakers of different dialects. There is almost nothing in common between spoken Cantonese, for example, thought by some to have preserved Tang dynasty pronunciation, and Mandarin. The government has promoted a simplified version of Mandarin (*putonghua*), with some success, as official Chinese, and in efforts to improve literacy introduced both a common system for writing the language with a Latin alphabet (romanization), known as *pinyin*, and a system for simplifying the most commonly used characters, now the

norm in mainland China. In their traditional form the characters are too complex and numerous for the majority of people to learn.

Massive characters on a column in the Forbidden City, Beijing

China was

Although China has the longest continuous civilization in history, it was nevertheless a relatively late starter. Current evidence suggests that the first organized Chinese state did not appear until several dynasties had already come and gone in ancient Egypt. Once under way, however, Chinese civilization has proved durable and, although it has occasionally been bruised and battered over the centuries, its basic foundations have proved rock-like.

PREHISTORY Little is yet known of Chinese prehistory. About 40,000 years ago it seems that the area was populated by people of the Mongoloidal type, and that a recognizably Chinese type with flatter features appeared 20,000 years later, perhaps in response to the freezing conditions of the era. However, it is only from 7,000 years ago that it is possible to trace the origins of the Chinese we know today.

CHINESE CIVILIZATION Although historians once thought that Chinese civilization was founded on influences from the Mediterranean, the spontaneous development of a separate culture is now accepted.

The first dynasty of which there is any concrete evidence is the Shang (there still exists considerable doubt about the legendary Xia, supposedly overthrown by the Shang in 1750BC), who probably ruled the areas of the North China plain around the Yellow River in the modern provinces of Shandong, Henan and Hebei, and

> ❏ Traditional accounts of the origins of Chinese civilization talk of various figures from whom all Chinese claim descent. The Yellow Emperor is the father of the Chinese but others include Yu the Great, said to have created China's waterways, and Shen Nong, the Divine Husbandman. ❏

parts of the provinces of Shanxi and Shaanxi. They were skilled and extremely well organized—excavated remains of a Shang city at Zhengzhou show walls 10m (33ft) in height extending around an area of some 3km (2 miles)—and used bronze, worked not with hammer and anvil, but cast in pottery moulds. Crucially, Shang architecture and family values

Bronze Shang ritual wine vessel

30

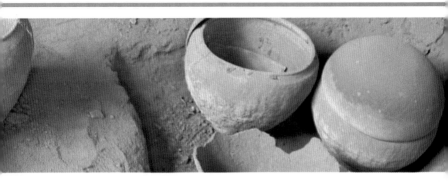

were to influence Chinese civilization to our own times.

There is no doubt that Shang influence spilled across its borders, but there was as yet no sense of Chinese statehood, and other states of varying degrees of power and cultural development operated around the Shang borders, sharing much of its culture but remaining politically independent. One such was the Zhou, who ruled an area not far to the west of Xi'an and who eventually overthrew the Shang in about 1050BC and extended the area of a cultural influence that was becoming recognizably Chinese.

THE ZHOU DYNASTY

The Zhou (1050–256BC) solved the problem of ruling what was now an extensive domain by establishing a feudal system in which relatives of the Zhou ruler were empowered to govern the various Zhou states. As for the Zhou ruler himself, he was seen as a Son of Heaven, and the supernatural influence he wielded (largely founded on the relationship to illustrious ancestors) was sufficiently powerful to linger even after the fall of the dynasty. Just how

great was the extent of the Zhou realm is hard to gauge—it seems to have extended through much of Shaanxi, Shanxi and Hebei, reaching the Gansu border in the west and Shandong in the east, and possibly the Yangtze valley. It was sufficiently large to warrant the construction of a secondary capital at Luoyang.

In 771BC, however, the western Zhou rulers met defeat at the hands of a mixture of barbarian invaders and disgruntled subjects, displaced by the eastern Zhou rulers. They moved east to Luoyang, but their vitality was sapped.

Top: neolithic pottery at Banpo
Left: a decorated ritual vessel, in the form of a stylized animal, dated to the Zhou dynasty

31

Although the Zhou lasted 800 years, its rule was largely nominal. Effective power lay with the nobles in far-flung regions of the kingdom, who frequently fought among themselves while continuing to defer to the Zhou king at Luoyang. Eventually, a newer, stronger state was to exploit this weakness.

32

The famous 'Flying Horse of Gansu', Eastern Han dynasty

FALL OF EASTERN ZHOU Echoes of the ritualistic deference shown to the Zhou king exist even today in public life, for some of the Zhou's administrative features lasted into the 20th century. The eastern Zhou, the second period of Zhou rule, is sub-divided into two, both named after the principal historical source books—the Spring and Autumn period (during which Confucius lived) and the Warring States period, characterized by internecine warfare among the various states, any one of which might finally have toppled the Zhou.

But it was the Qin, occupying the area around the original western

❏ The First Emperor believed his empire would last for 10,000 generations—in fact his own dynasty outlived him by only a few years, although the imperial structure he built lasted for 2,133 years.

The Emperor died in 210BC, on a trip away from the capital. His chief advisor, Li Ssu, returned the body in a sealed carriage to pre-empt revolt and changed the wording of the Emperor's will to the advantage of a younger, weaker son. The true heir committed suicide and the new emperor was murdered by Li Ssu, who was himself killed in the ensuing chaos. ❏

capital, that was to prove strongest, using its advantageous position on the fringes of the Chinese and uncultured worlds to expand to a point where it was able to defeat the Zhou in 256BC and the other states in 221BC.

THE MIGHTY QIN The Qin dynasty (221–206BC), although one of the shortest in Chinese history, was to prove one of the most influential. Its founder—Qin Shihuangdi, 'the Yellow Emperor'—brought to fruition an incipient sense of Chinese statehood. Qin ideology was not very innovative, but the adoption of the authoritarian tenets of Legalist philosophy ensured that the Qin triumphed. The emperor's principal aims were centralization, standardization and unification: China was divided into military regions and counties under central government; weights and measures and the written script were regularized; and intellectual opposition was ruthlessly suppressed. By 214BC, he had extended Chinese domains as far as Vietnam, but with his death in 210BC the dynasty fizzled out. His three short-lived successors were unable to cool the simmering resentments that resulted from the severity of the First Emperor's rule.

THE HAN The Han (206BC–AD220), though founded upon opposition to the Legalist framework that had been the key to Qin success, was left with a base upon which to develop into one of the greatest of Chinese dynasties. Confucianism became the state doctrine, absolute imperial power was enshrined as 'the Mandate from heaven', and a rudimentary examination system for selecting officials was introduced. It was a period of

cultural, scientific and foreign expansion and of consolidation of the Chinese identity. Many regions previously under nominal Chinese tutelage were better integrated, and the way west via the Silk Road, a conduit for Buddhism, was opened.

Although the Han fragmented into warring states, the idea of a united China never died. The demise of the Han can be attributed in part to economic factors. Before, the southern states had been no match for the Qin once it had acquired the prosperous northern plains. By the end of the Han, the wealth of the Yangtze valley and the Sichuan Basin was well developed and, when rebellions led to the fall of the Han, China split into three.

33

A 'Fairy Mountain' incense burner, as found in a Western Han tomb, made of bronze inlaid with gold

In China philosophy has played a role not unlike that of a religion. Most of the great Chinese philosophers emerged during a period of unrelenting instability, which was perhaps the inspiration for the quest to right human ills.

CONFUCIUS If a word had to be chosen to describe Chinese society for the last 2,000 years, that word might well be 'Confucian'.

Confucius was born in 551BC in the state of Lu (now Shandong province). Although his parents were probably minor nobility, he was concerned for the poor and dispossessed, and the belief that the goal of mankind was happiness. Each individual and each government, therefore, should desire happiness for others. Anyone could be

Top: Taoist monks. Below: the pagoda (here, at Tiger Hill, Suzhou) is a tribute to Chinese Buddhism

a good ruler, not just the high-born. All that was required was the right education, the will to learn and the desire to govern well. Together with his disciples he founded the first private school in China, accepting pupils of any background, providing they demonstrated intellectual curiosity.

Education had been confined to the well-born, or for those learning to become government officials. Confucian education also aimed to train people to govern but with a crucial difference. Confucius believed that public servants should play an active role in government, taking initiatives and criticizing bad policy.

34

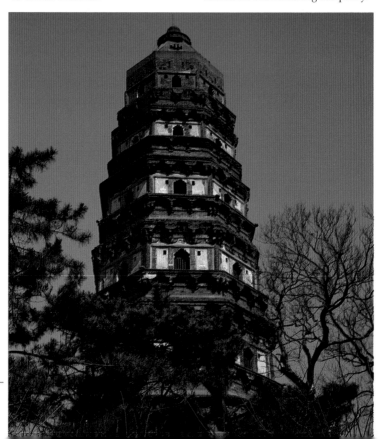

❏ 'One Chuang Chou (Zhuangzi) dreamed he was a butterfly. He did not know he had ever been anything but a butterfly, and was content to hover from flower to flower. Suddenly he woke and found to his astonishment that he was Chuang Chou. But it was hard to be sure whether he really was Chou and had only dreamt that he was a butterfly, or was really a butterfly, and was only dreaming he was Chou.'—Arthur Waley, *Three Ways of Thought in Ancient China*, 1939 ❏

In Confucian philosophy ritual was important but was deemed useless if it consisted of inflexible rules. It was the spirit of the ritual, not its mechanical application that was important.

While Confucius seems to have believed in a moral force called Heaven, he declined to tackle the question of life after death. One of his best-known responses to a question from one of his disciples was 'You do not yet understand life; how can you understand death?' Instead, he emphasized 'the Way' or the 'Golden Mean'. This was a way of action, which followers should be prepared to stand by, and die for if necessary. It taught that people should play an active role in society, observing conventions, yet not following the crowd. For Confucius, the concept of the well-rounded individual, rigorously intellectual yet emotionally balanced, was paramount.

Confucius's stress on universal government was too radical for most. Although he was eventually given a government post, he realized that it was a way of keeping him quiet and he soon resigned. He journeyed throughout China spreading his ideas, and died in 479BC.

TAOISM The other important Chinese philosophy was Taoism, in many ways complementing Confucianism. Its first major figure is Laozi (*c*570–490BC), a near contemporary of Confucius reputed to have written the *Daodejing*, which translates as 'The Way and its powers'. The nature of the *dao*, 'Way', which is the great underlying principle

Statue of Confucius, Confucian Temple, Beijing

of human and natural life, is never properly defined, but it might be said to be the bond that unites man with nature, with the concept of *wuwei* or 'no action' as its ethos. The second important Taoist figure is Zhuangzi (369–286BC) who wrote a volume of allegorical tales illustrating the tenets of Taoism. Taoism is a counter to the rigid propriety of Confucianism. It is still possible to see both points of view mirrored in the outlook of modern Chinese men and women.

The yin-yang *Taoist symbol*

35

After the fall of the Han, China divided into the three states known as the Wei, Shu and Wu. Constantly at war with each other over the following centuries, the three states eventually fragmented into a jigsaw of small dynasties. Two of China's greatest dynasties were to emerge from the chaos.

AFTER THE HAN Paradoxically, the era of confusion that followed the disintegration of the Han dynasty was also one of cultural flowering. The Tang dynasty (AD618–907) that followed is often considered the most accomplished of the Chinese dynasties.

THE TANG Its founder, a general, came from mixed Tartar and Chinese stock. He retained the

fundamental Confucian outlook, encouraged education and promoted contact with foreigners.

Unusually, the general abdicated to allow his son to succeed him when he felt that China was sufficiently stable.

THE GOOD LIFE Life in Tang China was cosmopolitan, vital and stimulating. Chang'an (Xi'an), the capital,

Above: Song dynasty mirror box

had an estimated 2 million people, probably the largest city in the world at the time. One of the hallmarks of the dynasty was its organization: elaborate laws were codified throughout the empire, which extended to Korea and Vietnam. On main roads there were post stations every 16km (10 miles) with hostels and restaurants. Confucianist schools were augmented by others specializing in law, mathematics and science. The development of the examination system, which was started in the Han, helped to create the first bureaucracy based on merit. Bills of exchange ('flying money') were introduced. The Tang was also notable for contact with the outside world, as Muslims and Jews, for example, found themselves among the traders in Canton and as Chinese influence re-established itself along the Silk Road.

Buddhism reached its apogee during this period, before its sudden decline as a result of official attacks on its influence. Painting and music flourished. For the first time central and south China vied in importance with the traditional northern heartland around the Yellow River. Confucian gentry began to earn money from the offices they held, rather than from land, heralding the burgeoning of a 'middle class'. Yet there were no exceptional or striking political innovations in the period and, ultimately, economic problems—such as the displacement of tax-paying peasants by land-hungry merchants, and the increasing wealth of the aristocracy—led to strife and disintegration.

THE SONG Five decades of bickering ensued before reunification under the Song (AD960–1279). This was to be another of the great Chinese dynasties, despite barbarian invasions that compelled the court to move south to Hangzhou from its capital in Kaifeng. During this period increasing urbanization brought about a commercial revolution, education and literacy improved, and a cultural renaissance was underway, noted for simple but beautiful glazed porcelain, and the finest painting in Chinese history.

FIRST INVASIONS The first Song emperor decided to centralize the bureaucracy, placing as many ministries under his personal control as possible, in order to consolidate reunification. But the threat of invasion was

Buddhist monks at Xi'an's Big Wild Goose Pagoda (left), built AD652

ever-present, and by 946 the Khitans, of Mongol origin, had reached Kaifeng. Over 3,000 courtiers were captured, and the Song, driven south, were forced to coexist with the 'barbarians', who occupied the north for 300 years.

This was, however, a period of progress. Foreign trade prospered and Chinese cities became more sophisticated. The Chinese genius for innovation inspired a series of inventions, including the compass and inoculations against smallpox; a less notable innovation was the fashion for binding girls' feet. It was also an era of decadence and military feebleness that accentuated the Chinese tendency to introspection. As Buddhism continued to atrophy due to government suppression during the Tang dynasty, neo-Confucianism dominated Chinese thought. Thus China remained, more or less, for a further eight centuries.

37

The Yuan was the first foreign dynasty to rule China, and although it was to last little more than a century it was to influence the Chinese outlook for hundreds of years to come.

THE KHANS The Mongols' success in taking China can be accredited partly to their use of the latest military technology, principally a mobile cavalry; added to this, lack of water in Central Asia finally forced the squabbling Mongol tribes to unite under a single dynamic leader, Ghengis Khan, with the aim of conquering less arid territory. In 1215, Beijing fell, but Ghengis did not live to see the full conquest of China; upon his death the Mongol empire was divided into four 'khanates' ruled by three sons and a grandson.

Ghenghis Khan's son Ogodai, who ruled from the Mongol capital of Karakorum, reinvaded China.

Genghis Khan's mausoleum, Ejin Horo Qi, Inner Mongolia

Although he conquered the Khitan rulers of the North China plain, he met stiffer opposition from the southern Song, who resisted all attempts at conquest for half a century. Finally they were overcome by Ghengis Khan's grandson, Kublai, in 1279.

Now ruler of all China, Kublai Khan took the Chinese name Yuan ('First Beginning') for his dynasty. The Mongols also pushed into Indochina and briefly reached Java, provoking huge migrations and indirectly contributing to political changes in adjoining lands as they did so. In 1260, the Mongol capital was moved from Karakorum to Beijing, with Xanadu (now Dolon Nor, in Inner Mongolia) then retained as a summer residence for the imperial family.

Left: lions on the Beijing bridge mentioned by Marco Polo. Top, opposite: the Forbidden City or, in Mongol days, the 'Great Within'

although he hired foreign contingents for Mongol armies, the Chinese were forbidden to carry arms.

Despite the changes, Confucian ideology and bureaucratic political life were maintained. To the disgust of the Chinese, however, Mongolian customs of dress, food, traditions and language were imposed. The Mongols did not use last names, for example, a barbarian custom to the family-conscious Chinese. But cultural and literary activity flourished, and with the abolition of the examinations, frustrated scholars had to find other uses for their literary skills. Popular drama also developed fast.

MONGOL CHINA Kublai Khan employed able men of all nationalities and listened to all philosophies. Dispensing with the civil service examinations, he streamlined the bureaucracy to four ministries—Justice, War, Rites, Finance—and

FOREIGN LINKS Expeditions were sent to find the source of the Yellow River, while links with the Muslim world inspired the introduction of Islamic design elements into Chinese art and architecture. China and Europe entered a new era of cultural exchange. Europeans began to arrive as adventurers or as representatives of European nation states, sent to export Christianity and perhaps find a powerful new ally against the Muslims. There was even a Mongolian counterpart to Marco Polo, a certain Rabban Sauma, a Nestorian monk who journeyed to Rome to meet the Pope. With the collapse of the Yuan, however, and the re-establishment of native rule under the Ming, the Catholic church lost the ground it had made in China, at least for the time being.

Eventually the Mongols lost their grip on their huge and unwieldy empire. None of Kublai's successors matched his ability. Distance and cultural divide wore down the conquerors. Once the Mongols began to lose their cultural identity, the familiar symptoms of dynastic decline appeared: famines, uncontrolled floods, excessive taxation and revolts. As is always the case, the rebellious chiefs were not able to unite, and it took a single strong Chinese general to seize control.

39

The Ming (which means 'brilliant') was to become the archetypal Chinese dynasty—peaceful, prosperous and stable, the image of traditional China ruled by the scholar-gentry on neo-Confucian principles. The Qing, another foreign dynasty, was to bring more than 2,000 years of imperial rule to a close.

Spirit Way, Nanjing, leads to the tomb of the first Ming emperor
Top: detail, Qing palace, Shenyang

THE MING Zhu Yuanzhang, the founder of the Ming dynasty (AD1368–1644), rose from a peasant background to become a general and then an emperor, driving out the Mongols and establishing the first Ming capital in Nanjing. Although Confucianism was revitalized, the emperor became increasingly autocratic. After his death, civil war broke out. His grandson and heir was usurped by his son, who had been ruling Beijing as Prince of Yan. He became the Yongle Emperor, the greatest of the Ming emperors.

GREAT WORKS Yongle relocated the capital to Beijing, creating his own power base close to the Mongol border. He oversaw the beginning of great public works, such as the reconstruction of the Great Wall, the mass movement of populations for colonization, and the reclamation of areas laid waste by war. This was an era of seaborne expeditions, led by a eunuch admiral hoping to promote Chinese prestige along new trade routes; at one stage 67 states, including Aden, were paying tribute to China and its emperor.

When these expeditions came to a sudden end—due to resentment against the eunuch leaders and fear of the Mongol menace—foreign relations went downhill. Pirate raids intensified on the coast and along the Yangtze. Chinese citizens were forbidden to travel abroad, and China turned in on itself. Despite this, Jesuit scientists were still tolerated, and cultural life flourished, albeit in a scarcely innovative way. Widespread printing allowed the dissemination of encyclopedias and treatises. Surprisingly, given the inhibiting effects of Confucianism, the novel flourished, and several classics were published at this time.

LAST YEARS After 300 years the Ming was in its death throes. The state eunuchs, in important ministerial positions at the palace, had become too powerful. Those close to the emperor and their families built up great estates, and dispossessed peasants joined together to form rebel bands that marched on Beijing. In response, the last Ming emperor committed suicide on Coal Hill, just behind the Forbidden City, but the peasant army did not enjoy the victory for long—taking advantage of the civil strife, a Manchu army swept down from the northeast to capture Beijing in 1644.

THE LAST DYNASTY The Manchus were a confederation of Jurchen tribes from central and southern Manchuria. Their leader was Nurhachi, who founded the Manchu state in 1616. He established his capital at Shenyang, and by adopting Confucianism won the support of the 3 million Chinese who lived in Manchuria. His son Abahai proclaimed the new Qing dynasty in 1636, captured Beijing in 1644, and over the next several decades established control over the whole of China. Unlike the Mongols before them, the Manchus decided to preserve the Chinese government structure while also enforcing some of their own traditions on the Chinese.

MANCHU CHINA Internal peace was maintained by military might, but the dynasty produced two notable emperors. The Kangxi Emperor (1661–1722) completed the agricultural reforms started under the Ming, initiated attempts to tame the Yellow River, supported scholarship and encouraged artistic talent. His grandson, the Qianlong Emperor (1735–95), extended the empire's boundaries despite several

unsuccessful military campaigns that were to leave the country undefended. But by 1800 there were already signs of cyclical decline. Peasant revolts and Western influence, which was taking hold in Canton despite disapproval in Beijing, could no longer be ignored.

Ming vase, with peacock and peony patterns

The decline and eventual fall of imperial China was a long, painful process. During the final 100 years of the Qing dynasty, influences were at work that traditional resources could not meet. One was the arrival of foreigners in unprecedented numbers, determined to force the Chinese government to enter free trade—a goal that was eventually accomplished through the Treaty of Nanjing, which opened certain treaty ports to foreign companies.

EUROPEAN BARBARIANS The reactions of Manchu rulers and Chinese intellectuals alike to the presence of foreigners on their soil were mixed. Some ignored them while others expressed interest in the new ideas offered by Westerners. Those who approved of Westernization could not agree on how to proceed. The official line taken by the Manchus was that the foreigners should be ignored; but they were not so easily disposed of, and there

Sun Yatsen, Father of the Republic

were other matters to consider. One of these was the Taiping 'Heavenly Peace' Rebellion (1850–64), the gravest of many uprisings at that time.

MESSIAH This rebellion lasted more than 20 years and cost at least 20 million lives. It began when a Hakka peasant, who had failed the official examinations, adopted Christianity, proclaiming himself the head of a new Confucian hierarchy with Christ as the Heavenly Elder Brother. He made considerable headway, taking Nanjing and even enjoying some limited,

> ❏ The Taiping Rebellion ended in ignominious failure but some of the ideas of its leader, Hong Xiuquan, were remarkable. He believed in state ownership of land and sharing food, clothing and money. Every 25 households were to be organized as 'comradeships' (*wu*), headed by a comrade leader (*wuzhang*). ❏

temporary Western support. A typical manifestation of the agrarian unrest of the time, the rebellion, although unsuccessful, showed how vulnerable the Chinese government really was when faced with a challenge.

NEED FOR CHANGE The British and French, in particular, frequently found excuses for acts of aggression. The weak Chinese government seemed powerless to prevent additional treaty ports being added to the list originally

Port of Shanghai in 1857 (top) and (above) The Shanghai Club—for foreign members only until 1949

DRAGON EMPRESS Predictably there were those who opposed any modernization. The imperial concubine Cixi (1835–1908), who acted as regent during the minority of her son, the nominated heir, became the *de facto* ruler for the rest of her life when he died in 1875, and was replaced by a four-year-old. Cixi ousted reformers but in 1898 the young emperor, attracted by foreign ideas, initiated the 'Hundred Days of Reform' movement. This proposed educational change included the foundation of a university in Beijing, and the reform of the Civil Service examination system. Cixi came out of retirement and ruthlessly put an end to it, but foreigners were now permitted to reside in Beijing. All this time, China's foreign residents continued to exploit the country but, strangely, this had an upside: maintaining trade relations with the outside world.

LAST DAYS Tensions finally culminated in the Boxer Rebellion of 1900–01. Initially anti-Manchu, it quickly became anti-foreign. Following its suppression by a powerful international army, more humiliating demands were made on the Chinese. Western influence also encouraged the appearance of several revolutionary groups, notably those led by Sun Yatsen (see page 229), who had been exposed to democratic ideals in Japan, America and Britain. Last-minute reforms by the government were too little too late; in 1912 Sun was elected President of the Republic of China after the abdication of the last emperor.

agreed to in 1842, under the Nanjing Treaty, or to halt the ruinous opium trade. Some in the Chinese government saw that reforms were necessary and minor changes were made—land tax was reduced and collected more efficiently, Chinese were sent abroad to learn Western technological skills, an office was established specifically to deal with foreign affairs, and there was some railway and telegraph construction and industrial development. The so-called 'self-strengthening' movement was undermined, however, by a determination to ignore the virtues of Western political systems.

During the 20th century China was shaken by a series of major upheavals, caused by the struggle to modernize the country after 2,000 years of backward-looking imperial rule. Inevitably the process was accompanied by ideological battles, notably between the conservative nationalists and the communists who believed in forging a new order based on the common ownership of property and resources.

THE FIRST REPUBLIC On 12 February 1912, the last Chinese emperor, the six-year-old Puyi (1906–67), was forced to abdicate and the first Chinese Republic was declared in Nanjing. Sun Yatsen, the leader of the reformist movement that opposed imperial rule, was duly elected Provisional President. His plans to create a more modern and

Top: Chiang Kaishek, Burma 1942
Below: a statue of Mao (in Shenyang), nowadays a rare sight

democratic state were thwarted, however, by Yuan Shikai. Yuan was the treacherous head of the imperial army who, despite his duty to protect the boy emperor, had actually orchestrated the emperor's abdication.

Yuan regarded Sun Yatsen as a challenge to his own bid for power but, in public at least, supported the republicans. In 1912, Sun Yatsen reluctantly agreed to stand aside for Yuan, who was unanimously declared President. Yuan dropped all pretence of republican sentiment in 1915 when he declared himself emperor, but his dictatorial ambitions came to nothing, as he died the next year. He paved the way for a grim period in Chinese history, when the various thuggish warlords, who controlled sections of the Chinese army, battled against each other for supremacy over North China and the possession of Beijing. All Sun Yatsen and his followers could do was work for much-needed reform from the distant southern Chinese capital in Guangzhou (Canton).

CHIANG KAISHEK At Sun Yatsen's death in 1925, his place as leader of the Nationalist Party (Guomindang) was taken by Chiang Kaishek (1887–1975). The party's main goal was to overthrow the Beijing-based warlords, thus reuniting China through military conquest under its leadership. In preparation for armed rebellion, the nationalists were trained by advisers from the newly created Soviet Union who were working to influence China's political situation. At the same time Soviet revolutionaries were active in Shanghai, where the Chinese Communist Party was formed in 1921.

In 1923, the communists joined forces with the nationalists, but strong tensions existed between the two parties, not least because Chiang Kaishek knew that his goals would not be achieved without the support of foreign governments and Chinese industrialists who were implacably opposed to Marxism. When Chiang led his army north in 1927 and declared a new nationalist government in Nanjing, his first act was to ban the Communist Party and to carry out a purge of left-wingers within his own ranks.

Many were killed and many imprisoned during this period, and communists all over China were harried by means of so-called 'encirclement campaigns' whereby the army tried to get rid of the forces in south central China. To escape the nationalists, the communists undertook an arduous 23,200km (14,400-mile) trek in 1935, heading through China's far west, an expedition that has gone down in history as the Long March (see page 111). Of the nearly 100,000 people who undertook the march, fewer than 10,000 survived. These veterans, including their leader Mao Zedong, would eventually form an élite within the Communist Party that would come to rule China and force its people into a series of equally heroic, if misguided, campaigns.

Now, however, the bitterest of enemies agreed to cease hostilities and put up a united front against the Japanese, who invaded those areas not already in their control in 1937. Until the surrender of the Japanese at the end of World War II, the communists kept up a constant guerrilla campaign from their bases in the west, while the nationalists, supported by the Western Allies, operated out of bases in the province of Sichuan.

Mao's Red Book, *symbol of Chinese communism*

Hostilities broke out again between communists and nationalists at the defeat of Japan in 1945. US envoys sought to find a compromise, and Stalin himself put pressure on the communists to cast aside differences with the nationalists, but Mao showed all the stubbornness and determination that were to be his hallmarks for the next 30 years.

Mao came from Chinese peasant stock (born in Shaoshan, in Hunan province, in 1893), and his master-stroke was to win the support of the mass of Chinese peasant farmers for his revolutionary ideals, unlike the university-educated intellectuals who led the urban-based Russian Revolution.

Eight years of war against the Japanese had taught the communists how to survive and win even in the face of extreme hardship. They out-classed and outwitted the nationalists at every stage of the bloody civil war that began in 1946 and ended in October 1949, when Mao finally stood with his supporters at the gates of the Forbidden City in Beijing. Chiang Kaishek fled to Taiwan where he set up a rival government.

THE PEOPLE'S REPUBLIC One of Mao's first acts was to redistribute all land (former landlords were often beaten up or killed), and by 1956 all industries had been nationalized. The West was prepared to accept Mao at first, but China was later ostracized for helping Communist North Korea invade the UN-supported South in the Korean War of 1950–53.

At first, China turned to the USSR for aid, and in cities such as Beijing and Shanghai the visible symbols of this era are the hotels and office build-ings constructed for and by Russian advisers. Increasingly, however, Mao began to develop his own idiosyn-cratic brand of communism, launching one mass-action campaign after another and seeming to exercise an extraordinary power to control the collective will of his people. In 1956, his cry was to let 'a hundred flowers blossom, a hundred schools of thought contend'. The aim was to revitalize Chinese culture, but the Party drew the line at criticism of its own role, and the campaign died in 1957 with the imprisonment of many dissidents.

Next came the Great Leap Forward of 1958–60, intended to mobilize the country into superhuman feats of agri-cultural and industrial productivity. Instead it resulted in mass starvation, as peasants spent more time in political debate than in physical work, a problem made worse by two years of poor harvests, floods and typhoons. When most in need of help, Mao then quarrelled with the Soviet Union, ostensibly in the name of Chinese 'self-reliance' but really out of pique because the Soviets would not share their nuclear technology with China.

Finally Mao lost all patience with his critics and turned to the young. In 1966, he launched the Cultural Revolution, encouraging armies of young Red Guards to wipe the slate of history clean and build a totally new China. This resulted in an orgy of iconoclasm, as the Red Guards smashed up historic buildings and museum displays, beat up intellectuals and teachers, and turned on their own parents. Three years of terror and anarchy and 10 years of repression were unleashed.

China's travails only came to an end with Mao's death in 1976. Mao's wife, Jiang Qing, tried to seize power but she, and the other members of the so-called 'Gang of Four', were arrested within a month. Deng Xiaoping, Mao's long-time opponent, then emerged as China's new leader. His pragmatic form of communism, and his econ-omic reforms to encourage foreign investment, led to a period of calm and the gradual strengthening of the economy. Democracy still remains a distant dream, however, as proved by army intervention in Tiananmen Square in 1989.

Since then a comparatively free market has enabled some Chinese to buy themselves material independence but without the personal freedom to enjoy it. China remains an essentially autocratic state in which dissident views are not tolerated and where the rights of minority peoples are consistently violated (most notably in Tibet, but also among the Muslims of Xinjiang). Religion has been allowed to flourish, yet those who worship are still exposed to harassment. Power is still centralized and, increasingly, riddled with corruption, leaving many Chinese frustrated and powerless.

Mao (below, as seen on the Tiananmen Gate) is depicted greeting the People's Army

Beijing

Beijing

Shopping facilities are burgeoning in Beijing, adding to an already extensive range of places to purchase both international and locally made products

THE NORTH During China's long history there have been many capital cities. Some were no more than regional capitals for dynasties that did not control the whole of the country. Others, like Xi'an, were state capitals for the earlier dynasties. Beijing was the last of the imperial capitals and has remained the capital since 1949. What is left of its ancient glories derives mostly from the last two dynasties, the Ming and Qing, but it has been a capital on and off for some 3,000 years.

EARLY DAYS Before the unification of China in 221BC, Beijing was Jicheng or Yanjing, the capital of the Kingdom of Yan found to the east of the current site. It remained a provincial town of some significance during the Tang, but became a secondary capital in AD947 under the Liao rulers who controlled the north. The only reminders of this period are the Tianningsi pagoda near Guang'anmen and a stele in the Western Hills. During the 12th century, the Jin rulers named the city Zhongdu and made it their main capital. The most splendid relics from that period are the Marco Polo Bridge and a group of pagodas at Changping.

In 1215, Zhongdu was razed by the Mongols. By 1260, when all of northern China had been conquered, the Mongol leader Kublai Khan, the grandson of Genghis Khan, moved his capital from Karakorum to Zhongdu, rebuilt the city, and called it Khanbaliq (Khan's Town), or Dadu (Great Capital) in Chinese. The focal point was today's Beihai Park; before that the city's focus was the area of Guang'anmen. The principal streets ran mostly north–south and the intersecting *hutongs* (from the Mongolian word *hottog* meaning 'waterwell'), or lanes, ran east–west. Some of these lanes still exist.

Peking Opera: dramatic, noisy and very Chinese

The glazed pagoda at Xiangshan, Beijing

MING AND QING The Mongol Empire began to crumble after Kublai's death in 1297 and was replaced in 1368 by the Ming dynasty. The first Ming emperor chose to move the capital to Nanjing ('Southern Capital'). One of his sons was made ruler of the principality of Yan, with Dadu, now renamed Beiping ('Northern Peace'), as its capital. In 1403, when the prince became the third Ming emperor, Beiping was called Beijing ('Northern Capital') and became capital of China once again. It was rebuilt mostly on the foundations of Dadu, although it was larger, and the basic dimensions of today's central area date from this period, as do its principal monuments, the Forbidden City and the Temple of Heaven.

During the Qing dynasty, which lasted from 1644 to 1911, the city's layout was altered and additional palaces were built in and around the central area. In the main, however, Beijing retained its Ming quality.

BEIJING TODAY Modern Beijing is no longer a classically beautiful city—mindless destruction, planned or politically inspired, has seen to that. But its extraordinary history has bequeathed to it a certain grandeur, and there is no doubt that it impresses. The Forbidden City, one of the most magnificent architectural structures in the world, and the other snippets of the past that linger here and there, still make a visit essential.

Map labels:

Palace | Gate of Divine Prowess (Shenwumen) | Moat

Watchtower

Shunzhen Gate

Hall of Imperial Peace

Hall of Arts and Crafts of the Ming and Qing Dynasties

Watchtower

Imperial Garden

Exhibition of Original State Palace

Gate of Terrestrial Tranquillity

Exhibition Halls of Imperial Treasure

Hall of Ceramics

Palace of Terrestrial Tranquillity

Palace of Peaceful Old Age

Hall of Heavenly and Terrestrial Union

Hall of Bronzes

Hall of Imperial Supremacy (Art Gallery)

Hall of Mental Cultivation

Palace of Heavenly Purity

Gate of Peaceful Old Age

Palace of Peace and Tranquillity

Imperial Clock Collection

Gate of Heavenly Purity

Gate of Flourishing Fortune

Nine Dragon Screen

Gate of Peace and Tranquillity

Gate of Imperial Prosperity

Garden of Peace and Tranquillity

Hall of Preserving Harmony

Archery Pavilion

Hall of Middle Harmony

Central Right Gate

Central Left Gate

Hall of Supreme Harmony (closed until end of 2007)

Tower of Enhanced Righteousness

Tower of Manifest Benevolence

Imperial Library

Hall of Martial Valour

Hall of Literary Glory

West Flowery Gate

Gate of Martial Valour

Gate of Supreme Harmony

East Flowery Gate

Gate of Literary Glory

Gate of Prosperous Harmony

Gate of Harmony

Golden Water Bridges

Imperial Archives

Watchtower

Watchtower

Meridian Gate

0 100 200 300 m
0 100 200 300 yards

Palace Moat

Zhongshan

Right Imperial Gate

Left Imperial Gate

Park

52

Walk

Forbidden City

The description of the Forbidden City on pages 53–55 guides you on a walk, starting at the South (Meridian) Gate, along the main central axis to the exit at the Gate of Divine Prowess (Shenwumen). You will pass all the major ceremonial pavilions used by the emperors, the imperial bedrooms and, by taking a couple of diversions, the former residence of the imperial concubines, the imperial treasure exhibition rooms, the painting exhibition and the Imperial Clock Collection.

▶▶▶ Beihai (North Lake) Park   49D3
(Beihai Gongyuan)

Open: daily 6–9pm. Admission: inexpensive
Xianmen Dajie. Buses 5, 13, 100

If you have time, visit this park and classical garden just northwest of the Forbidden City. The area, which was the heart of the Mongol capital, Dadu, retains from the Mongol period only the jade bowl in the **Tuancheng** (**Round City**, just inside the main entrance on Wenjin Jie). Several buildings in the Tuancheng, and the **Dragon Screen** on the north bank of the lake, date from the Ming. The **White Dagoba** was built in 1651 to commemorate a visit by the Dalai Lama. Most of the pavilions on the east side were the Qing-dynasty pleasure gardens. On Qionghua Island is the **Fangshan Fandian**, which serves dishes once created for the Dowager Empress Cixi. The park is said to have been a preferred spot of Jiang Qing, wife of Mao and one of the 'Gang of Four'.

▶▶▶ Forbidden City (Zijincheng)   49D3

Open: 8.30–5 (last entry 3.30). Admission: moderate
Xichang'an Jie. Buses 1, 5, 54, 101

The heart of Beijing is dominated by the imperial yellow roofs and vermilion walls of the Forbidden City, sometimes called the Imperial Museum or Palace Museum (Gugong). In Mongol times it was the 'Great Within'. Under the Ming and Qing, Beijing was divided into walled sections or cities—the Forbidden City was the innermost and the most important, because it was the residence of the emperor, the focal point of the empire and the middle of the 'Middle Kingdom' (i.e. China). Entry was forbidden to all but those on imperial business until 1911, when the last emperor, Puyi, was overthrown. It occupies 720,000sq m (775,000sq ft), there are, allegedly, 9,999 rooms and it is surrounded by a moat and a 10m (33ft)-high wall with a perimeter of 6km (4 miles).

Entry to the Forbidden City is on foot only and is via the south or north gates; the south (Wumen or Meridian Gate) is preferable, because the audio-guided tour (extra charge) takes you that way. It is accessed by Tiananmen Gate.

The Hall of Supreme Harmony in the Forbidden City

53

BOXER MURDER
In Zhongshan Park is a memorial to Baron Clement August von Kettler, a 19th-century German minister to China. He was murdered by a mob on 20 June 1900, on his way to the Chinese Foreign Office to protest at the violence of the Boxers (an anti-Manchu and anti-foreign sect, see page 43).

The White Dagoba in Beihai Park

Beijing

54

BIRTH OF AN EMPEROR
When Dowager Empress Cixi was a 'virtuous imperial concubine', she became pregnant. Cixi was permitted to select six maids to help her at the birth, as well as the two midwives and two doctors. As a reward for producing a son, Cixi was promoted and given 300 taels of silver and 70 bolts of top-quality fabric.

Flying cranes on a glazed panel in the Imperial Garden

HAIR-LOOM
Preserving the hair of ancestors has long been a sign of respect in China. In the Forbidden City there is a solid gold stupa built by Emperor Qianlong to store his mother's fallen hair.

Golden characters on a column in the Forbidden City

The main structure is made up of two groups of three palaces, mostly 18th-century, situated one after the other on a central axis called the Meridian Line. Behind them, at the north end, is the Imperial Garden. Alongside the palaces to the northwest are the former apartments of the concubines; to the northeast are the palaces of Emperor Qianlong and Empress Cixi.

The first group of three palaces (the outer court) were for official functions; the second three (the inner court) were for private ones. Before you reach them, you pass the **Meridian Gate**, reserved for the emperor, and so-named because it was here that the new lunar calendars were distributed. Each morning the principal officials would wait atop the gate for the emperor's arrival, which was announced by the drums and bells in the pavilions on either side of the gate. Beyond is a magnificent courtyard across which runs the **Golden Water Stream** spanned by the five **Inner Golden Water Bridges**. The **Taihemen (Gate of Supreme Harmony)** follows, and to the right is a group of buildings devoted to Confucian studies and containing the imperial library. To the left is the **Hall of Martial Valour** where the Ming empresses received their female subjects. After Taihemen is a courtyard and the three main palaces of the 'outer court'.

The first of these is the **Taihedian (Hall of Supreme Harmony)**, once the tallest building in Beijing, where the emperor ascended the throne, received high officials and celebrated important festivals. It has 55 rooms, a room being the space between four pillars. No commoner was permitted to build higher than this hall. Roofs were accorded rank, too, and naturally this was of the highest, built in the *wudian* (thatched hall) style with four fully hipped double roofs with curved, overhanging eaves. At each end of the ridge are giant dragon heads (the dragon was the imperial symbol); the mythological figures running down the side ridges ward off calamity, particularly fire. The marble ramp leading up to the terrace was for the emperor's sole use. On the terrace are a sundial and grain measure, testifying to the imperial concern for the harvest, four incense burners in the form of tortoises and cranes, symbols of longevity, and bronze cauldrons for water in the event of fire. The Hall of Supreme Harmony is closed for renovations, but is due to reopen at the end of 2007.

After Taihedian comes **Zhonghedian (Hall of Middle Harmony)**, venue for rehearsals and receptions for officials from the Ministry of Rites. Then comes the **Baohedian (Hall of Preserving Harmony)**, where the emperor gave banquets to princes from vassal states on Lunar New Year's Eve. Here, during the Qing, the emperor supervised the final stage of the civil service examinations (see panel, page 67).

As you leave the Baohedian, before you, protected by two gilded lions, is the **Qianqingmen (Gate of Heavenly Purity)**, the gateway to the inner court, in many ways the true seat of power. Proceed through here and come to the **Qianqinggong (Palace of Heavenly Purity)**, the emperor's bedroom and also the office of quotidian administration. Large banquets were given here on festival days. Behind it is the smaller **Jiaotaidian (Hall of Heavenly and Terrestrial Union)**, which was used for lesser ceremonies. The empress raised silk-worms here to demonstrate her industry, and the building was also used to house the imperial seals. You then come to the **Kunninggong (Palace of Terrestrial Tranquillity**, symbol of the earth), the empress' bedroom and, under the Qing, the emperor's bridal chamber. Behind the palaces is the **Imperial Garden** and the north exit, the **Shenwumen (Gate of Divine Prowess)**.

Two longer routes also bring you to the Shenwumen. Turn left before the Qianqingmen and then right, and walk along an alley to the left of the Qianqinggong; a gateway on the left leads to the concubines' quarters. Among them is the **Yangxindian (Hall of Mental Cultivation)**, the residence of the emperors from 1723. Within, to the right, is the **Dongnuange (East Chamber of Warmth)**. Here the boy emperors were told how to conduct affairs of state by the dowager empresses, who sat behind a screen.

Turn right before Qianqingmen, pass under a portico, bear diagonally left to a doorway and emerge into a courtyard. On the left is a building housing the **Imperial Clock Collection**. This was where Emperor Qianlong lived after his retirement. Return through the doorway, turn left and left again, and you come to the **Nine Dragon Screen**. Opposite is a doorway. Go as straight as you can, pass on the left the painting exhibition, and eventually reach the exhibition halls of imperial treasure. From here you can easily find your way to the exit gate.

A Forbidden City dragon, symbol of the emperor, chasing the 'flaming pearl'

55

GREAT WALL INFO

• In China, the Great Wall is also known as the '10,000 Li Wall', *li* being an ancient Chinese measure of distance, while the figure 10,000 simply expresses the magnitude of the project.

• It is a matter for debate whether the wall was ever truly successful as a means of defending the country. It is likely that its main functions were to provide a convenient conduit across difficult terrain and as a means of passing information.

Keeping the 'barbarians' out of the Middle Kingdom: a restored section of the Great Wall at Badaling, north of Beijing

▶▶▶ The Great Wall (Changcheng)   *Off 48C5*

Open: daily 7.30–7. Admission: moderate

The Great Wall is a symbol of Chinese genius. Although the present wall dates mainly from the Ming dynasty, at least 20 states and dynasties were involved in its construction over a period of 2,000 years, following different routes or building extensions according to need. Stretching 6,000km (3,730 miles), the wall was garrisoned by up to 1 million soldiers and was complemented by over 1,000 fortified passes and 10,000 beacon towers. Walls were first built as barriers between states during the Spring and Autumn period—the oldest was built by the Kingdom of Qi in 500BC and extended for 480km (298 miles). When China was finally united in 221BC under the Qin, the existing walls were linked together to protect the new China from invaders from the north. Different building materials were used according to the terrain—rammed earth or stone and brick (as in the Ming wall). Thousands of conscripts were involved in the project, many of whom died of exhaustion and malnutrition. The Han emperor extended the wall, but it was not until the Ming dynasty in the 14th century that an imperial regime was to have total control over its entire length again. The early Ming emperors almost entirely rebuilt the wall, extending it westwards over 6,400km (3,975 miles) from Shanhaiguan to Jiayuguan. It was never to play such a significant role in again—with the advent of the Manchus, who controlled the territory on both sides, the wall fell into disrepair.

Visitors head for the restored section at **Badaling**, 72km (45 miles) northwest of Beijing. You need a ticket to climb on to the wall; you will find the less crowded (but steeper) side to the left. Another access point is at **Mutianyu**, (80km/50 miles northeast), which is less crowded but not

TOURS FROM BEIJING

Many hotels organize tours to the Great Wall. Otherwise, tourist buses regularly depart for Badaling from Qianmen, Beijing Railway Station, Dongdaqiao and Beijing Zoo. For Mutianyu, buses leave from Dongzhimen Bus Station or by the Great Hall of the People. Tourist minibus No. 1 for the Ming Tombs leaves regularly from Qianmen.

as well preserved. A cable-car operates at Badaling to ease congestion. Other sections open to foreigners are at **Simatai**, **Huanghua** and **Jinshanling** and are much less commercialized.

▶ The Ming Tombs (Shisanling)   *Off 48C5*

Open: daily 7.30–6. Admission: expensive

The tombs of the Ming emperors are about 24km (15 miles) from the Great Wall and 50km (31 miles) north of Beijing. Only 13 of the 16 emperors are buried here—the first Ming emperor is buried at Nanjing. The second emperor's whereabouts are unknown, and the seventh emperor is buried somewhere in Beijing. Three tombs are open: **Dingling**, tomb of the 13th emperor (died 1620), and the only excavated tomb; **Changling**, the largest, tomb of the third emperor (reigned 1403–24); and **Zhaoling**.

The search for a burial site, based on the rules of geomancy (or *feng shui*, wind and water), was started by the third emperor in 1407. Rolling hills form a screen to the north, Dragon Hill and Tiger Hill stand to the south, and the Wenyu river provides the water element. The tomb area, once surrounded by a 40km (25-mile) wall, is approached via a sacred way. It begins at a commemorative gateway (perhaps the finest in China) erected in 1541, passes through a vermilion gatehouse and then between stone animal and human figures. After another gatehouse, the road diverges to the tombs, each marked with a yellow-roofed 'visible tower'. The vault at Dingling has vases, marble thrones and doors, and reconstructed coffins. Some of the treasure is exhibited above ground. Changling, although unexcavated, is grander, and has an exhibition of some of the treasures found at Dingling in the magnificent main hall.

Changling ('Long-lasting Tomb'), one of 13 tombs of the Ming emperors occupying a burial site north of Beijing

57

Guards in mock Ming period costume stand sentinel on the Great Wall at Badaling

CHINESE NURSERY RHYME
The Emperor of Qin Shihuangdi
Built a wall
From the hills to the sea.
He built it wide,
He built it stout
To keep his subjects in
And the Tartars out,
The Emperor of Qin.

Since 1949, Beijing has experienced destruction, both deliberate (zealous town planning) and spontaneous (Cultural Revolution). But pockets of magnificence survive amid a network of anaemic boulevards.

URBAN CHINA
The old walled city was considered a perfect example of Chinese town-planning theory, which extends back to the Warring States Period (475–221BC). It is rectangular, surrounded by a wall; its palace, close to government ministries, is in the middle. It is also excellently situated according to geomantic criteria—open to the south and east, with water at the front and well screened by mountains to the north, to protect the city from evil.

58

The great tower gate at Dongbianmen, a reminder of the city wall's former grandeur

Imperial cities Beijing still exudes greatness, partly because the street-plan devised under the Ming remains to remind the visitor of its 'celestial geometry'. But as recently as the 1950s Beijing would have looked like a very different place.

Under the Manchus (the Qing dynasty), Beijing was divided in four. The innermost city was the walled Forbidden City. Outside the Forbidden City lay the Imperial City, where government officials resided. This, too, lay behind a wall, the remains of which still stand (by the north side of Tiananmen Square) and behind which today's government officials continue their work. The whole was surrounded by the 15th-century city wall. During the Qing, this wall enclosed what foreigners called the Tartar City, the northern part of Beijing reserved for Manchus, particularly troops. The southernmost point of the Tartar City wall was the southern margin of Tiananmen Square, today marked by two ancient towers, which were part of the northern wall of the Chinese City. The latter was where the Chinese were compelled to live; its walls extended originally south to beyond the Temple of Heaven. This was the business area of the city. The attempt to separate Manchu and Chinese inevitably failed—although the walls survived until the 1950s, their purpose had long been forgotten.

The streets outside the areas of the Imperial Court ran north–south and east–west, and were lined with low buildings in grey brick that surrounded family courtyards. At strategic points throughout the city were the imperial temples, visited by the emperor at certain propitious times of year (the Temple of Heaven was one, but there were also the Temples of the Earth, Sun and Moon, which still survive).

The city walls The city walls, of rammed earth

with a carapace of grey brick, were thought to be the finest and grandest in the world. They were an astounding 40km (25 miles) in length and up to 4m (13ft) in height. There were 16 gateways, each surmounted by a tower, and the whole was surrounded by a moat. In winter its frozen water was cut out and preserved underground to be used in the summer. The streets within the walls were a riot of hues and movement—silken pennants hung outside stores and offices, and all manner of noises and smells mingled together in the bustle of activity. It is still possible to experience something of this atmosphere by walking through what is left of the old shopping district of Qianmen, to the south of Tiananmen Square, especially along Dazhalan. Sections of the walls have been rebuilt.

PLEASURE DOMES
After the Japanese took control of Beijing in 1937 opium dens were openly allowed in parts of the city. Attendants brought smokers opium, a pipe, an oil lamp and a pin. Addicts speared the opium on the pin and heated it before inhaling the fumes.

Beijing's Bell Tower, a little way north of the Forbidden City

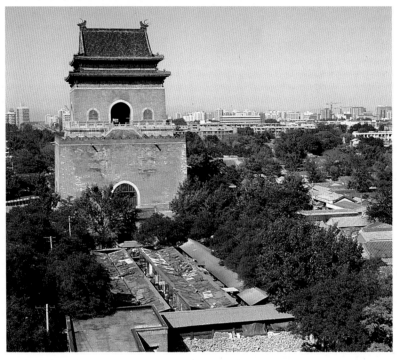

59

The Legation Oddly enough, one of the areas of the city that still retains the sort of charm that comes with continuity is not really Chinese at all, but European. Many of the buildings of the old Legation area east of Tiananmen Square still stand and provide a sort of leafy graciousness absent elsewhere in the city. In the late 19th century the Legation area was less compact, but following the Boxer Rebellion of 1900 it was decided it was safer to group the legations together in a compound, with its own crenellated wall.

Beijing was also celebrated for its *hutongs*, the network of alleys and traditional courtyards, most of which have now disappeared. However, the areas between Wangfujing and the east wall of the Forbidden City, or the areas between Wangfujing and Dongdan, still give much of the character of old Beijing.

HIGH FLYERS
In the past, kite-flying was a preferred pastime, frequently to be seen all over the city and particularly at New Year, when markets sold a multitude of kites made of bamboo and paper in a variety of shapes, including birds, goldfish and mythical characters. Nowadays, kites are still flown in Tiananmen Square—an uplifting sight.

The Summer Palace

The walk through the Summer Palace, described in detail on pages 61–63, is essentially scenic. Enter through the East Palace Gate, then bear right, and carry straight on to pass near the main halls that were used by the last emperors. Walk along the Long Corridor, the covered walkway that runs beside Kunming Lake, visiting more of the pavilions to the right. A detour at the beginning will take you to the Garden of Harmonious Interest with its own miniature lake. You can return to the entrance by taking a ferry from close to the Marble Boat.

Taking a rest in the Long Corridor

These women in Qing costume are attendants at the museum of performance in the Summer Palace

▶▶▶ Summer Palace (Yiheyuan)   48A5

Open: daily 9–7. Admission: moderate

The buildings of the Summer Palace, known as Yiheyuan, date back only to the turn of the 20th century. The site, however, goes back to the 12th century when the first Jin ruler built his Gold Mountain Travelling Palace on what is now Longevity Hill. The water from the Jade Spring was diverted to form the Gold Sea, an early Kunming Lake. During the Yuan dynasty, the Gold Mountain was renamed Jug Mountain, and the lake was enlarged. Another palace was built here under the Ming, but the area was transformed during the reign of the Qianlong Emperor. Longevity Hill was named to commemorate the 60th birthday of Qianlong's mother, and the Kunming Lake in memory of a lake near Xi'an that the Han emperors used for naval exercises.

In 1764, the area became the Park of Pure Ripples (Qingyiyuan) and was part of a grand plan to build a set of pleasure grounds in the lee of the Western Hills. Aside from Qingyiyuan, there was to be Jingmingyuan at Yuquanshan, Jingyiyuan at Xiangshan, Changchunyuan

BENEFICENT BOVINE
At the mainland end of the Seventeen-Arch Bridge in the Summer Palace is the Bronze Ox, which has been guarding Kunming Lake for more than 200 years. Its presence is based on the legend that said that the Great Yu tamed lakes and rivers by throwing oxen made of iron into the water.

EXCLUSIVE PEKING
Non cuivis Homini Contingit adire Corinthium. It is the lot of few to go to Pekin.—John Barrow, Lord Macartney's Private Secretary. *Travels in China*, 1801

Beijing

THE GARDEN OF PURE BRIGHTNESS
Although all that is left of the Yuanmingyuan are romantic ruins, it once included a labyrinth, an aviary, a gazebo, palaces with fountains, and representations of the countryside of Turkestan with moving scenery. Engravings of the pleasure dome by the Jesuits are to be found in the British Museum, London, and the Bibliothèque Nationale, Paris.

and Yuanmingyuan. The last mentioned, the Park of Perfection and Brightness, was the original Qing dynasty Summer Palace, destroyed in 1860 by the British and French; by 1895 a replacement was constructed in the Park of Pure Ripples, but when the Anglo-French force reinvaded Beijing in 1900, the new Summer Palace was destroyed. Reconstruction began in 1902, and the result is what we see today. The Summer Palace became a classical Chinese garden, the south face of Longevity Hill laid out in vague imitation of Hangzhou's West Lake, the north face following the architectural style of Suzhou. After 1908, the palace was no longer used by the imperial family, and in 1924, it became a public park.

The main entrance is at **Donggongmen (East Palace Gate)**, which leads to the **Renshoudian (Hall of Benevolence and Longevity**, derived from an old saying 'Benevolent people live long lives'), where affairs of state were conducted by Cixi. The grey-roofed buildings between the gate and the hall were the waiting rooms for officials on duty. The bronze *qilin* (a legendary beast with dragon's head, lion's tail, deer's antlers, ox's hooves and fish-scaled body) in front of the hall was at the original Summer Palace.

To the right of the Renshoudian is the **Deheyuan (Court of Virtuous Harmony)** with its theatre, the largest in China, where Cixi watched performances of Peking Opera. Trapdoors in the ceilings and floors of its three levels were designed for the entrances and exits of supernatural characters. Beyond the Renshoudian is the former residential area; here the first and principal building is the **Leshoutang (Hall of Joyful Longevity)**, the residence of the Dowager Empress between May and November. South of the Leshoutang, at the waterfront and to the rear of the Renshoudian, is the **Yulantang (Hall of Jade Billows)**, named after a poem by Lu Ji, a third-century poet, the former residence of the Guangxu Emperor. The interiors of the Leshoutang and Yulantang have been preserved intact. The side halls of the Yulantang were blocked off in 1898 on the instructions of Cixi, thereby confining the Guangxu Emperor to house arrest for his involvement in the 1898 'Hundred Days of Reform' movement.

A remnant of the south façade of the waterworks at Yuanmingyuan, the Old Summer Palace

Farther west along Kunming Lake is the famous **Changlang (Long Corridor)**, a covered walkway 730m (2,395ft) long, painted with views of the famous West Lake in Hangzhou and scenes from Chinese legend, history or literature. It breaks into two halves at the **Paiyundian (Cloud Dispelling Hall,** from a poem by the third-century poet Guo Pu), where Cixi celebrated her birthdays. Built on the site of an earlier Ming temple, the tower above is called the **Foxiangge (Pagoda of Buddhist Fragrance)**. Behind the pagoda is the **Zhihuihai (Sea of Wisdom Temple)**, covered in religious statues, many disfigured by troops in 1860. To the east of the pagoda is the **Zhuanluncang (Revolving Scripture Repository)**, containing a tablet inscribed with an essay on Kunming Lake in the hand of the Qianlong Emperor.

The Long Corridor continues and passes the **Tingliguan (Pavilion for Listening to Orioles)** on the right, the site of a restaurant and shop. The corridor comes to an end at the corner of the lake. In front of you to the right is the **Marble Boat**, an ironic reminder that the funds appropriated by the Dowager Empress to reconstruct the Summer Palace had been earmarked for the Chinese navy. During the summer, pleasure cruises run from here back to the entrance. You can hire rowing-boats from the nearby jetty.

The way to the **West Palace Gate** lies beyond the Marble Boat. An old Japanese-built steamboat, formerly part of the Chinese navy, lies in dry dock near the old boat-houses. Beyond is a beautiful arched bridge in the south China style.

The north and northeast areas of the palace gardens are in quiet contrast to the showy areas at the lakeside. In the northeast corner is the **Xiequyuan (Garden of Harmonious Interest)**, a series of small pavilions around a landscaped miniature lake. Opposite its entrance is a staircase up the hill to **Jinfuge (Tower of Great Fortune)**, which has a fine view to South Lake Isle and the magnificent Seventeen-Arch Bridge. The area of the **North Palace Gate** was badly affected by the French and British invasion. Following the restoration work in 1998, the tea-houses and shops at Suzhou Creek are now open, revitalizing a part of the Summer Palace that had fallen into decay and which was hardly ever visited. In addition, there is a **Cultural Relics' Hall**, housing the palace's collection of Qing dynasty art.

Also in the northwest suburbs (Bus 375) are the remains of the **Old Summer Palace▶**, Yuanmingyuan, razed by the British and French in 1860. This is mostly still in ruins, but a brick maze with a central pavilion has been restored.

An imperial folly: the Marble Boat on Kunming Lake

LAKE OF POETICAL INSPIRATION
Kunming Lake in the Summer Palace is as famous as the West Lake in Hangzhou. The Ming poet Wen Zheng wrote: 'The sun sets on blue waters of the spring lake. Sky-high pavilions are reflected down below. The *tenli* green hills are like a scroll painting. Two white birds fly high in a scene of watery land.'

IMPERIAL STAFF
The Dowager Empress liked to travel with a retinue of at least 1,000. Her arrival at the rebuilt Summer Palace in 1905 was met by 458 eunuchs, and her two main meals consisted of 100 dishes.

Beijing

64

MAO'S MEMORIAL HALL
Mao's resting place was built by 70,000 volunteers in 10 months between October 1976 and August 1977. It is screened by pine trees from Yan'an, recalling the 13 years Mao spent there. Within is an air-conditioned hush, a white statue of a seated Mao gazing prophetically in front of a giant landscape tapestry based on a design by the contemporary painter Huang Yongyu. Mao himself lies in state in a crystal coffin.

HEROIC WORK
The granite obelisk known as the Monument to the People's Heroes is inscribed with the calligraphy of Chairman Mao. It reads 'The people's heroes are invincible'.

Tiananmen Square, backed by the Gate of Heavenly Peace

▶▶▶ Temple of Heaven (Tiantan) Park 49D1

Open: daily 8–5. Admission: moderate

Built in 1420, Tiantan became part of the city during the Qing, when the Manchus extended the city walls. It is China's most famous temple and stands within 270ha (667 acres) of park. Entrance was originally through the west gate, but is now via the north or south gates.

The whole area is enclosed by a wall, the northern portion of which is round (heaven) and the southern half square (earth). The principal buildings are at either end of the Cinnabar Stairway Bridge. **Qiniandian (Hall of Prayer for Good Harvests)** is to the north and is an 1890 replica of the building destroyed by lightning the preceding year.

It was here that the emperor came to pray for a good harvest during the first lunar month each year. The day before the main ceremony was devoted to minor rituals, after which the emperor fasted in the Hall of Abstinence, west of the causeway. The sacrifice to heaven was made in the Qiniandian. Constructed without nails, this has wooden mortise and tenon joints and wooden brackets on supporting pillars. The 28 pillars (representing the constellations) are made of *nannu* hardwood. The four large ones represent the seasons, the 12 inner pillars are the months of the lunar calendar and the outer 12 are the two-hour periods into which the day was traditionally divided. Together they become the 24 solar periods of the year.

At the end of the causeway is the **Echo Wall**, inside which is the **Huangqiongyu (Imperial Vault of Heaven)**. This was where the spirit tablet of the Supreme Ruler of Heaven was stored, which, during the ceremony of the winter solstice, was moved to the vast round Altar of Heaven to the south.

▶▶▶ Tiananmen (Gate of Heavenly Peace) Square (Guangchang) 49D2

Today's vast, grandiose space, scene of tragic student demonstrations in 1989, bears little resemblance to its imperial ancestor. During the Ming and Qing, it was narrower, and in addition to the Tiananmen Gate to the

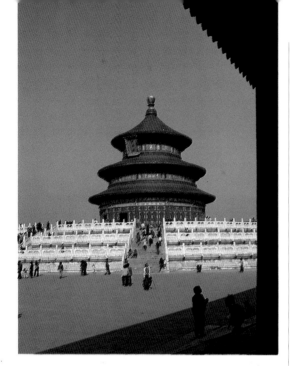

ECHO CHAMBER
The Temple of Heaven is renowned for its acoustic qualities. Most famous is the Echo Wall, where your whispered words are amplified to a listener opposite. In the same compound is the Imperial Vault of Heaven, before which are several flagstones—depending upon where you stand on them, the sound made by clapping your hands will echo once, twice or three times. If you speak in the middle of the Imperial Altar, your voice will echo back louder.

The Hall of Prayer for Good Harvests, Temple of Heaven

A watchful 'lion' atop one of the ceremonial columns (huabiao) *in front of the Tiananmen Gate*

Imperial City (which still stands), there were two more gates on today's Chang'an Avenue and another, to the south, where the Qianmen now stands. It was surrounded by a vermilion wall beside which ran a covered corridor for use by officials. To the east and west were the imperial ministries. After 1949, most of this was torn down and replaced with what you see today. Each sunrise the national flag is hoisted with military precision. The square is now open to the public.

The **Tiananmen Gate** has survived since 1651. The central bridge over the Outer Golden Water Stream forms part of the Imperial Way, used on ceremonial occasions and over which only the emperor could pass. Two columns are surmounted by dishes containing a stone lion-like creature. The dishes were to catch the 'jade dew' imbibed by the emperor to ensure longevity; the lions were to watch over him if he were away from the palace.

Along the spine of the square, north to south, are the **Monument to the People's Heroes** (1958), **Chairman Mao's Memorial Hall**, where Mao lies in state (*Open* Tue, Thu, Sat 8–11.30, 2–5, Wed, Fri 8–11.30. *Admission free*), the **Arrow Tower** and **Qianmen**. On the west side is the **Great Hall of the People**—opposite is the revamped **Museum of the Chinese Revolution** and the **Museum of Chinese History** (*Open* Tue–Sun 8.30–3.30. *Admission: inexpensive*), one of the most important in China.

Beijing

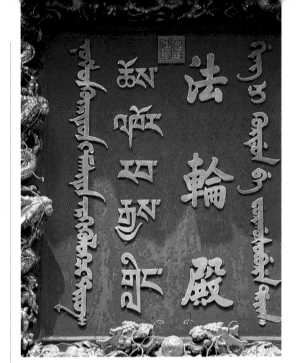

EAST IS BEST
Before the break with the
USSR in 1960, Mao was
confident of a shared,
bright future. In Moscow
in 1957 he said: 'I believe
it is characteristic of the
situation today that the
East Wind is prevailing
over the West Wind. That
is to say, the forces of
socialism have become
overwhelmingly superior
to the forces of imperial-
ism.'

*Polyglot inscriptions in
Mongolian, Manchurian,
Tibetan and Chinese
welcome visitors to the
Lama Temple*

*An equinoctial sphere,
one of the beautiful
scientific instruments
to be seen at the Ancient
Observatory*

Other sights

Lama Temple (Yonghegong)▶▶ (Andingmen Dong Lu.
Open daily 9–4.30. *Admission: inexpensive*). Built in 1694 by
the Kangxi Emperor as a residence for his son, Yinzhen,
Yonghegong was partly turned over to the Lamaists for
scripture recitation when Yinzhen became emperor. It is
an extravagant building of some beauty, with remarkable
examples of joinery and craftsmanship, and consists of a
series of courtyards and pavilions, many with statues of
the various incarnations of the Buddha. In the middle of
the **Hall of Infinite Happiness (Wanfuge)**, at the rear,
stands the grandest statue, a 26m (85ft) Tathagata
(Maitreya) Buddha, made from a single sandalwood
trunk. Tibet's China-appointed Panchen Lama was sworn
in here in 1995.

The Western Hills (Xi Shan)▶▶ This is an area of recreation and worship, excellent both for sightseeing and
strolling (*Temples open* daily 8.30–5). Here you may visit the
Temple of the Reclining Buddha (Wofosi), where a bronze
Buddha instructs his disciples from his deathbed. Weighing
250,000kg (550,000lb), it dates from the Yuan dynasty. The
Temple of Azure Clouds (Biyunsi) dates back 600 years. In
the **Hall of Arhats** are 500 statues of Buddha's disciples, and
at the rear is the **Sun Yatsen Memorial Hall**, where Sun
Yatsen, the revolutionary and former Provisional President,
lay in state after his death in 1925 (see page 229).

Part of the area is known as the **Fragrant Hills Park
(Xiangshan Gongyuan)**, formerly the emperor's pleasure
park. Now it is a recreation area with a cable-car.

Churches▶ The Jesuits, who became active in China
during the Ming dynasty, bequeathed several churches.
The grandest (Nantang) is found at 181 Qianmen Xidajie.

A building was erected on the site in the 16th century, but the current version is from 1904. Another church is at 74 Wangfujing. The North Cathedral is on Xishiku.

The Ancient Observatory (Guanxiangtai)▶ (*Open* Wed–Sun 9.30–11.30, 1–4.30. *Admission: inexpensive*). Not far from the Friendship Store, mounted on a section of old wall just off Jianguomenwai Dajie, are the remnants of an observatory which can be traced back to the Yuan dynasty. It was built between 1437 and 1446 to provide astrological predictions. Within is a display of navigational equipment, reproductions of ancient Chinese maps and other items relating to the stars. Outside, on the parapet, are instruments designed by the Jesuits, who in 1601 gained permission to work with Chinese scientists eager to learn about European firearms. The emperor, impressed by the Jesuits' scientific knowledge, later appointed them court astronomers in place of his Muslim advisers. The instruments are not all original but are of considerable beauty. There is also a small museum.

Beijing Zoo▶ (Xizhimenwei Dajie. *Open* daily 7.30–6. *Admission: inexpensive*). The zoo itself is not representative of enlightened animal management, but the animals look healthy, and there are several examples of China's rarities, notably pandas (giant and red) and golden monkeys.

Underground City▶ A network of tunnels honeycombs Beijing's subterranean depths, a result of the fear in the 1960s of a Soviet attack. Part of the system now includes shops and even a hotel, but the main interest lies in the entrances, several of which are concealed beneath sliding floors in busy shops above ground.

Other temples▶ The ruins of the former imperial temples can still be seen in Beijing—in the north is **Ditan (Temple of the Earth)**; to the south is **Taoranting (Happy Pavilion Park)**; to the east is **Ritan (Temple of the Sun)**; and to the west is **Yuetan (Temple of the Moon)**. Although these resemble parks more than temples, hints of their past abound, and they are interesting places to observe Chinese

EXAMINATION HALL
Opposite the Ming observatory, to the north, were the former imperial examination halls—8,500 brick cells where, every three years, candidates were locked in for three days and two nights to take the first stage of the civil service examinations that led to high office. In operation for over 2,000 years, these examinations ceased in 1900, and the halls were demolished in 1913.

67

Beitang, the North Cathedral, with its defiantly European façade, stands stiff behind curving Chinese roof profiles

Listening in at the Echo Wall, Temple of Heaven

HANDFULS OF DUST
One of the quirks of Beijing weather in the spring is the dust that arrives in clouds from the Gobi Desert.

The open space of Longtan Park provides a peaceful setting for early morning meditation

life, especially in the early morning. The **Confucian Temple (Kongmiao)** (*Open* daily 8.30–5. *Admission: inexpensive*) is on Guozijian Jie, an interesting street spanned by commemorative arches. The **Baiyun Temple (White Cloud Temple)** (*Open* daily 9–4. *Admission: expensive*), on Binhe Lu near the southwest corner of the old city was once the heart of Taoism, while the **Niujie Mosque** is in a Muslim area in the southwest of Beijing. The **Five Pagoda Temple (Wutasi)** is northwest of the zoo, while the **Great Bell Temple (Dazhongsi)**, on Beisanhuan Xi Road, has a 47.5-tonne bell, cast in 1406.

West of Beijing (Bus 336) is the ancient **Tanzhi Buddhist Temple►►** (*Admission: inexpensive*), the largest in the area. It dates back to the 3rd century AD and contains decorative features not found elsewhere in Beijing.

Marco Polo Bridge (Lugouqiao)► This bridge 16km (10 miles) southwest of Beijing (Bus 339), mentioned by the Italian explorer, dates back to the late 12th century, but most of the present edifice is from the 17th century.

Qing Tombs► The tombs of the Qing emperors are divided into two groups: Western Qing (Xiling) and Eastern Qing (Dongling). The former are 113km (70 miles) southwest of Beijing and include the excavated tomb of Emperor Guangxu at Chongling, the last to be built (between 1905 and 1915). The latter are 129km (80 miles) east of Beijing and are more impressive, having a 'spirit way', or avenue lined with bridges and statues to guard the tomb. The tombs of Emperor Qianlong and Dowager Empress Cixi are open.

Other parks► Beijing boasts a number of parks. The **Longtan Park (Longtanyuan)** is east of the Temple of Heaven; the **Purple Bamboo Park (Zizhuyuan)** is west of the zoo; and the **Yuyuantan Park** is in the west of the city. The area around the moat of the Forbidden City is also popular.

Other museums and galleries► The **Soong Qingling Museum (Soong Qingling Guju)** is the former residence of the wife of Sun Yatsen, the founder of the Republic of China. The **China Art Gallery (Zhongguo Meishuguan)** is of interest, particularly when there are temporary exhibitions. The **Lu Xun Museum (Lu Xun Bowuguan)** is dedicated to the career of the revolutionary writer.

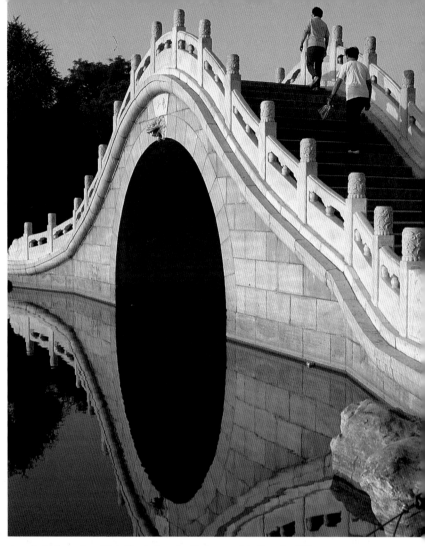

A perfectly formed marble bridge in Longtan Park, east of the Temple of Heaven

Cycle ride

From Tiananmen Square

See *highlighted route*, page 49. Bicycles can be hired from most hotels very cheaply. Start near Tiananmen Square and go up Beiheyan Street, just east of the Forbidden City. At a main intersection (Wusi Street), turn left and then right, by Jingshan Park. Follow the road as it goes left, then turn right along Di'anmennei, cross an intersection and continue to the old Drum Tower. Bear right, then left and then take the second lane on the left to bring you to Jiugulou, near the Bamboo Garden Hotel (Zhuyuan Binguan), former home of a Qing official. Turn south down Jiugulou, then right, then left along narrow streets to cross Qianhai Lake. Go left, to Di'anmen Xi Street; turn right and then left and follow streets south beside Beihai Lake and Nanhai Lake to return to Tiananmen Square.

The garden of the Fragrant Hills Hotel outside Beijing, designed by Chinese-American architect I. M. Pei

The five-star Guoji (International), typical of Beijing's modern hotels

Hotels

The standard of hotels is now high in Beijing. The number of top-end hotels is expanding fast, fuelled by China's booming economy, surging inbound tourism and the 2008 Olympics. More affordable mid-range and budget hotels are also opening. The Beijing Municipal Tourism Bureau is aiming for more than 800 star-rated hotels with 130,000 rooms by the Olympics—double the number in 2000.

A central location is somewhat less important in Beijing than in other major cities, as many of the principal sights are outside the city, and heavy traffic can make a journey across Beijing frustratingly long. However, several hotels are within walking distance of Tiananmen Square, one being the former Beijing Hotel, which reopened in June 2006 after a six-month refurbishment as the Raffles Beijing Hotel. Originally the Wagon Lits Hotel, the century-old landmark building's elegant, restored interior has French and Oriental influences, five Grand suites and four stylish, pricey restaurants. The adjacent Grand Hotel Beijing has a bar overlooking the Forbidden City. The Holiday Inn on Wangfujing and nearby luxury Peninsula Palace also enjoy excellent central locations. Other quality central Beijing hotels include the Guoji (International), New Otani, Gloria Plaza, Shangri La's China World Hotel, the Novotel Peace Hotel and the Taiwan.

Several luxury hotels are in Beijing's northeast corner. The Great Wall Sheraton, with its striking exterior, is efficient, expensive, comfortable, and rather soulless. Nearby are the Kunlun, the Kempinski and the Hilton. In the same area is the Zhaolong, which was reborn as a five-star hotel in 2002 after extensive renovations. The Shangri La Beijing, in the northwest of the city, is adding a new tower with 150 rooms, a health club connected to a separate floor of

HOUSING SHORTAGE
When Beijing first opened to foreigners, there was a severe shortage of hotels. As tourism expanded in the early 1980s, things got out of hand. Groups of tourists landed at Beijing airport only to be placed on the next flight out because there was nowhere to accommodate them. Or they arrived to be told that they were staying in Tianjin (several hours away) and would be driven to Beijing each day for sightseeing.

luxury spa suites, conference facilities, and a rooftop garden with a jogging track. The Jianguo is reasonably central, near the Friendship Store. It was the first foreign-designed hotel to appear in Beijing (in 1982) and remains one of the best. The Jinglun next-door (formerly the Beijing Toronto) is of equal standard.

Among new hotels to debut in 2007 is the Park Hyatt, with 237 rooms between the 47th and 54th floors of a 63-storey twin tower building capped by a glass Chinese lantern-style roof soaring four floors and incorporating the 60th-floor lobby, restaurants and bars.

Outside the city there is the luxurious Fragrant Hills Hotel (Xianshan Hotel) in the park of the same name. It is convenient for the Summer Palace and Great Wall, though somewhat less so for the city.

The Lido Holiday Inn is not in the luxury bracket, but is comfortable enough and is well placed for Beijing's airport, although less convenient for the city centre. There is a Mövenpick hotel at the airport itself, and the airport has a hotel desk, beyond customs.

Beijing has a number of less expensive hotels built in the 1950s, before the open-door policy. The Friendship Hotel, a sprawling building on the road to the Summer Palace, was originally constructed for Russian experts, but now houses many of the new wave of 'foreign experts', and is reasonably comfortable. The Qianmen (Front Gate) is another modernized hotel dating from the Russian period, and has a good location on Yong'an Lu in a vibrant part of Beijing.

At the cheaper end of the market there are a few reasonable propositions, among them the three-star Haoyuan, tucked away down a hutong alley east of Wanfujing. There are also hotels and hostels with triples or dormitory-style rooms, such as the Jinghua, Xiluoyuan Nanli, Yongdingmenwai (tel: 8781 2211) and Leo Hostel, 750m (820 yards) south of Tiananmen Square (tel: 6303 1595). They are inexpensive but the barrack-like rooms, although likely to be clean, provide no privacy.

…traditional style—the Bamboo Garden

East meets West: Coca-Cola—made in China

Food and drink

In Beijing, it is now possible to sample most styles of Chinese and foreign cooking but it remains difficult to categorize the average restaurant for quality—most reliable restaurants are still to be found in the main hotels, although Beijing Tourism Administration is placing plaques on the doors of those restaurants it recommends. On the whole it is fairly difficult to eat badly, even in some of the shabbier establishments. Many ordinary restaurants have two floors—a utilitarian ground floor and an upper floor where the food usually will be more sophisticated, better presented and more expensive. If you want a full meal, then upstairs is a better proposition; if a snack, then confine yourself to the ground floor. The streets, meanwhile, are still filled with vendors selling tasty, inexpensive food.

Although Beijing cuisine is in the robust and rustic northern tradition, it has been subject to many influences throughout its long history and also has its own particular dishes, the most famous of which is 'Peking Duck'. Air is blown between the duck's skin and flesh, and then boiling water. The skin is covered in a malty solution after which the duck is hung and then roasted in a fruitwood oven. Strips are eaten wrapped in a pancake, with spring onions (scallions) and a bean sauce (*tianjiang*). There are a number of restaurants specializing in this dish, notably the Qianmen and Hepingmen branches of the Quanjude Kaoyadian, and also the Jiuhuashan on Zhengguang Lu. The Bianyifang Roast Duck Restaurant, at 2 Chongwenmenwai Dajie, has long been popular and is sworn to be the best in town by many Beijing residents. It's not at all expensive, offering a choice of fixed-menu-style service, preferred by many locals, or a more expensive à la carte selection. Similarly, the Dadong Roast Duck Restaurant, at 3 Tuanjiehu Beikou, Dongsanhuan, is one of the oldest and most highly recommended 'Peking Duck' restaurants in the city.

'Do-it-yourself' dining: one of the Mongols' tangible legacies, the Hotpot

'Peking Duck', complete with pancakes, scallions and tianjiang *sauce*

Another dish characteristic of Beijing (in winter) is the Mongolian Hotpot. Patrons cook thinly sliced mutton with vegetables and other ingredients at the table in a pot with a vertical funnel containing burning charcoal, which keeps the cooking liquid constantly boiling. The Hongbinlou and the Nengrenju restaurants are famous for this dish.

Another famous Chinese restaurant is Fangshan. It was established in 1925 by a former imperial cook on the site of an imperial dining room, which once stood on the island in the lake at Beihai Park. It specializes in imperial-style banquets or Manchu-Han feasts, which include 'all known or available delicacies from land and sea'. For example, the Eight Marine Delicacies include shark's fin and sea cucumber, the Eight Mountain Delicacies camel's hump and deer tendons. Advance bookings are essential.

Other recommended restaurants are the Fengzeyuan at 83 Zhushikou Xidajie, famous for seafood, soups and Beijing-style cooking; and the Duyichu at 36 Qianmen Street, specializing in steamed dumplings (*baozi*). The Sichuan at 14 Liuyin Jie, popular among high-level government officials, is housed in the palatial former mansion of a Qing prince and serves the excellent spicy food of Sichuan province.

Also recommended are the Cuihualou (Shandong), the Laozhengxing (Beijing and Shanghai style), the Xiheyaju Canting (Beijing style) and the Guangdong (Cantonese). The Kaorouji, which is just north of Beihai Park on the east bank of Qian Lake, specializes in Mongolian barbecued food. The Weiguncun Uighur Village on Baishiqiao Lu specializes in noodles and grilled mutton. The Bamboo Garden Hotel on Xiaoshiqiao Jiugulou Lu serves good Chinese food in a classical garden.

The standard of the best Chinese restaurants in the hotels is very high, with good service and presentation and prices to match. European and American food is of varying standard and often disappointing but all types are represented, mostly in the hotels. Otherwise, most hotels have coffee shops, some of which stay open until 11pm or later. There are many branches of McDonald's, KFC and Pizza Hut as American-style fast food becomes increasingly common.

PROVERB
An enigmatic saying in China goes: 'If you rattle your chopsticks against the bowl, you and your descendants will always be poor.'

FEAST FOOD
Imperial hospitality, like many things in old China, was rigorously graded. Dukes were to be treated to three morning meals and three evening banquets; counts to two in the morning and two in the evening; barons to one in the morning and one in the evening. Morning banquets were usually simply a matter of protocol; but in the evening guests were expected to 'remove their shoes and drink until wine-rapt'.

Beijing

WATCH OUT
It is worth keeping an eye out for interesting fob watches in antiques shops. Many were left by foreign residents living in China before 1949, and although a good one will be expensive, the price may compare well with the cost at home.

Guanyuan bird market in northwest Beijing

Shopping

Not long ago, the only place where you could buy high-quality goods was the Friendship Store on Jianguomen-wai Dajie. It remains one of the best shops in China, with three floors of beautiful merchandise. Within are two excellent food areas, one a supermarket and the other selling foreign and domestic-produced foods and drinks.

There has been a shopping revolution of late. The once-gloomy traditional shopping streets have been transformed into emporiums filled with the latest consumer goods. Try the local shops along Wangfujing that sell cotton and silk clothes at reasonable prices, toys, antiques and crafts. The Foreign Languages Bookstore is at No. 235, and No. 275 is the excellent Beijing Department Store Toy Shop. Other shops sell more pedestrian items, but

74

you may be able to buy some things cheaper than at the Friendship Store.

Atmospheric Liulichang Jie, lined with 18th-century antiques and crafts shops, was restored in 1981 and has just been renovated again. It has high-quality goods but few bargains.

The Qianmen area, south of Tiananmen Square, is the nearest you will get to the distinctive lanes of old Beijing. Many shops retain their original facades, carved or decorated with wrought iron, especially along the narrow lane of Dazhalan. Here are shops selling stationery, silks, Mongolian 'hot pots' and everyday clothes, and pharmacies with selections of traditional medicines using fungus, deer antlers and other unusual items—the best known is Tongrentang on Dazhalan.

Shops specializing in certain goods dot the city. The most famous shop for silk is the Yuanlong Silk Store at 55 Tiantan Lu. For teas, try the Zhangyiyuan Tea Company, with locations including 22 Dazhalan. For carpets, visit the Beijing Curio City at 21 Dongsanhuan Nanlu. For theatrical Peking Opera costumes and props, try the shop at 32 Xichaoshi Jie.

Although Beijing's street markets are not the most vibrant in China, it is still worth looking around them. The best market for antiques and curios is Panjiayuan (Sat–Sun 4.30am–5pm). At the northeast corner of the Temple of Heaven is the Hongqiao antiques market. The bird and fish market (*niao shi*), near the zoo on Xizhengmen, west of the Pinglani junction, is now indoors; while Shichahai Market on the south side of Houhai deals in flowers and birds. The original outdoor Silk Alley (Xiushui) clothes market was demolished in 2004 because of its reputation for knock-offs of branded goods. A sanitized, five-storey indoor version, with higher prices, has replaced it.

Western-style malls are also revolutionizing Beijing's shopping scene. The Golden Resources Shopping Mall became the world's largest when it opened in 2004. Other malls include the Lufthansa Centre in the Kempinski Hotel and the New World Shopping Centre at Fuchengmenwei, with some 200 shops. Fast-food outlets abound, and you can buy imported food from the supermarkets.

'I climbed the Great Wall' is the ubiquitous T-shirt slogan

SECOND-HAND SHOPS
State-owned commission shops were once the only official outlet for surplus or second-hand items. But changes in the law and higher living standards made them less popular and the shops have now all but disappeared. The best option today is a market, such as Panjiayuan, or shops along Liulichang Jie.

Liulichang, a short distance south of Tiananmen Square, is renowned for its antiques shops

Peking Opera is an ingenious and distinctive combination of elements from many sources: traditional music, poetry, singing, recitation, dancing, acrobatics and martial arts. In China there are more than a hundred types of traditional performance, with singing their common feature—it is a kind of singing drama, yet has little in common with Western opera.

Peking Opera: fascinating as a spectacle, it can sound unusual to Western ears

STAR LACKING SPARKLE
One of the greatest practitioners of Peking Opera was Mei Lanfang, who died in 1961. As a student he felt that his eyes were insufficiently lustrous for stardom. To remedy this, he exercised his eyes relentlessly by gazing at the flickers of an incense flame in a darkened room, by staring at soaring kites against a blue sky and by keeping pigeons so he could follow their flight. This, he concluded, gave him a pair of bright, keen, expressive eyes.

History Each type of Chinese opera uses the dialect of a particular area; Peking Opera is one such and grew out of several types of opera being staged in Beijing some 200 years ago. The demands for the performer are great—he or she must be attractive in make-up, of pleasing physical proportions, and have a pair of expressive eyes and a rich variety of facial expressions. A professional must train for up to 12 years.

Gestures and symbols Symbolism is all-important in Peking Opera, because the stage is generally bare. Gestures signify the opening of a door, entering or leaving a room, climbing a mountain or crossing a stream. Riding in a carriage is suggested by attendants standing on each side of the performer and holding flags painted with a wheel design. Walking in a circle indicates a long journey; a spotlight on two men somersaulting represents a fight at night, and so on. A Chinese proverb goes: 'Small as the stage is, a few steps will bring you far beyond heaven.'

The action is accompanied by continuous percussive music from the wings. The main instruments are gongs and drums, and clappers of hardwood and bamboo. A distinctively strong rhythmic pattern is produced; and the drummer, who is also the conductor, suggests emotions in co-ordination with the performer. The stringed instruments are the *jinghu* (Beijing fiddle) and the *erhu* (fiddle); the *yueqin* (moon-shaped mandolin); the *pipa* (a four-stringed lute) and *xianzi* (three-stringed lute). Sometimes a horn and a flute are used.

The words are both spoken (stylized) and sung (high-pitched). The spoken parts use Beijing dialect for clowns, frivolous females and children, and the dialect of Hubei and Anhui for grander, more serious roles. The melodies are set to a fixed pattern and are adapted from provincial folk songs, arranged to suit the action.

Roles The characters are classified according to age and personality. Female roles are *dan* and subdivided into 'quiet and gentle', 'vivacious or dissolute' and so on. Male roles are *sheng* and subdivided into 'old', 'young' and 'warrior'. The third role is *jing* (the painted face), people who are rustic and simple, or devious or dangerous. These are subdivided into principal, minor, civilian and warrior and are distinguishable by the hues and patterns of their make-up (rather heavy because originally opera was an open-air event) and costumes (based on those of the Ming dynasty). The clown (*chou*) is depicted by a dab of white on his face. Thus the moral standing of the characters is immediately obivous. The plot is insignificant—the appeal of the drama lies in the spectacle and the skill of the performers.

Action Some Westerners may find Peking Opera hard to endure at first. The spectacle is impressive and the reactions of the audience fascinating (there is no formality and much movement and comment), but the singing can seem unmelodious to the untrained ear. It is not without its subtleties, however, and is an integral part of the drama itself. Peking Opera is special in another way, too, because many of the dramas contain spectacular tumbling acrobatics.

Where to see Peking Opera Performances are held frequently in Beijing at the Liyuan Theatre, in the Qianmen Hotel; also at Prince Gong's Palace, the Lao She tea-house on Qianmen Dajie and at the ancient wooden playhouse, Zhengyici Daxilou, on Xiheyan Dajie.

Treading the boards: a performer in Chinese opera

Poster for a Chinese film being shown with English subtitles, starring Gong Li. Zhang Yimou is one of China's top film director

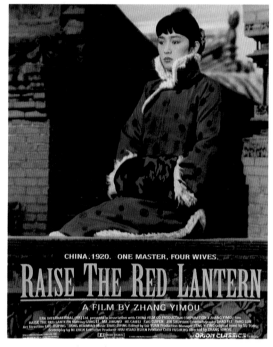

Nose-to-tail bicycle parking in Wangfujing

Entertainment and practical matters

Entertainment Beijing is not famous for its evening entertainment, although the situation has improved. For the casual visitor interested in sampling traditional culture, however, there is plenty to satisfy. Find out what is going on in *The China Daily* (the English-language newspaper) or the quarterly *Welcome to China, Beijing*; the monthly *Beijing This Month, Metrozine* and *That's Beijing*; or the weeklies *Beijing Weekend* and *Beijing Scene*, available at hotels.

There are many venues in Beijing, although the Guanghe Theatre at 24 Qianmen Dajie is the only old one. Performances are inexpensive, likely to cost just a few *yuan*, particularly if tickets are bought directly from the venue itself. At any one time Beijing's venues are likely to have on offer Peking Opera (frequently in the Zhengyici Daxilou and the auditorium of the Qianmen Hotel); a dance drama, in which a traditional story is told in dance and music; concerts ranging from classical Western music to ethnic music and dance, Chinese pop music or a mixture of all of the above. Acrobatics (presented nightly at the Poly Plaza on Baoli Dasha Juyuan) and puppetry are also on offer. A new feature is a revival of a Chinese music-hall at the Tianqiao Happy Tea Garden. The cinema is popular and some of the films produced in China have received international acclaim, among them *Yellow Earth* (1984), *Farewell My Concubine* (1993), *Red Sorghum* (1987), *Raise the Red Lantern* (1991) and *Crouching Tiger, Hidden Dragon* (2000). Chinese films are shown with English subtitles at Cherry Lane Movies on Liang Ma Qiao Lu.

Most of the major hotels have discos, and karaoke bars abound. Other discos include Island Club, 16 Tuanjiehu

Nanli, JJ's at 74 Xinjiekou Bei Dajie and the Blue Jays, 1km (0.5 miles) west of the Language and Cultural University opposite Wudaokou Market. Independent bars along Sanlitun Lu and by the Wudaokou Workers Club in Haidon often have live music. The International Club has tennis courts, a swimming pool, billiards and table tennis. There is a golf club near the Ming Tombs and, oddly, a rifle-range.

Practical matters The best way to get around is by taxi. There are different price scales more or less according to size—but the least expensive taxis are the so called '*xiali*' taxis. Hail and make sure that the meter is in use. You are advised not to use the pedicabs, certainly not without agreeing on a fare in advance. To obtain a taxi in advance, call the Capital Taxi Company (tel: 6232 8701). To hire a car with driver, call 8827 2020 or the Beijing Limo Company (tel: 6540 1588). The local bus service is comprehensive and inexpensive, but the buses are often very crowded (Nos 1, 4, 37 and 52 run east–west along Chang'an Avenue). Also, special double-decker buses travel continuous routes around the city's central area. Beijing is more than doubling the number of subway lines by 2010, including routes to the Olympic Village and Capital International Airport. The most useful is the circle line with stops at Beijing Railway Station, Qianmen (Tiananmen), the zoo and the Lama Temple.

Hiring a bicycle is feasible, but increasingly dangerous; it is advisable to spend a little time observing the traffic first.

Emergency numbers are 110 (Police), 119 (Fire) and 120 (Ambulance). Many hotels have clinics, and there is a First Aid Centre at 103 Qianmen Xi Dajie Among several hospitals the best is the Beijing Union Medical Hospital (Xiehe Yiyuan), 1 Shuaifuyuan, Wangfujing, tel: 6529 6114. Beijing International (SOS) Clinic, 1 Xingfu Sancun Bei Jie, tel: 6462 9100, offers 24-hour medical treatment.

Although most postal matters can usually be taken care of in hotels, some services may require a post office—the main one is on Yabao Lu, north of Jianguomen overpass.

The office of China International Travel Service (CITS), now known as Beijing Tourism Group, is at 28 Jianguomenwai Dajie, tel: 6515 8562.

MEDICAL WARNING
One of the less pleasant stories to come out of money-mad Peking in the 1980s was one concerning nurses who, it was alleged, were extorting high payments from patients before offering treatment. This situation has now changed but do check in advance how much you may be expected to pay.

79

Pedicabs, prolific in most Chinese cities, can be useful in heavy traffic, but be sure to agree on the fare in advance

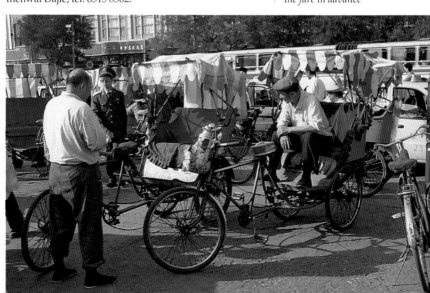

The North

MGL

0 100 200 300 400 km

0 100 200 miles

Duolun

Taibus Qi

Bayan
Óbo

NEI MENGGU ZIZHIQU

Yin Shan

Qahar
Youyi
Houqi

Zhangbei

Jining

Zhangjiakou

Xuanhua

**BEIJING
SHI**

Lang Shan

Wuyuan

Linhe

Hohhot

Baotou

Datong

Fengzhen

Yungang
Caves

**BEIJING
(PEKING)**

Dengkou

Huang He (Yellow)

(INNER MONGOLIA)

Dongsheng

Shuoxian

Hanging
Temple

Baoding

Wuhai

Helan Shan

Shizuishan

3556m

Yinchuan

Mu Us Shamo
(Ordos)

Shenmu

Shuoxian

Wutaishan

H E B E I

Yuanping

Zhengding

Hengshui

Dezhou

Shijiazhuang

Great Wall

S H A N X I

Taihang Shan

Wuzhong

Yulin

Taiyuan

Yangquan

Zhongwei

Dingbian

Suide

Lishi

Jinci

Yuci

Fen He

Xingtai

**NINGXIA
HUIZU
ZIZHIQU**

Luo He

Shuanglin

Pingyao

Jiexiu

Handan

Liupan Shan

Guyuan

Qingyang

Yan'an

Changzhi

Linxian

Anyang

Pingliang

Hancheng

Linfen

Wei He

Tongchuan

Yuncheng

Houma

Jiaozuo

Xinxiang

Tianshui

Tang Tombs

Xianyang

Weinan 2160m

Luoyang

Gongyi

Zhengzhou

Kaifeng

Baoji

Wei He

Xi'an

Huashan

Sanmenxia

Shaolin

Shangqiu

Han Tombs

Huaqing Hot Springs

Banpo

Shangxian

**Longmen
Caves**

Song Tombs

Xuchang

Bozhou

3767m

Qin Ling

Luanchuan

Pingdingshan

Luohe

Zhoukou

G A N S U

2192m

H E N A N

Hanzhong

S H A A N X I

Yunxian

Nanyang

Zhumadian

Fuyang

Xixiang

Danjiangkou
Sk

Huaibin

Guangyuan

Ankang

Shiyan

Laohekou

Luoshan

Wudang Shan

Fangxian

Xiangfan

Xinyang

Daba Shan

Suizhou

Anlu

Dabie Shan

S I C H U A N

Jialing Jiang

Han Shui

Macheng

Daxian

Yunyang

Fengjie Wushan

Zigui

H U B E I

Nanchong

Wanxian

Badong

Yichang

Jingmen

Tianmen

WUHAN

Jingmen

Huang He (Yellow River)

Da Yunhe (Grand Canal)

Zhengding

Linqing

Hengshui

Dezhou

Luan H

80

▶▶▶ REGION HIGHLIGHTS

Chengde Palace
page 85

**Longmen Buddhist
Caves** *page 93*

Taishan *pages 98–99*

Terracotta Warriors
pages 108–109

Xi'an *pages 105–107*

Yungang Caves *page 86*

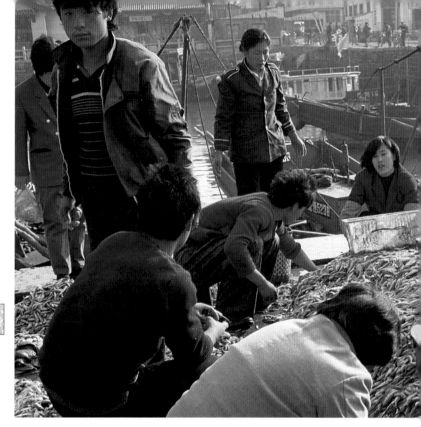

THE NORTH China—not counting Tibet, Xinjiang and Inner Mongolia—can be broadly divided into two: the area north of the Yangtze and that south of the Yangtze. Since the geographical and cultural reality is more complicated than that, 'the north' is generally taken to mean the area comprising the floodplain of the Yellow River (Huang He), where Chinese civilization is believed to have started. The Yellow River is known as 'China's Sorrow' because of its tendency to produce drastic floods. The north's boundaries are the Yangtze Valley in the south, Inner Mongolia to the north, Manchuria to the northeast and Gansu province, which is the corridor to the desert areas, in the northwest. It is composed of the provinces of Hebei, Shanxi, Henan, Shaanxi, Shandong and parts of Jiangsu and Anhui.

CROPS AND THE CLIMATE Climatically, the region is one of extremes. Summers are very hot, with average temperatures of 25°C (77°F) during July (more than 38°C/100°F is not uncommon). Winters, however, are long and cold (state housing is provided with heating in the north, but not in the south), with average January temperatures well below freezing. Snow is a rarity, but in spring northerly winds bring in sand from the Mongolian Gobi. The short autumn from September to October is the most pleasant time to visit.

Despite the heat, rice is not grown in the north because of the relative absence of water—instead wheat, millet and barley are cultivated, and cotton is grown after the harvest of winter wheat in June. Other crops include sorghum, sweet potatoes and seasonal vegetables, especially cabbages, beans, peppers, leeks and onions. Mulberry bushes are grown for the manufacture of silk, tobacco is an important cash crop, orchards are noted for apples, persimmons, pears and pomegranates, while rape, sunflower, sesame and peanuts are grown for oil.

Houses are traditionally of one floor with all the windows facing on to a courtyard. In the cities, these have largely been replaced by high-rise flats, but in the countryside many traditional-style homes survive and are still being built.

THE CHARACTER OF THE REGION The northern areas of China are still mostly Han (or ethnic Chinese)—with the exception of the Muslim Hui people, there are no minorities in the region. The north, with the capital Beijing, is still the focus of political power in China. Compared to the south, which has had links with the outside world for centuries, the north has been highly resistant to change.

But the north shares many characteristics with the rest of China, because the culture of the Han Chinese has been remarkably successful in maintaining continuity over the entire area of China for many centuries. That character was formed in the north of China, and it was under the leadership of a northern state, the Qin, that China was unified. It was further shaped by the constant threat of the barbarians from beyond the northern frontiers and by the fickle nature of the Yellow River.

Penglai, Shandong province: early morning shrimp harvest…

…and temple guardian figure

The North

THE LAST IMPERIAL GENERAL

Yuan Shikai, who tried to restore the Qing dynasty with himself as emperor in 1915, is buried just outside Anyang. A traitor through and through, he betrayed the 1898 One Hundred Days of Reform movement to the Dowager Empress Cixi and then, realigning himself with progressive factions, was appointed President in 1911, before declaring himself Hongxian Emperor. He died in 1916. His tomb is in the style of that of Ulysses S. Grant.

Fine ceramic figure on the Putuozongsheng, one of the collection of temples at Chengde, the Qing emperors' summer palace

▶ Anyang   80C2

Anyang, in the north of Henan province, is close to the site of the last capital of the Shang dynasty and has a well-preserved old quarter with alleyways, courtyards and low-eaved houses. In 1899, ancient oracle bones with engraved marks, which were used to predict the future, were found here, and later excavations confirmed the existence of a 3,000-year-old city. There are few upstanding remains at the site of Yin, just the merest outline of a city, but the original excavations produced much from the tombs. A possible excursion from Anyang is to the **Red Flag Canal**. Built by hand during the Cultural Revolution as part of a project to irrigate the region, the 1,450km (900-mile) canal was also intended to show the feasibility of a self-reliant China.

▶ Beidaihe   81D4

China's foremost beach resort is a five-hour train ride from Beijing. It first became famous at the end of the 19th century when it was patronized by foreigners living in Tianjin's concession areas or the legations of Beijing. Much of the architecture, with its European villas, reflects the period. Kiessling's restaurant still exists, serving desserts and bread. The sea water is clear and the **three beaches ▶** (formerly divided into one for foreigners, one for Communist Party officials, the third for everyone else) are clean. There are a number of scenic spots in the area with unusual rock formations and views. The train from Beijing stops about 15km (9 miles) from the resort, but there is a bus link.

A GLUT OF PALACES

The Manchu rulers of the last imperial Chinese dynasty were spoilt for choice as far as summer palaces were concerned. There were the two on the outskirts of Beijing, as well as Chengde, also called the Summer Palace. The first two were preferred near the end of the dynasty, but during the 17th and 18th centuries the court spent most of the summer at Chengde. Local tours cost much less than those arranged from Beijing.

85

Tibetan-style roof ornament at Chengde

▶▶ Chengde   81D4

Formerly known as Jehol, Chengde was the 18th-century summer palace of the Qing emperors, close to the mountains and forests of their northern homeland. It has the largest imperial gardens in China and is only six hours by train from Beijing. It is now a UNESCO World Heritage site.

At first a country seat, it soon became an important seat of government. Many of the pavilions were built in the style of the religious architecture of the minority peoples in China, especially the Mongolians and Tibetans, partly to impress their envoys and partly to use Lamaism to control these potentially troublesome peoples.

In the mid-19th century, Jehol witnessed many dramatic events as hostilities between China and the foreign powers increased. It was abandoned as a summer retreat in 1820 following the death of the Jiaqing Emperor, but in 1860 as the British and French forces approached Beijing, the Xianfeng Emperor fled here accompanied by his esteemed concubine, the ambitious Cixi. Concerned that the emperor might die without naming their son as heir, she forced her way into his bedroom to extract the promise that was to make her the most powerful person in China. The emperor died shortly afterwards.

The palace▶▶▶ (*Open* daily 7–6. *Admission: expensive*) consists of a villa within a park and several outer temples. The entrance through the Lizhengmen (main gate) takes you to the Front Palace, now a museum of imperial memorabilia. Beyond is the Misty Rain Tower (Yanyulou), an imperial study. The Wenjin Chamber (Wenjinge) housed the Sikuquanshu (Complete Library of the Four Treasures of Knowledge), an anthology of literature and philosophy. Outside the main park are the **Eight Outer Temples** (*Open* daily 8.30–4.30. *Admission: expensive*), built between 1750 and 1780. The largest and most impressive is the Putuozongsheng, a miniature facsimile of the Potala in Tibet, although the most interesting is the Pule, built for Mongolian envoys in a style that is partly Buddhist and partly Islamic.

Yungang Caves: the broken-hearted son of Emperor Daiwu, represented as a Buddha in Cave 20

Detail on Yungang cave façade of a mythical creature supposed to warn sinners

ANCIENT PAGODA
Not surprisingly there are few original wooden pagodas still standing in China today. The earliest is the Yingxian pagoda some 64km (40 miles) south of Datong. It was built in 1056 and is 67m (220ft) high.

▶▶ **Datong**   80C4

Datong is an industrial city with a coal-mining heritage in Shanxi province. It lies west of Beijing, not far from the Mongolian border on the route of the Great Wall (of which there are several decaying remains in the vicinity) and the railway line to Mongolia and Siberia. This once grimy city is interesting because of its Buddhist shrines, created in the fifth century when Datong was briefly capital of the Northern Wei. During this period, the town prospered and the Buddhist religion, actively fostered by the Wei rulers, flourished, producing some of China's finest Buddhist art, and more than 51,000 stone carvings still exist.

The **Yungang Caves**▶▶▶ (*Open* daily 8.30–5.30. *Admission: expensive*) are west of the city. Originally the entrance to each was concealed by pagoda-like buildings. The idea of sculpting the rock into Buddhist shrines came from India, and there is plenty of evidence of Indian, Persian and even Mediterranean influence in the decorative features of the caves. The peculiarly Chinese styles are seen in the bodhisattvas, dragons and apsaras (angel- or nymph-like creatures). The original caves were carved with images of the first Northern Wei emperors, but the site was abandoned after the imperial capital was moved to Luoyang. Caves 5 and 6 are the most impressive, the first containing a 17m (56ft) Buddha, the second with the life story of Buddha carved on the east, south and west walls. The statue in Cave 19 is of the Daiwu Emperor, a one-time champion of Buddhism who later came to reject it and turned to Taoism, even persecuting Buddhists in the process. Cave 20 has the best view of a Buddha statue, supposed to represent the son of the Daiwu Emperor, who died of a broken heart as a result of the misdeeds of his father.

Datong has an interesting **old central area**▶, one of the better preserved old towns in China, which is worth a stroll even if you have no particular desire to see the two monasteries or the dragon screen. The **Huayan Monastery**▶▶ (*Open* daily 8.30–5. *Admission: inexpensive*) is the more interesting of the monasteries, with an atmosphere of antiquity that can be lacking in some others. Its main attraction is the Bojiajiaocang Hall, with architecture and 31 clay figures dating from the Liao period (AD907–1125). The **Shanhua Monastery** (*Open* daily 8.30–5.30. *Admission: inexpensive*) has Ming sculpture in its main hall. **The Nine Dragon Screen**, built in 1392 on Dadong Jie and one of only three in China, was supposed to have offered protection to the mansion of the 13th son of the first Ming emperor, Hongwu, who was viceroy of Shanxi.

A worthwhile day trip from Datong is to the **Hanging Temple (Xuankongsi)▶▶** (*Open* daily 9–5. *Admission: moderate*), constructed on the side of a cliff, about three hours' drive from the city. The temple's precarious location is spectacular enough, but the loess landscape and the villages passed through on the way there are worth seeing in their own right.

▶ Gongxian/Gongyi City 80C2

Gongxian County, now called Gongyi City, is famous for the Buddhist caves at the foot of Dalishan dating back to AD517 and, above all, the **Song Tombs** (*Open* daily 7–10. *Admission: free*) of seven of the nine Northern Song emperors. Here, 700 stone statues of animals, military and court officials line the sacred avenues that lead to the ruined tomb buildings, which are scattered over a large area. Stylistically, there are several clear distinctions, varying from Tang influence to the naturalistic features of the later Song.

The gravity-defying Hanging Temple (Xuankongsi), well worth the three-hour journey from Datong

87

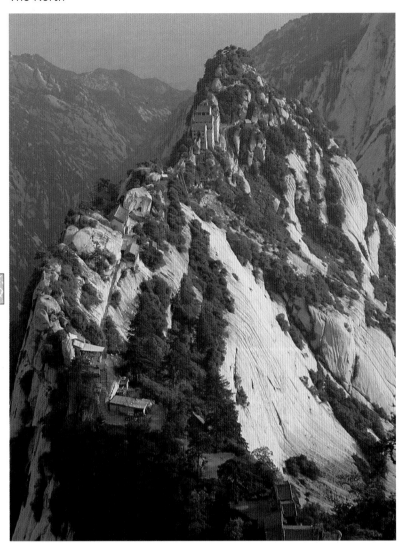

Huashan Mountain is one of China's five holy Taoist mountains

▶ **Huashan**   *80B2*

Open: daily 7–7. Admission: expensive

Huashan (Flowery Mountain), 2,200m (7,218ft) high and east of Xi'an, is one of the five mountains in China sacred to Taoism and, to some extent, later adopted by the imported religion of Buddhism. There are three routes to the top which can be followed in a day, as well as a cable-car. You can find places to stay also at the summit. The mountain is composed of five peaks; the Middle Peak has the best view of the 'Sea of Clouds' at sunrise.

▶ **Jinan**   *81D3*

As capital of Shandong province, Jinan is an important political and industrial city. It is well known for its springs—Gushing-from-the-Ground Spring, Black Tiger Spring, Pearl Spring and Five Dragon Pool—surrounded by gardens. The **Shandong Provincial Museum**▶▶ (*Open daily 9–5. Admission: inexpensive*) has a fine collection of sculptures and artefacts from Longshan, and an exhibition of musical instruments.

The **Four Gate Pagoda (Simenta)**▶, the oldest stone pag-oda in China, dating from the seventh century, is 35km (22 miles) from Jinan. Beyond Simenta is the Song-dynasty **Dragon Tiger Pagoda (Longhuta)**, which is surrounded by a small forest of *stupas* (reliquaries) built as a memorial to the monks who lived at the nearby Shentong Monastery. The **Thousand Buddha Mountain (Qianfo shan)**, served by a cable-car, has good views and statues from the Sui dynasty.

Lively detail from the glazed tiles that face the Iron Pagoda in Kaifeng

▶▶ Kaifeng 80C2

An imperial capital during the Northern Song dynasty, Kaifeng is interesting because of the former presence of a Jewish community, one of several in China before the establishment of the foreign concessions in the major ports in the 19th century. Although the presence of a Jewish community in Kaifeng is well documented, its origins are a mystery. The heart of the Jewish quarter was **Beitun Jie**, where some of the streets bear Jewish names. In the middle of the old town a street of Song-style buildings has been constructed.

One of Kaifeng's principal attractions is the **Xiangguo Monastery (Xiangguosi)**▶▶ (*Open daily 8–6.30. Admission: moderate*). Founded in AD555, the original buildings were destroyed in the deliberate flooding of the Yellow River in 1642. The current buildings date back only to 1766. There is a magnificent bronze bell and a gingko wood statue of Guanyin of a *Thousand Arms and Eyes*.

The **Iron Pagoda (Tieta)**▶▶ (*Open daily 7–7. Admission: inexpensive*), built in the year 1049 and 54m (177ft) high, is said to house relics of the Buddha.

The **Dragon Pavilion (Longting)**, a fine Qing hall on the site of the old imperial palace, was the only building not destroyed by the flood of 1642.

King Yu's Terrace (Yuwangtai), southeast of the old wall, was the haunt of Tang musicians and poets. The nearby **Fan Bo Pagoda**, built in 977, is the oldest building in Kaifeng. Just northeast is **Long Temple**, containing an iron rhinoceros from 1466, supposed to guard against flooding.

Near the **Liuyuankou Ferry** is a look-out point across the Yellow River, 8km (5 miles) to the north of the city.

The metallic sheen of the glazed bricks that cover the Iron Pagoda in Kaifeng give it its name

The Yellow River (Huang He) is 5,487km (3,410 miles) long and the second longest river in China. The birthplace of Chinese civilization, this temperamental waterway—named after the hue of its silty waters—has earned itself the epithet 'China's Sorrow'.

OLD TRICK
Almost 300 years after the Ming officials at Kaifeng deliberately breached the Yellow River to halt the Manchus, the nationalist leader, Chiang Kaishek, did the same at Zhengzhou, when he tried, but failed, to prevent the Japanese invaders from utilizing the railway in 1937. Hundreds of thousands of Chinese died.

Riverside ox at Zhengzhou, meant to placate the river

Route The Yellow River emerges from the Bayan Har Mountains in Qinghai. When it reaches Lanzhou it is already of considerable size; then it winds across north China, bunches up into Inner Mongolia, returns to China proper, and ends in the Gulf of Bo Hai in the Yellow Sea.

Heavy water The Yellow River is infamously temperamental. The quantity of water that it carries varies drastically from season to season and from year to year, a reflection of the strongly seasonal rainfall of north China, three-quarters of which occurs between June and August. The rainfall is supplemented by snow melting in Qinghai as late as June. The river's characteristic hue is produced by thick deposits of filtered soil (loess) picked up in Gansu, Shaanxi and Shanxi, blown there from the deserts of Central Asia. When the river reaches the sea, the water is tinted in all directions by the same dark yellow paste, and indeed the coastline is constantly expanding farther northeast as the silt finally settles.

No ships Despite its size, the Yellow River has never been important as a waterway. The density of the silt, the erratic water flow, and the difficulty of mapping the shifting shoals have made this impractical. Even in areas quite close to the mouth, the river is shallow, and in the severe northern winters it often freezes. So it tends to be used for local fishing, ferries from bank to bank and some commerce over short, sure distances. This lack of commercial potential has been compensated for by the smaller **Huai** River to the south, which is navigable; the artificial **Grand Canal**; and the **Wei**, the Yellow River's principal tributary, navigable almost as far as west Xi'an.

Temperament The Yellow River has been most important as a source of irrigation, but at a price. When it floods, it does so with a vengeance. Whole towns have been washed away, and even now it is not remarkable to see the bodies of animals, and occasionally of humans, bobbing through the middle of Lanzhou. On the whole, however, the construction of dikes has kept the river in check.

In 1855, severe flooding altered the course of the river near its mouth, shifting it some 354km (220 miles) to the north. For 500 years previously it had joined the Huai in Jiangsu province, to flow with it to the sea. This change, which had the effect of almost emptying stretches of the Grand Canal, was by no means the first, for from the seventh century BC until AD11 the river

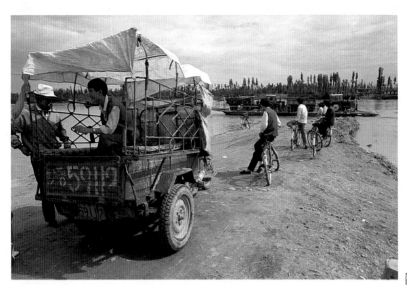

in its lower reaches became a series of divided channels, all of which flowed into the sea to the north of the mouth today. Construction of dikes at that time created a single major channel and reduced the frequency of floods but accelerated the deposit of silt. This made the floods, when they came, far worse, because the water between the dikes was higher than the surrounding plain. Records indicate that the river burst its banks on some 1,500 occasions during the last 3,000 years.

The silt made the area attractive to the first Chinese cultures. Traces of neolithic settlements are legion along the river's banks, and the first recorded dynasty, the Shang, had an early capital near Zhengzhou.

In recent years, flooding has not been the only problem. On the contrary, there have been water shortages and in 1997 the Yellow River ran dry 965km (600 miles) short of the sea for nine months.

Ferry crossing point at Zhongwei in the Autonomous Hui Region of Ningxia

The Yellow River at Huaxuankou, near Zhengzhou. Mao's words 'Control the Yellow River' are inscribed on the wall

Laoshan water

DROPPING OUT
During the 12th century, Luoyang was famous for the 'Seven sages of the Bamboo Grove', a group of scholars who abandoned politics to follow a bohemian lifestyle: discussing Taoism, writing poetry, playing music and drinking wine. According to legend, one of them was constantly shadowed by a servant bearing wine flagons and a spade for his burial in case he dropped dead.

The residence of the former German governor in Qingdao

► **Laoshan**   **81D3**
Open: daily. Admission: expensive
To the east of Qingdao, in Shandong province, Laoshan is an attractive mountain area famous for its mineral water, which is used in the production of China's best-known beer, Qingdao (Tsingtao). The mountain is also noted for its **Taiqing Palace**, a Taoist monastery from the Song dynasty. A cable-car can take you half-way up.

►► **Luoyang**   **80B2**
Although a major city historically and industrially, Luoyang is comparatively little visited. There is, however, plenty to see in the vicinity. The site, strategically placed with hills on three sides and bisected by four rivers, was inhabited from neolithic times. In 771BC, it became the main Zhou capital, and legend has it that Confucius studied here and Laozi was the keeper of archives. Capital again under the Later Han, it was the starting point of the Silk Road. Buddhism was introduced into China from India via Luoyang, and it hosted a number of Chinese inventions, including paper.

After the fall of the Han, the city remained capital for several dynasties and was the scene of a cultural flowering. The Northern Wei dynasty moved its capital from Datong to Luoyang and carved its monuments to Buddhism at nearby Longmen. But the Wei rulers suddenly abandoned the city in 534; it lay in ruins for about 70 years before becoming the capital again, under the Sui. It was a secondary capital under the Tang, too, after which the focus of Chinese life moved elsewhere, and Luoyang, though capital of Henan province, became a backwater until its industrial revival after 1949.

Luoyang is not beautiful, but a walk in the old town, around **Zhongzhou Donglu**, with its well-preserved timbered houses and market atmosphere, pleasantly evokes the past. Luoyang is famous for its peonies, which bloom in early April particularly in Wangcheng Park or Zhiwuyuan. It is said that in AD800 Empress Wu Zetian, angry that peonies refused to bow to her command to bloom in the snow, banished them from Xi'an.

Most of what has been uncovered of Luoyang's past is in the **museum**►► (*Open daily 8–5.30. Admission: inexpensive*), near Wangcheng Park, where there are some fine examples of work, notably the famous Tang polychromatic figures and models of the Sui dynasty grain silos discovered north of the old town. From the park, a pair of Han tombs and one from the Jin with interesting murals have been moved to the **Museum of Ancient Tombs** (*Open* daily 8.30–5.30. *Admission: inexpensive*), on Jichang Lu.

The **Longmen Buddhist Caves**▶▶▶ (*Open* daily 7–6.30. *Admission: expensive*) are among the finest in China. On a splendid site by the Yi River, outside the town, the earliest caves were carved soon after AD493, although the majority date from the Tang. There is a spectacular array of niches, statues, carved pagodas and inscriptions, among which the most striking is the 17m (56ft) Buddha flanked by statues of leering guardians.

The Han dynasty **Baimasi (White Horse Temple)**▶, 10km (6 miles) from Luoyang, is China's earliest Buddhist temple. Its foundation during the first century AD dates back to a journey made by envoys of the Han who went west in search of Buddhist scriptures, and who returned with them on the backs of a pair of white horses. The structures you see now date from the Ming and Qing dynasties (*Open* daily 7–7. *Admission: moderate*).

▶ **Qingdao** 81D2

See following page for town map and walk

China's interesting fourth port was no more than a fishing village in 1897 when the Germans annexed it to compete with other Western powers. It was returned to China only in 1922. It is a popular beach resort and is home to China's most famous **brewery**▶ (*Open* daily 8.30–4.30. *Admission: expensive*), which can be visited through CITS. There is a modern Qingdao but the well-preserved **German Concession**▶▶, with its cathedral, and the former German governor's residence are worth a visit for their European atmosphere. The **Qingdao Museum**▶ has a good collection of paintings and large stone Buddhas. There are also several parks. A day excursion to **Laoshan** from Qingdao is possible from here by boat or by bus.

Heavenly guard and demon warrior on Fengxian Temple; Longmen Buddhist Caves near Luoyang

The heart of Qingdao

Begin at the No. 1 Bathing Beach and walk to the middle of town along the waterfront. Pass the **Marine Museum and Aquarium▶** and Lu Xun Park and continue to the pier with the Huilan Pavilion perched at the end.

Opposite the pier is Zhongshan Road, the main street. Walk along it for a short distance and turn left along Guangxi Road to see the busy station and famous reconstructed clock tower.

Retrace your steps to Zhongshan Road, continue past the many shops, visit the **Catholic Cathedral** on the right, and then continue past the skyscraper department store opposite the Jianglinglu alley to Jingchen market on the right.

Walk through the market and bear right up a rising street; then bear left and then right. Once at the main street turn left, and at a junction by an old church turn right into the heart of the old but well-preserved **German Concession area**.

Continue downhill, keep to the left of a small park and then at a clearing bear to the right in the direction of another church and then left before you reach it, down Longkou Road.

Cross another intersection which has an ancient Chinese wall on the left, climb up the hill and then bear right by some trees.

Follow the road as it curls left around a building with a tower, and then right keeping the tower to the left. This road will eventually bring you back to the waterfront.

► Qufu   81D2

Qufu is famed as the birthplace of Confucius and as the home of his clan, the Kong. The **Kong Mansion**►► (*Open daily 8–5. Admission: expensive*), built during the Ming dynasty, was home to the clan until 1948 and is one of the finest examples of an aristocratic mansion in China.

The **Kongmiao (Temple of Confucius)**►► (*Open daily 8–5. Admission: inexpensive*) dominates the town. Across the moat is the Guiwenge, which used to contain the Confucian library. In the Great Courtyard is a tree, allegedly planted by Confucius, the Xingtan Pavilion, and the Dachengdian, built during the Qing dynasty and one of the largest wooden structures in the world.

The **Konglin**►►► (*Open daily 8–5. Admission: expensive*) is the family graveyard, set amid trees outside the town that contains Confucius' simple, dignified grave. Confucius' birthday is celebrated on 28 September in Qufu. South of Qufu is **Zouxian**, birthplace of the philosopher Mencius.

POPE'S VIEW
The master's fame reached far and wide. 'Superior and alone, Confucius stood. Who taught that useful science, to be good.'— Alexander Pope, *The Temple of Fame*, 1715.

95

Wine from Qufu: Confucian wine improves the mind

POLITICALLY INCORRECT
The opinions of Confucius, who was himself fairly high-born, on women and the lower classes would be given short shrift these days. 'Women and people of low birth are very hard to deal with,' he said. 'If you are friendly with them, they get out of hand, and if you keep your distance, they resent it.'

One of the residential rooms in the Kong Mansion, Qufu, family seat of Confucius' clan, the Kong

China's railway system is of particular interest for a number of reasons, not least because China's withdrawal from the world stage for so many years aroused curiosity among train buffs, who tend to have an insatiable desire for detail.

'Hard seat class' on a train in Inner Mongolia

REVOLUTION AND THE RAILWAYS

It is possible that the railways in China played a contributory role in the downfall of the last dynasty. Railway construction in the decade up to 1911 had been financed largely by foreign organizations in co-operation with provincial governments, but it was less profitable than before. The Chinese government, already badly short of funds, was compelled to service railway debts and consequently took control of the system. Resentment of this action in the provinces led to rallies among all enemies of the state, sparking the 1911 revolution.

A difficult start The history of China's early railway system is characterized by Chinese intransigence and imperial artifice. The first attempt to introduce railways to China, by a consortium of Chinese and foreign companies in 1863, was refused because of the Taiping Rebellion. In 1864, another application was made to the governor of Jiangsu, Li Hongzhang, a man aware of the advantages that dealing with foreigners could bring to China. But he felt that the time was not yet right, despite agreeing that the railways were a key to prosperity. This did not stop the illegal laying of a track from Shanghai to Wusong in 1876 (after negotiations with landowners and families with ancestral graves in its path), which was subsequently torn up.

Official approval The Chinese slowly warmed to the idea, and the next line to be built, with official approval, was for a coalmine near Tianjin. Mule power was soon replaced by steam traction, as Beijing's government recognized its military possibilities. Indeed, it was fear of Russian and Japanese aggression that led to plans for new lines in Manchuria and between Beijing and Guangzhou (Canton). From then on, railway construction became more entangled with the fates of the Western powers, whose presence in China was increasingly unwelcome.

Foreign pressure China was constantly caught in the struggles between countries wanting to carve it up between them and those that disagreed. In some ways this was to China's advantage. Railways were built, but usually under some sort of foreign pressure, because the Chinese government had no money. The first contract was signed in 1896, with France, for a railway near the Vietnamese frontier; this was followed by more with other countries. The eagerness to build railways was founded less on the desire to make money than on the need of each power to obtain concessions before rivals did.

Shortfall After the Boxer Rebellion, China's enthusiasm for railways increased, and various agreements with foreign powers were ratified. In 1911, major lines were brought under central government control. Sun Yatsen strove to standardize the railway systems, which reflected the technology current in the countries that built them. Apart from the logistical challenge, standardization was difficult because of China's climatic and geographical extremes.

Wars Civil war and invasion by the Japanese halted further progress over the next 40 years. Improvements to the system followed, with the help of private Chinese capital and the Boxer Indemnity Fund, but mostly using revenues generated by the railways themselves, and with the communist victory in 1949 railways once again became a priority. Collaboration with the USSR produced many more lines and a railway bridge across the Yangtze at Wuhan. After the split in 1960, security concerns led to the construction of still more lines and the Yangtze Bridge at Nanjing.

Today, the emphasis is on electrification and new lines to remoter areas. They include lines from Kunming to Dali and Nanning and the first railway line to Tibet, a 27 billion RMB project from Golmud to Lhasa which began trial operations in July 2006. There are already plans to extend it to Xigaze by 2010. High-speed trains are another key development area. The world's first magnetic levitation, high-speed line opened in 2004, linking Shanghai with Pudong Airport. A second maglev line will link Shanghai with Hangzhou, 177km (110 miles) away. A 1,320km (820-mile) high-speed line between Shanghai and Beijing has also been approved. Trains will run at up to 350kph (220mph), cutting journey times from 12 to 5 hours. The Beijing South Railway Station closed in mid-2006 to turn it into a high-speed terminus in a 6.3 billion RMB project due to be completed in 2007.

Until 1989, steam locomotives were produced just for the home market
Opposite, top: a steam train in the desert at Dongsheng
Above: Manchurian steam in Heilongjiang

97

Beijing Railway Station, in central Beijing, built in the grandiose style that characterized Mao's China

The 17th-century town gate of Shanhaiguan, inscribed 'First Pass Under Heaven'

SACRED PEAKS
The five holy mountains represent the five directions sacred to the Chinese (north, south, east, west and middle), hence the link with the emperor who was viewed as the son of heaven and who lived in the middle of his kingdom.

▶ Shanhaiguan (The Pass between the Mountains and the Sea) 81D4

Shanhaiguan is where the Great Wall meets the East China Sea. The 1639 **town gate** is inscribed 'First Pass Under Heaven'. A temple about 6km (4 miles) out of town is dedicated to Meng Qiangnu. The wife of a man conscripted under the Qin to build the Great Wall, she followed him only to find that he had died. Her tears are said to have brought the wall down to reveal his skeleton within.

▶ Shaolin 80C2

The **Shaolin Monastery▶** (*Open* daily 8–6. *Admission: expensive*), west of Zhengzhou, was founded in AD495. It was said to have been visited by the founder of Zen Buddhism, Bodhidharma, in AD527. Having crossed the Yellow River on a reed, he contemplated a wall for nine years. He rejected doctrine for meditation, and Shaolin is best known for *gong-fu*, a martial art followed by its monks and developed to enhance meditation, which has found fame in films. Shaolin is also noted for its Ming frescoes, as well as its forests of stupas (reliquaries) and its collection of stelae, one of which dates back to AD683. *Gong-fu* classes are possible at the Shaolin Monastery Wushu Institute.

The 'Forest of Stupas', or ancient reliquaries, near the Shaolin Monastery, Shaolin

▶ Shijiazhuang 80C3

The capital of Hebei province is an important railway crossing and the burial place of the Canadian doctor Norman Bethune, honoured by the Chinese communists. He arrived in China in 1938 and died a year later.

North is Zhengding, site of the **Longxing Temple**, famous for its 22m (72ft) bronze of Guanyin. Southeast is China's oldest bridge, the Zhauzhou Bridge (Zhauzhou Qiao), which was built 1,400 years ago.

MASSACRE OF MISSIONARIES
Taiyuan was a major focus for anti-foreign Boxer activity in 1900. Xenophobia reached a climax when the local governor rounded up all the foreign missionaries in the area and publicly executed them.

▶▶▶ Taishan 81D2

Open: 24 hours. Admission: expensive

Taishan is perhaps the holiest of the five Chinese holy mountains devoted to Taoism and the cult of the emperor. Of the two possible routes to the summit, the middle one is the most popular. Make your way through the **Daizongfang** and begin the five-hour, 1,515m (4,970ft) climb up the 5,500 steps. You can also take a bus to Zhongtianmen, about half-way up, where there is a cable-car to the top. There is a hotel at the summit.

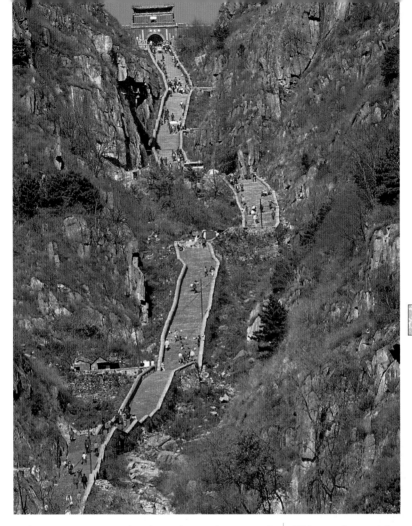

The mountain is covered with temples, scenic spots, and tourists or pilgrims. A circuitous western route back also has excellent views over the mountainside.

The **Taishan Temple** at the foot of the mountain is one of China's great, ancient palace-style buildings.

Visitors to the mountain of Taishan, the holiest of China's holy Taoist mountains, must climb thousands of steps to reach the summit

▶ Taiyuan   80B3

The capital of Shanxi province is an industrial city with several interesting sights. The **Shuangta Temple▶▶** (*Open daily 8–6. Admission: inexpensive*) is one of China's finest examples of Ming architecture, while the **Chongshan Temple▶** (*Open daily 8–5. Admission: inexpensive*) was once part of the largest Buddhist monastery in China. The **Shanxi Provincial Museum▶** (*Open daily 9–5. Admission: inexpensive*) has reopened in a former Confucian Temple. Other temples include the **Jinci▶▶**, southwest of Taiyuan, with some fine examples of Song architecture. Also dating from the Song dynasty, 90km (56 miles) south, is the **Shuanglin Monastery▶▶** (*Open daily 8.30–6. Admission: moderate*) while only 1.5 hours southwest of Taiyuan is Pingyao, one of the few remaining towns with a complete city wall.

YELLOW EARTH

The provinces of Shanxi and Shaanxi not only have similar names but are both covered in thick deposits of yellow loess, sometimes to a depth of more than 100m (325ft). In some places, troglodyte cave-houses have been cut into the perpendicular valley sides. Though primitive, the cave-houses are cool in the summer and warm in winter.

'*Qi*' in Chinese denotes a vital breath within us that also animates the cosmos. Although it is a loose term, according to Chinese philosophy—notably Taoism—the secret of inner strength lies in harnessing this mysterious force.

Gong-fu is about self-discipline, both as a form of exercise (above, taijiquan) and as a martial art

Natural alliance The secret of outer strength lies in using *qi* to unleash latent power that depends not on physical strength but on knowledge. *Gong-fu* is the cultivation of *qi* and its use as a fighting technique.

Taoism claims to be able to demonstrate its superiority through movement, based on the notion that the human body is the universe in miniature. But the movements themselves are to be based on acquiescence, not confrontation, with nature.

In martial arts there are two categories of movement, external and internal. Both forms aim to tap into the flow of *qi*. Of the former, karate, concerned with skills of defending the body, is a well-known example. Internal forms are more concerned with the body as a vehicle of spiritual development; among these *taijiquan*, or shadow-boxing, is the best known.

Meditation Meditation concentrates the mind so movements made are in tune with it. Meditation in action is considered essential by Taoists because it involves the whole human being, body and soul. The practitioner must be aware of his or her actions, so the weapon, whether it be hand or sword, is directed to strike but does so almost intuitively, having sensed in advance the movement of an opponent. The mind is flowing, and this is *qi*. The relationship between the two types of breathing, physical and spiritual, is vital. Perhaps this could be described as 'tranquil', but the word is inadequate because it fails to imply the level of alertness essential for success. *Taijiquan* is supposed to be able to teach both the calmness necessary in everyday life and the added awareness needed for fighting.

Rhythms In *taijiquan* the spine should be erect, the abdomen relaxed and the point of balance lowered. The breath must be allowed to find its source in an area just below the navel and identify with the inner breath of *qi*; to concentrate on control of physical breathing alone is to inhibit one's natural, instinctive strength. There must be no strain, for to strain is to go against nature. Energy should be stored and only unleashed at the right moment, as the arrow from the bow. Observing the Chinese people will show that these lessons have been absorbed and used in ordinary life, for the Chinese are rhythmical in everything they do until speed is called for, in which case the reaction is often intense and accurate.

In some ways *qi* might be thought of as the combination of concentration and self-discipline. But for Taoists, *qi* is something more; it is the essence of essences, an innate, though invisible, power shared by all human beings.

The martial artist's concentration of *qi* should produce the innocent mental state of a child—no preconceptions, focused only on the immediate circumstances but within the larger framework of the universe. This state is illustrated by the following account of a *gong-fu* contest taken from Peter Ralston's *Consciousness and the Martial Arts*: 'For example I would start to move and my opponent would throw a kick and I would realise that I was moving out of the way of a kick. But I was doing it before I knew why! I just moved, and they would throw a kick and miss!'

Gong-fu as an aid to meditation: sculptures in the temple at Shaolin Monastery portray 13 monks practising their art before the Tang Emperor Li Shimin in the seventh century AD, and (top, opposite), Nine Dragons glazed wall screen

A WORLD OF SHADOW BOXERS
David Rice, in his book *The Dragon's Brood: Conversations with Young Chinese*, describes Chinese shadow boxing: 'From five o'clock in the morning, in every street-corner park, in front of every apartment block, and in the woods around the Temple of Heaven, there were thousands of people, some in groups, some alone, all performing what seemed to be slow-motion ballet, making strange, slow, graceful movements with limbs and torso.'

Walk

Tianjin's foreign concessions

A stroll through the foreign concessions reveals a surprising degree of Westernization. Walk from the east railway station to the river.

Cross Liberation Bridge and continue along Jiefang Road, passing the old Imperial Hotel on the right. Continue through the former **French Concession** to the Fine Arts Museum. Yingkou Road marked the beginning of the **British Concession**, but continue along Jiefang Bei Road to the Astor Hotel and the former Victoria Park. Turn left to the river and return along the waterfront, passing the old French and British consulates and the Customs House.

▶▶ Tianjin (Tientsin)   81D3

Tianjin was one of the treaty ports controlled by the Western 'great powers' from the 19th century. In 1976, it was hit by an earthquake, but has since recovered to become China's third-largest city, with the status of autonomous municipality (as Beijing, Chongqing and Shanghai), which is similar to that of a province.

Tianjin has retained much of its European atmosphere, although the various concessions granted to the foreign powers in 1860 never merged, as they did in Shanghai, to form an International Settlement. Each concession preserves a distinctive quality, particularly the British, French and German ones. The old Chinese town is to the north of the city, the concessions to the south.

Other than the **concessions▶ ▶**, there are several places of interest. The **Dabeiyuan (Great Compassion Temple)** (*Open* daily 9–4.30. *Admission: inexpensive*), is a Buddhist temple that used to contain the cranium of Xuanzang, the seventh-century monk who made a celebrated journey to India. **Wenhua Jie (Ancient Culture Street)▶** is an area of restored traditional Chinese shops, just west of the river. It is close to the **Tianhougong (Hall of the Heavenly Empress)**, originally a temple, now a **Folk Museum▶** (*Open* daily 9–5. *Admission: inexpensive*) with many examples of the mud craft peculiar to Tianjin and of the woodblocks made in the nearby village of Yangliuqing. The **Fine Arts Museum▶** at 77 Jiefang Bei Road has old and new paintings. The 18th-century **Great Mosque (Qingzhen Da Si)▶** is in the old Chinese city. The old **French cathedral▶** is interesting. Also worth a look is the southern-style **Guangdong Guildhall (Guangdong Huiguan)▶**, built in the 1920s for traders from that province. Tianjin is famous for its annual Kite Festival, and its fascinating, daily **antiques market** on Shenyang Dao. The **TV Tower (Dianshi Ta)**, which you can climb for 50 RMB, was built in the 1990s.

French Concession architecture along the former rue de France, Tianjin's old banking district

103

▶ Wutaishan   *80C3*

Wutaishan, in the north of Shanxi province, is one of the five holy mountains of Chinese Buddhism. It is a cluster of five peaks, the highest reaching just over 3,000m (9,800ft). There is an abundance of temples, many concentrated at the town of **Taihuai**. The Yuan-dynasty **Nanshan Temple** is decorated with frescoes of the classic 'Journey to the West' made by the monk Xuanzang, who travelled to India. The **Luohou Temple** contains an imposing wooden lotus flower on a mechanism that, when rotated, opens the petals to reveal carved Buddhist figures.

STRENGTH THROUGH WISDOM
Wutaishan is supposed to have been the home of the Bodhisattva Manjusri, the god of wisdom. Riding on the back of a lion, he carries a sword used to fight ignorance.

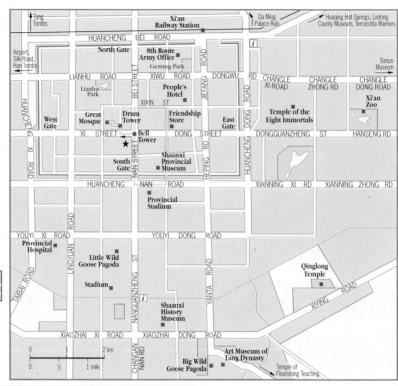

Walk

Xi'an, taking in the Muslim quarter

The Bell Tower near the middle of the city is a good place to start. From here, head west along Xi Street until you arrive at the **Drum Tower** at the beginning of the Muslim quarter. Turn right beneath the tower, turn left along a narrow street lined with street traders and follow it as it bears right, and then turn left again to the **Great Mosque**. After that return to the main road and walk left along it, passing a number of attractive traditional houses. At the top bear right along Xixin Street until you finally come to the old main square. A little farther on is the People's Hotel. Return to the square and turn south, walk past the Friendship Store and continue on until you get to the **Shaanxi Provincial Museum**. Turn right to the South Gate and then right back to the Bell Tower.

Ready to worship at the Great Mosque in Xi'an's Muslim quarter

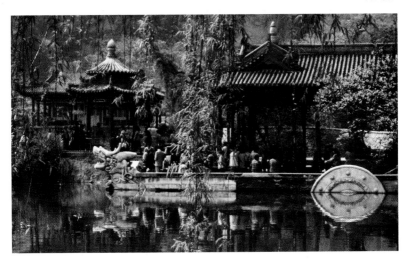

▶▶▶ **Xi'an** 80A2

One of the greatest cities in the history of civilization, Xi'an (Sian) had declined to a provincial backwater before the discovery of the Terracotta Warriors in 1974. Since then it has become one of the most important tourist destinations in the world. A capital during the early Zhou dynasty, it became the first capital of a united China under the First Emperor, Qin Shihuang. During the Tang dynasty, Xi'an became the focus of the greatest flowering of Chinese culture. It is thought that the population may have reached 2 million, at a time when commerce with the outside world reached unprecedented levels. The modern city, however, is based on the Ming street plan.

Although the **Terracotta Warriors▶▶▶** (see pages 108–109) must be the highlight of the visit, there is much else to see around the city. The **city wall and moat▶▶▶** (*Open* daily 8–6. *Admission: moderate*), over 15km (9 miles) in perimeter, dates from the early Ming. Made of rammed loess on a base of earth, lime and glutinous rice, faced with grey brick, it was completely restored during the 1980s and is an awesome sight, particularly in the misty early morning or at sunset. It is possible to mount the wall at different points. Long-term renovations of the wall, moat and heritage streets and houses will last until 2020.

The old **Shaanxi Provincial Museum** was housed in the former Confucian Temple at the foot of the wall in the south of the city. Part of it still is; the rest is now in a new museum on Xiaozhai Donglu. The **Beilin Museum▶▶** (*Open* daily 8–6. *Admission: moderate)* houses the famed Forest of Stelae, a collection founded in 1090 of inscribed stone tablets, some dating back to the Han. Some have pictures of scenery or illustrations; others carry the text of the 13 Classics. One testifies to the arrival in Xi'an of a Nestorian Christian priest and the foundation in 781 of a chapel.

The **History Museum▶▶▶** (*Open* daily 8.30–5.30. *Admission: moderate*) has a display of locally discovered Zhou bronzes, fine Tang ornaments and a variety of stone sculptures, including four of the carved horse reliefs from the tomb of Li Shimin, founder of the Tang dynasty. Two of these are now in the Metropolitan Museum in New York.

The tranquil Huaqing Hot Springs

FOLK ART
The brightly hued quilted jackets embroidered with stylized designs that are now for sale all over China originate from the countryside around Xi'an. A more recent development is the art in naïve style from Huxian, a nearby town. The vivid paintings of agricultural themes became popular in the late 1950s and are now widely sold in the area.

INFORMATION AGE
For many years CITS (China International Travel Service) was regarded as more of an obstacle than an aid to obtaining information about China. Things have improved only slowly but in Xi'an there is now a Tourist Information Centre (tel: 745 5043; *open* daily 7.30am–8pm) close to the railway station which offers helpful and friendly service.

The North

*Part of the Forest of
Stelae in Shaanxi
Provincial Museum*

THE JOURNEY WEST
The 'Journey to the West'
(*Xiyouji*) is the name of a
fable written during the
Ming dynasty. The fable is
based on the pilgrimage to
India made by the Tang
monk Xuanzang, in
memory of whom the Xi'an
Big Wild Goose Pagoda
was built. In the story of
his adventures, he is
accompanied by a pig,
symbol of intelligence and
greed, and a magician
monkey. There are many
stories based on the characters, some of which
appear in a television
series.

*Ancient guardian of
Huaqing Hot Springs,
near Xi'an, where
Chiang Kaishek was
captured by his own
generals in 1936*

The city's symbol is the 60m (197ft) **Big Wild Goose Pagoda (Dayanta)▶▶▶** (*Open* daily 8–6. *Admission: moderate*), first built in AD652 to house the sutras collected from India by Xuanzang, the wandering monk. The top has fine views of the city. The **Little Wild Goose Pagoda (Xiaoyanta)▶** (*Open* daily 7.30–6.30. *Admission: inexpensive*) is a similar, smaller, more delicate structure from 707.

Xi'an's Muslim population numbers 30,000, a legacy of the Silk Road. On Huajue Xi'ang, in the Muslim quarter, is the **Great Mosque (Qingzhensi)▶▶** (*Open* daily 8–7. *Admission: inexpensive*). It was founded in 742, though the heavily restored present buildings are in Ming style. It is a charming place, particularly the garden and prayer hall.

Near the Mosque is the **Drum Tower▶**, and its twin, the **Bell Tower▶**, just to the southeast. Moved here in 1582, Bell Tower was built in 1384 and originally stood in the middle of the Tang city, two blocks west. Music performances take place daily (*Towers open* daily. *Admission: inexpensive*).

The route to the Terracotta Warriors takes visitors past several places of interest. The area around Xi'an has been

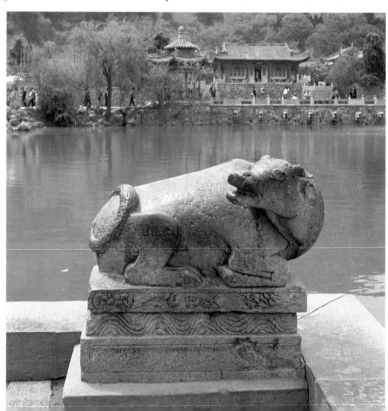

important from the earliest times. **Banpo**▶▶▶ (*Open daily 8–5.30. Admission: inexpensive*), discovered in 1953, is a covered excavation that clearly shows the layout of a neolithic village of the Yangshao culture. The foundations of several dwellings (thatched roofs supported by timber columns) and kilns and graves, some of which were filled with urns containing the bones of children, can all be viewed. The pottery discovered there shows an interesting progression of pattern from representations of man and fish to more abstract geometric design.

The **Huaqing Hot Springs**▶ (*Open daily 7–7. Admission: expensive*), a scenic spot in the shadow of Li Mountain, have been patronized for their mineral content since the Zhou dynasty, but they are particularly associated with the Tang emperor Xuanzong and his concubine Yang Guifei, whose fate is a perennial subject of Chinese art: Xuanzong was forced to order Yang Guifei's execution by royal guards in AD756. The baths are being reconstructed in the Tang style. The springs are also associated with the 'Xi'an incident' of 1936. Chiang Kaishek had come to Xi'an to continue his offensive against the communists, ignoring pleas for a united front against the invading Japanese. A warlord, Zhang Xueliang, though allied to Chiang's nationalists, saw the urgency of the situation and captured him here, chasing him from his office (which still stands just above the spring) up the hillside. Chiang was forced into an alliance, though he later obtained his revenge on Zhang by imprisoning him.

Not far from Huaqing is **Lintong County museum**▶, with an interesting display of Buddhist relics discovered on Li Mountain and other sites in the area. Close to Xi'an is **Xianyang museum**▶ (*Open daily 8–6. Admission: inexpensive*), with 3,000 miniature soldiers excavated in 1965.

There are several worthwhile sites not normally included in a visit to Xi'an. The **Han dynasty Tombs**▶ (none of which have been excavated) are west of Xi'an. The most interesting is that of Huo Qubing, which has a series of fine stone animals that would once have graced the spirit (or royal) way and are now under cover. Near by is the tomb of the Tang concubine Yang Guifei. The main **Tang Tombs**▶▶, however, are some 80km (50 miles) northwest of Xi'an. The grandest is **Qianling** (unexcavated), the tomb of the third Tang emperor and his wife Wu Zetian, one of the three notorious women rulers of Chinese history, who assumed power on the death of her husband.

The location of the tomb, on a natural hill, is impressive. It is approached along a 'spirit' or royal way running between two mounds, flanked by a succession of winged horses, birds, human figures and stelae. Beyond is a congregation of headless statues—the foreign envoys who attended the emperor's funeral. Near by are several lesser tombs, some excavated, notably those of Princess Yongtai and Prince Zhanghuai, and covered with beautiful court paintings. East of Qianling is the **Zhaoling** group of tombs—it was from the tomb of Taizong, the second Tang emperor, that the famous horse panels now displayed in the provincial museum were taken.

The **Temple of Flourishing Teaching (Xingjiaosi)**▶, 25km (16 miles) southeast of Xi'an, is spectacularly set on the side of a hill, overlooking a village and a tree-studded plain. It is famed as the burial place of the monk Xuanzang.

107

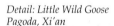

Detail: Little Wild Goose Pagoda, Xi'an

The discovery of the Terracotta Warriors in 1974 by local farmers who were digging a well turned out to be one of the most significant finds of the 20th century.

FROM EMPEROR TO QUEEN
Such is the beauty of the bronze chariots on exhibition at the site of the Terracotta Warriors that Queen Elizabeth II of Britain was given an exact copy of one of them when she visited in 1987. She is also one of the few foreigners ever to have been allowed to stand in the pit among the warriors.

Construction The First Emperor, Qin Shihuang, whose unexcavated mausoleum lies beneath a hill 2km (1 mile) from the site, was a figure of almost legendary stature. The scale and nature of this find reveals a level of civilization remarkable for its self-confidence.

Work was begun on the mausoleum in 246BC, as soon as the First Emperor became ruler of Qin, and involved a workforce of nearly 750,000 conscripts. According to historical records, the mausoleum itself was filled with models of palaces and a China in miniature where the 'waters' of the Yellow and Yangtze rivers were made of mercury and could even be made to flow by means of a special mechanism. The site was protected by automatic crossbows. Outside the mausoleum there was a perimeter fence and villas once occupied by guards.

The army So far interest has focused on the army of life-size terracotta soldiers arrayed in pits to the east. The largest, Pit 1, is now protected under a vast hangar. It consists of 11 parallel underground corridors from which earthen ramps lead to the surface. Each was paved with bricks and protected by a wooden roof covered in straw matting and clay. The mausoleum was sacked by rebel soldiers after the First Emperor's death, probably as a result of the tell-tale mounds of excavated earth.

The soldiers stand in military formation in infantry battle order facing east. They have some body protection but no helmets (which were reserved for officers). The vanguard at the east end consists of bowmen who are

The celebrated Terracotta Army, in battle formation in the vast Pit 1

separated from the foot soldiers by chariots, and mobile infantry unprotected for rapid deployment. Body protection was unnecessary, since ferocity and bravery were considered sufficient protection for infantry men. Thus, in the narrow north and south corridors, soldiers guarding the flanks face out, shieldless. The Terracotta Warriors did, however, carry real arms, made of bronze, many of which were removed by the rampaging rebel army.

Sculpture The statues themselves were made of local clay. No two faces are alike—each is a personal portrait. Each body was made separately. The legs are solid, but the torsos are hollow. Hands and head were added later. Individual details such as beards and ears were sculpted last, then the whole statue was brightly painted. It is uncertain why so much trouble was taken, but one theory is that the different faces, many of which belong to what have become minority races, are a celebration of the first unification of China. Another argues that the warriors demonstrate the power of the ordinary citizen, a view that smacks more of 20th-century Marxism than serious empirical analysis. But certainly these men were clearly highly esteemed by the First Emperor, even if their presence here represents no more than the egotism of a powerful man.

Exhibitions Pit 2 contains a unit of cavalry and war chariots; Pit 3 contains a war chariot, 68 warriors and numerous bronze weapons; and Pit 4 is empty. Pits 1, 2 and 3 are currently open to the public (*Open daily 8.30–5. Admission: expensive*).

Separate exhibition halls display examples of the soldiers under glass, and in yet another hall you can see a pair of scaled-down bronze chariots of remarkable precision, discovered in 1980 just west of the tomb itself.

It is forbidden to photograph or video the exhibits in Pits 1, 2 and 3, a rule that is vigorously enforced. Photography is permitted elsewhere, however. There is an interesting market outside the site gates.

Each of the life-size warriors is said to be an individual portrait

109

ROYAL RAGE
The First Emperor was a driven man. In about 218BC he found crossing the Yangtze difficult because of a gale. He blamed the river goddess whose temple was on a nearby mountain and so, to punish her for inconveniencing him, he ordered 3,000 slaves to fell all the trees on its slopes.

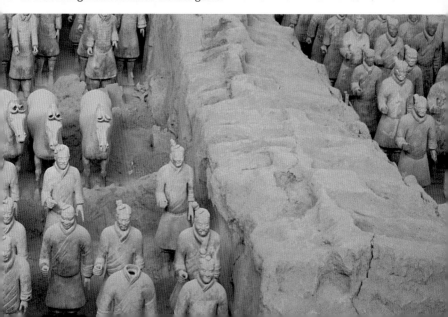

A deserted back street near the waterfront in the old part of the port city of Yantai, Shandong province

▶ Yan'an (Yenan)   *80B2*

Yan'an (Shaanxi province), the communists' headquarters during the Anti-Japanese War, holds a special place in Chinese history as it was also the end point of the Long March. The area is notable for its cave architecture, and for **Qingliangshan** (*Open* daily 7–7. *Admission: moderate*), a park with the Ten Thousand Buddha Cave, the name given to any

shrine filled with Buddhist statuary. Miraculously, many of the statues survived the Cultural Revolution.

▶ Yantai   *81E3*

Known as 'Chefoo' to 19th-century foreigners, Yantai is a fishing port, notable for its **Yantai Museum▶** (*Open* daily 8.30–4.30. *Admission: inexpensive*), built by traders from Fujian in 1884.

▶ Yulin   *80B3*

This small town in Northern Shaanxi has interesting architecture and an almost complete Ming wall.

▶ Zhengzhou   *80C2*

The capital of Henan province is thought to have been a Shang dynasty capital. A city of middling importance for the next 3,000 years, it only recently regained its stature, but as a rather ugly manufacturing city. Here in 1938 Chiang Kaishek breached the Yellow River dikes to hold back the Japanese, killing vast numbers of Chinese in the process. There is a commemorative tablet at Huaxuankou. The new **Henan Provincial Museum▶▶** (*Open* daily 9–4.30. *Admission: inexpensive*), in Nongye Lu, has a remarkable display of local finds from the neolithic to Ming periods. The Ming-dynasty **Temple of the City God (Chenghuangmiao)▶** is dedicated to the city protector, while at the east end of the same street are the remains of the **Shang city wall**.

RAILWAY STRIKE
In Communist folklore, Zhengzhou is inextricably linked to the revolution because of the strike which started on the railway in 1923. This arose because of the local warlord's opposition to the establishment of a united trade union, not least because the railway line was vital, he felt, to the movement of his troops. Thirty-five workers were shot, and the strike that followed is considered to be one of the first major steps taken by the Workers' Movement.

The Long March

In 1930, Mao Zedong, with the assistance of Zhu De, founder of the Chinese Red Army, and others destined to play a considerable role in the New China, founded a Chinese soviet republic in the mountains of Jiangxi, in southeast China.

Breakout Chiang Kaishek, aware of the growing threat to his nationalists posed by the communists in southern China, mounted five campaigns against them in 1931–34. Only on the fifth occasion were Mao's forces compelled to break out. The communists decided to retreat from Jiangxi to Yan'an, a remote town in the northwest, in Shaanxi province. From October 1934, for two years, almost 100,000 marchers lived off the countryside, making their way over difficult terrain to Yan'an, a distance of almost 13,000km (8,000 miles). Peasants were converted to the cause *en route*, but the ordeal and battles with local warlords took their toll, and only a fraction of the original number completed the journey.

The march, however, was an important milestone in Mao's career—it enabled him finally to achieve the leadership he sought, and in 1935 he was elected chairman of the Party's Central Committee. Simultaneously, the march temporarily benefited the nationalists, because much of the burden of fighting was passed on to the warlords. At the same time there was a good deal of factional fighting among the communists themselves; it was only Mao's emergence as leader that settled those differences once and for all. Once the communists had arrived in Yan'an, it became their capital until 1945.

Revolutionary base areas

	1934
	1935
	1936
	Guerrilla zones

Long March routes

→	First Front Army
→	Second Front Army
→	Fourth Front Army
→	Sixth Army Group
→	25th Army Corps

1 Central Soviet Area
2 Hunan-Jiangxi
3 Hunan-Hubei-Sichuan-Guizhou
4 Sichuan-Shaanxi
5 Fujian-Zhejiang-Jiangxi
6 Hunan-Hubei-Jiangxi
7 Hubei-Henan-Anhui
8 Hubei-Henan-Shaanxi
9 Shaanxi-Gansu-Ningxia

111

The Northeast

RUS

Mohe (Xilinji)
Tahe
Huma
Heihe
Ergun He
Ergun Zuoqi
Jagdaqi
Manzhouli
Hailar He
Hulun Nur
Hailar
NEI MENGGU ZIZHIQU
Nenjiang
Wudalianchi
Bei'an
Laha
Yichun
Tongjiang
Hegang Fujin
Zalantun
Qiqihar
Zhalong **HEILONGJIANG**
Daqing
Anda
Suihua
Jiamusi
Shuangyashan
Ulanhot
Zhaodong
Jiang
Yilan
Qitaihe
Hulin
Baicheng
Da'an
Songhua
Harbin
Shangzhi
Linkou
Mishan
Jixi
Taonan
Fuyu
Xingkai Hu
(INNER MONGOLIA)
Da Hinggan Ling
Wanda Shan
JILIN
Mudan Jiang
Mudanjiang
Changchun
Jilin
Jingpo Hu
Tongliao
Shuangliao
Siping
Songhua Hu
Dunhua
Tumen
Liaoyuan
Yanji
Chifeng
Meihekou
Tumen Jiang
Fuxin
Liao He
Tieling
Hunjiang
2750m
SHENYANG
Fushun
Changbaishan
Chaoyang
Benxi
Tonghua
LIAONING
Jinzhou
Anshan
Liaoyang
Jinxi
Yingkou
Fengcheng
Yalu Jiang
Qinhuangdao
HEBEI
Liaodong Wan
Bingyu
Dandong
Xinjin
Liaodong
Bandao
KP
Bo Hai
Dalian
Xiao Hinggan Ling
Nen Jiang
Heilong Jiang
Wusuli Jiang

Hinggan Ling

MGL

| 0 | 100 | 200 | 300 km |
| 0 | | 100 | 200 miles |

Women workers shovel snow off the streets of Harbin

Right: the Throne Room of the Manchurian Imperial Palace, Shenyang

A detail from the walls of the Imperial Palace, Shenyang

114

MIGHTY MANCHUS
Such was the Manchus' prestige when they took control of China in 1644, that the then Dalai Lama journeyed in person from Lhasa to Beijing to acknowledge the suzerainty of the new Qing dynasty. He ordered the building of the White Dagoba there in 1651 (it still stands today in Beihai Park).

THE NORTHEAST Although the northeast region of China has much in common with north China, it nevertheless has its own character, a mixture of China, Manchuria, Siberia and Korea.

This is partly because the frontier here has fluctuated considerably over the centuries. Indeed, it is only during the last 30 years that agreement has finally been reached between the Chinese and the Russians to prevent the sniping across the banks of the Heilongjiang (Amur) River that had previously been a characteristic of the region. Residents of this region may now go about their daily business without fear of invasion, and foreigners also benefit since they may travel more freely here.

The region is the northernmost part of China proper and consists of the provinces of Liaoning, Jilin and Heilongjiang. It borders Siberia in the north, Korea in the southeast, and Chinese Inner Mongolia in the west, and is washed by the Yellow Sea to the south. The area is a marked contrast to the rest of China because of its freezing winters, fir-clad hills and mountains, rivers and lakes, as well as its minority peoples. These days its major cities are vital components in China's industrial life.

OFF THE BEATEN TRACK From the visitor's point of view, the northeast is usually considered a fringe attraction. This does not mean, however, that it is devoid of interest, only that it demands more research and more effort. For the nature lover, particularly, the northeast has much to offer; but the determined visitor can discover much else. After all, China was ruled by people from this region for the last 300 years of its imperial history.

Its history, as might be expected in frontier country, is a varied one and rather obscure. Of the many peoples to have made their home in the northeast, perhaps the best known are the Manchus or Manchurians, who gave a political shape to the region. They, it seems, were originally a Jürchen tribe of Tungusic stock. The Tungus inhabited the northeast, living by a mixture of hunting and agriculture. The Manchu dynasty arose out of the Aisin Gioro clan, which held the hereditary chieftainship of one of the Jürchen tribes. By the usual tactics of marriage into and alliance with other tribes, Nurhaci, the leader of the Manchus (whose son subsequently inaugurated the Qing dynasty), developed a power base in the Liaodong peninsula and created a united front against the Chinese, with whom relations had for long been uneasy.

By the time Nurhaci was sufficiently powerful to invade China, he had inculcated a sense of statehood into his people. The economy was solidly based on ginseng and horses, while the state bureaucracy, no doubt influenced by that of China, was conducted using a new script based on the Mongol alphabet. Shenyang became the capital of the new Manchurian state, which was then absorbed into China.

The Manchurian state was later reincarnated briefly and ingloriously in the 1930s as Manchukuo, a spurious attempt by the invading Japanese to give legal substance to their own ambitions.

The ginseng and the horses remain, and so do some 8 million Manchurians, one of China's 55 minority peoples. The northeast is not China's heartland but is none the less an integral part of the modern Chinese state.

CHINA IN A MODERN WORLD
A fascinating aspect of China is its contradictions: a socialist country that encourages its citizens to earn more; a country that pioneered great inventions (gunpowder, the magnetic compass, printing) yet lags behind modern technology; and a country that has strict measures for population control yet relies on manual methods of agricultural production.

115

A winter vendor of yams in Harbin where January temperatures plummet

The Northeast

ASSIMILATED RULERS
China's last dynasty, the Qing, were Manchurians, from the part of China known as Dongbei, or the Northeast. Like the Mongols, they were foreign conquerors but with a crucial difference—they did not impose their own traditions on the Chinese, but instead adopted the Confucian customs and structures of Han China. At the same time, the Manchu maintained their own identity, by continuing to wear their traditional dress and insisting that men wear their hair in a long braid. They also protected their power base by employing both Chinese and Manchu in influential political posts.

Dalian is one of China's most important ports. The maritime climate here means that the waters never freeze

▶ Anshan   112A1

Anshan produces over 20 per cent of China's steel but has little aesthetic appeal. To the southeast, some 10km (6 miles) away, are the **Tanggangzi Hot Springs** (*Open daily 8–12. Admission: moderate*), where Puyi, the Last Emperor, used to go to bathe with his empresses. About 19km (12 miles) to the southeast is **Mount Qian (Thousand Lotuses Hill)**▶, a well-known beauty spot of green peaks and Taoist and Buddhist monasteries dating back to the Ming dynasty.

▶▶▶ Changbaishan   112B1

Open: daily. Admission: expensive

China's largest nature reserve, a vast area of dense forest and tundra, is noted for its varieties of plant and animal life, from wild ginseng to Manchurian tigers. It is within the Yanbian Korean Autonomous Prefecture, and its most famous beauty spot is the volcanic crater lake of **Tianchi (Heavenly Lake)**▶▶, at a height of over 2,000m (6,500ft). With an average depth of 205m (670ft), Tianchi is the deepest lake in China. Formed by an eruption in 1702, it glistens in the shadow of wild peaks and is a 1- or 2-hour climb from a 60m (200ft) waterfall, the point where most visitors arrive. At other times of year the area is only accessible by snowmobile.

▶ Changchun   112B2

Between 1933 and 1945, Changchun, the capital of Jilin province, was the capital of Manchukuo, the artificial state created by the Japanese to be ruled over by the puppet Last Emperor, Puyi (see pages 118–119). His former **imperial residence**▶▶ (*Open daily 8.30–4.20 in summer; 8.30–3.40 in winter. Admission: inexpensive*) has become a museum and exhibition hall. Otherwise,

Changchun is famous for its car factory (which produced the Red Flag limousine used by Party dignitaries) and for its film studio. Tours of both can be arranged by CITS.

▶ Dalian

112A1

Formerly known as Dairen and Luda, Dalian is the only real port in the northeast. It is clean and uncrowded and, as an Open Coastal City, has an air of prosperity seldom found in most of the rest of China. Strategically important because of its deep-water, ice-free port, it was a rival to Hong Kong under the Japanese. Before that, Dalian was of interest to the Russians, who wanted an alternative to Vladivostok, which becomes ice-bound. Under the Yalta agreement in 1945, the Japanese gave Dalian to the Soviet Union, whose occupation ceased only in the 1950s. The occasional Russian street sign is a reminder of that time, and there are interesting examples of neoclassical architecture, like the People's Cultural Hall on Zhongshan Square.

It is not an exciting place to visit, however. A tour of the port is possible, and there are some excellent beaches at Jinshitan and Fujiazhuang. The shopping streets are lively, and the **Natural History Museum▶** (*Open* daily 9-4.30. *Admission: moderate*) is of interest, but Dalian's main attraction is its fish restaurants. These establishments specialize in sea-cucumber stew, yellow croaker in sweet-and-sour sauce, pike in soy bean sauce, soft-fried sea conches and phoenix shark's fin.

About 200km (125 miles) to the northeast of Dalian is the **Bingyu (Ice Valley)▶▶**, which winds through a 4,900ha (12,000-acre) primeval forest, and a river meanders through a landscape of sheer rock formations. Places of interest in the valley include the Skylark Peak, Xiaoyu (Small Valley), the Yingna River, and the Longhua (Dragon Splendour) and Huaguo (Orchard) Mountains.

ORE DOWN UNDER

Iron was first discovered in China in about 600BC, followed quickly by the development of cast iron. There was a flourishing iron and steel industry by the Han dynasty. China still has huge reserves of untapped iron ore, mostly of low quality with an iron content of about 30 per cent. A great deal of high-grade ore is imported from abroad. To secure supplies, the China Metallurgical Import and Export Corporation bought a 40 per cent stake in a mine at Channar in Western Australia.

117

Steel works at Anshan, Liaoning province. The smoking furnaces highlight China's serious pollution problem

The tragi-comic life of the Last Emperor has been vividly brought to world attention by the Italian director Bernardo Bertolucci in his film The Last Emperor. *Puyi's story was a travesty, but in many ways he personified the decline and fall of a once-great civilization.*

REFORMATION
For the Western reader, the first part of Puyi's autobiography (on which the film was largely based) is fascinating for its insight into the way of life inside the Forbidden City. The second part, dealing with his re-education, is less compelling. None the less, it too is of interest because it shows how Puyi was used as an example to the people: the book closes with the words, 'Only today, with the Communist Party and the policy of remoulding criminals, have I learnt the significance of this magnificent word ["man"] and become a real man.'

One man's life, two ways of living

NOW THE SUBJECT OF A MAJOR FILM

From Emperor to Citizen

THE AUTOBIOGRAPHY OF PUYI
THE LAST EMPEROR OF CHINA

Early start Puyi was born in Beijing on 7 February 1906, in the mansion of his father, Prince Chun, who inherited the title from Puyi's grandfather, the seventh son of the Emperor Daoguang (reigned 1821–50). He was not yet three when, in November 1908, he was made emperor at the behest of the dying Dowager Empress Cixi, in whose shaky hands the destiny of China had lain for several uneventful decades.

Puyi ascended the throne as the eleventh and last emperor of the Qing dynasty on 2 December. On 12 February 1912, he was forced to abdicate by the newly installed revolutionary government, but his retirement was not to be a quiet one.

Premature retirement The years after his abdication are of greater interest than those of his juvenile reign. His life under the Republic was at first governed by the 'Articles providing for the Favourable Treatment of the Great Qing Emperor after his Abdication'. His title of dignity was to be retained; he was to receive an annual allowance of 4 million taels; he was to continue to live, temporarily, in the Forbidden City; the sacrifices at his ancestral temples and imperial tombs would be maintained forever; the uncompleted tomb of the Emperor Guangxu would be finished according to the original plan; although no further eunuchs were to be engaged, all persons of imperial grade would continue to be employed at the palace; the former emperor's private property would enjoy the protection of the state; and the existing palace guard would become part of the Republican Army.

Palatial existence Puyi remained in the Forbidden City, complete with imperial retinue, until 1924 when the nationalists, concerned at the threat of restoration, forced him to leave. It was as if he lived in a continuous theatrical production—outside, the China that had sustained dynastic rule for 2,000 years was attempting to come to terms with notions of incipient democracy, something altogether at odds with Chinese tradition; while, simultaneously, Puyi lived a barely diluted imperial existence in the palace. Everywhere he went, whether it was to study, carry out imperial duties or to stroll in the garden, he was pursued by his staff of eunuchs and attendants. He called this 'the daily pomp'.

Restoration There was surprisingly widespread support for the monarchy in early Republican China, and Puyi was restored to the throne for just 12 days in 1917. The idea of restoration was never entirely relinquished, particularly by the Japanese, who thought that popular support for an emperor might play a useful role in their own ambitions for a Pan-Asian empire.

After his expulsion from the Forbidden City in 1924, Puyi took refuge in the Japanese Legation. He was later made puppet emperor of Manchukuo, the artificial empire created in northeast China by the invading Japanese. After the war he was captured by Soviet troops and lived in Russia until Mao's victory in 1949. After his return he underwent political indoctrination before becoming a gardener in the Botanical Gardens in Beijing. He was publicly humiliated during the Cultural Revolution, and died in 1967.

Above: a scene from the film The Last Emperor, *directed by Bernardo Bertolucci*

119

The much-decorated last representative of 2,000 years of imperial rule looks out at a rapidly changing world

The Northeast

► Dandong 112B1

A border town with North Korea, Dandong, in the province of Liaoning, is one of the most important ports in the region and a focus of light industry. A visa is required to visit North Korea, however, it is possible to see into North Korea without a visa by taking a speed-boat ride along the Yalu River, or by going up the hill in Jinjiangshan Park. A visit to the town's Museum to Commemorate US Aggression (*Open* daily 8–5. *Admission: moderate*), offers an insight into the Cold War. About 50km (30 miles) from Dandong is **Fengcheng**, where the 840m (2,756ft) Fenghuang Mountain is dotted with temples from various dynasties.

Autumn mists on Taoist Fenghuang Mountain, near Dandong

►► Harbin 112B2

Architecturally speaking, Harbin, in Heilongjiang province, is unique in China. This is because of Russian influence—not from the alliance with the Soviet Union in the 1950s, but from the days when Harbin was an important junction on the Russian Manchurian Railway. As a result, Harbin's skyline is shaped by the onion domes and traditional roofs of a pre-revolutionary Russian town, although these are gradually being eclipsed by high-rise buildings.

Before the 1890s, Harbin was a moderately sized fishing village on the Songhua River. The construction of the railway brought many Russian engineers and merchants, followed by Chinese in search of work. After 1917, the population swelled to 200,000 as refugees from the revolution in Russia escaped over the border.

There are still a few Russian residents left in Harbin, but their numbers are dwindling fast, to be replaced by crowds of Russian citizens who cross the border to go shopping. Their influence can be seen most clearly in the *Continued on page 122*

Walk

Harbin

Take a ferry to **Sun Island** and then return, walking east through the Stalin Park, noting the **Flood Control**

Monument, to Shangzhi Street on the right. Walk, keeping Zhaolin Park on the left. At the crossing turn right, then right again up Zhongyang Street with the Modern Hotel on your right. At the top turn left, then take the first left to the intersection with Jingwei Street. Take the second left for the **cathedral**, then go south to Fendou Road and Dong Da Zhi Street in the city centre.

Harbin: winter in China's far north

One of the glowing ice sculptures, London's St. Paul's Cathedral, created for Harbin's extraordinary ice festival held in Zhaolin Park every year

Continued from page 120
Daoliqu▶▶ area, near Zhongyang Dajie, which is also of interest for its shops and markets on the banks of the river. Nearby is the restored Church of St. Sophia.

During World War II, Harbin was home to a Japanese Germ Warfare Experimental Base, which is now a museum, some 32km (20 miles) away in the town of Pingfang. The museum (*Open* daily 9–11.30, 1–4. *Admission: inexpensive*) shows the sadism of the experiments carried out on Chinese, Soviet, British and Korean prisoners of war, who suffered unspeakable horrors.

A more cheerful reason to visit Harbin is for the **ice festival**▶▶▶ in January to March. Artists create ice and snow sculptures that are wrapped around lanterns so dragons, bridges and traditional pavilions glow in the dark. The sculptures are concentrated mostly in Zhaolin Park. There is also a ballroom dancing competition, a food sampling fair, as well as the chance to ride on sledges and snowmobiles.

Sun Island is a sandbank on the Songhua River that is popular with sunbathers in the summer. A snow-sculpture competition is held there in January. It is also has parks and gardens, including **Siberia Tiger Park** (*Open* daily May–Oct 8.30–5; Nov–Apr 8.30–4. *Admission: moderate*), where Siberian tigers are bred.

▶ Heilongjiang (Heilong or Black Dragon River)
112B3

This river, which has given its name to the province, is more familiar by its Russian name—Amur. It forms the border between China and Russia and has been the scene of border disputes and skirmishes. Now that the border has been settled once and for all, the area is open to foreign visitors. Boat tours run between **Heihe**, **Huma** and **Tongjiang**. This is a region of minority peoples: the Hezhen, numbering about 1,500 at the last count, live by fishing and, like their Inuit cousins, use dog sledges.

COLD COMFORT
Although the people of Harbin are well known for their warmth, the city has a typical Siberian climate. In the winter temperatures fall to –38°C (–36°F) but in the summer can climb to more than 30°C (85°F).

Nowadays, however, the Hezhen wear woven clothing instead of animal hides. Another minority people, with a population of just over 4,000, are the Oroqens, who also live across the border in Inner Mongolia. Although many live settled lives now, they are by tradition nomadic forest hunters, raising reindeer and making their utensils from birch bark.

Mohe is China's most northerly town, from which the aurora borealis can be viewed.

A NORTHEASTERN TREASURY
The three treasures of the northeast are antlers, furs and ginseng. There is also frog oil, which is extracted from the female frog's ovary and, when served in soup or with chicken, is supposed to have curative properties.

▶ Jiamusi   112C3

A large manufacturing town, Jiamusi is of interest for the farms where ginseng is grown and also where red deer are bred for their antlers, which are used in Chinese medicine.

▶ Jilin   112B2

A major chemical-producing city with a population of more than 1 million, Jilin (formerly Kirin) has nearby ski slopes, a **ginseng farm▶**, and the **Jilin City Museum** (*Open daily 8.30–4.30. Admission moderate*), containing the world's

biggest meteorite, weighing 1,770kg (3,900lb), which fell in 1976. The **Wen Confucian Temple** (*Open daily 8–4. Admission: inexpensive*) with an exhibition about the old imperial examinations, is worth a visit.

Songhua Lake is 13km (8 miles) southeast of Jilin, in a scenic area of 544sq km (210sq miles).

Manchurian ginseng and tree fungus, used in traditional Chinese medicine

▶ Jingpo Lake   112B2

Some 113km (70 miles) from the town of Mudanjiang is this S-shaped lake surrounded by high mountains. A good place for fishing (equipment may be hired), it is the result of a volcanic lava flow that dammed up a gully. The area is a **national park▶▶**, with volcanic craters, karst caves and waterfalls, including 40m (130ft) wide Diaoshuilou. Sadly, the area is beginning to be spoiled by insensitive tourist development but visits in spring or autumn are comfortable and comparatively tourist-free.

▶▶ Shenyang

A city of 6 million and the Liaoning province capital, at the beginning of the 17th century Shenyang was the capital of the Manchurian empire. In that same century, the Manchus overran China, making Beijing their capital, relegating Shenyang (formerly Mukden) to a secondary position. By the 20th century, it was a Russian railway town; then it alternated between China and Japan during the first Russo-Japanese War (1904–05). During the next 45 years, it was in the hands of various warlords, the Japanese, the Russians, the Guomindang and finally the communists. Nowadays Shenyang's thriving industrial output includes aircraft and textiles.

The city's main sites are the **Imperial Palace▶▶**, the **Qing tombs▶▶** and the **Shisheng Temple▶**. The **Imperial City** (*Open* daily 8.30–4.30. *Admission: moderate*) is a Manchu version in miniature of the Forbidden City in Beijing. Originally the Palace of the Prosperous Capital (Shenjing Gong), it was renamed the Travelling Palace of Upholding Heaven after Beijing became the capital in 1644. The palace was completed between 1625 and 1636, and additions were made during the 18th century. Contained by its walls are some 300 rooms and 10 courtyards, set on three axes—middle, eastern and western. The arrangement of the eastern axis is most typically Manchu. On the western axis is the

124

Stately birds and elegant lotus blossoms adorn an ornamental feature in the Imperial Palace in Shenyang, Liaoning province

Map of Shenyang

Wensuge (Hall of the Source of Culture), built in 1782 to house the 3,450 classical works that made up the Complete Library of the Four Treasures of Knowledge. The Liaoning Provincial Museum opened in late 2004 in the Heping District and includes displays of Qing calligraphy, paintings and porcelain.

The **Tomb of Nurhaci (Dongling or Fuling)**, founder of the Manchu nation, is northeast of Shenyang. An avenue of stone animals leads to a wall enclosing a tower and a mound, in which are buried the emperor and his empresses and concubines (*Open* daily 7.30–5.30. *Admission: moderate*).

Beiling or **Zhaoling** (*Open* daily 6–6. *Admission: inexpensive*), in a wooded park in the northern part of the city, is the tomb of Huang Taiji (Abahai), son of Nurhaci, and his wife. It is better preserved than Dongling, with stone horses and lions, bridges, and a fine *pailou* (canopied gateway) in black stone, as well as a stele bearing Abahai's calligraphy.

The **Shisheng Temple**, on Heping Lu, was built in 1638 and was the main Lamaist temple in the city.

▶ Wudalianchi 112B3

This nature reserve comprises five linked lakes, formed in 1720 when volcanic activity forced lava into the Bei River. The mineral springs are said to cure almost any ailment.

▶▶ Zhalong 112B3

Open: daily 8–6. Admission: inexpensive

Zhalong is at the edge of a vast area of marshland that lies on a bird migration route from the Arctic to southeast Asia. Some 180 species of birds pass through between April and October, among them the almost extinct red-crowned crane, the traditional Chinese symbol of longevity.

Roofscape, Imperial Palace, Shenyang

STOCKS AND SHARES
In 1986, Shenyang was the first city in China since 1949 to boast a stock exchange. In the same year, a Shenyang company declared bankruptcy, unheard of in a socialist economy.

CHARISMATIC CRANES
For the Chinese, animals are to be either eaten or venerated. Such was the reverence accorded the red-crowned crane by Duke Yi of Wei that he paid them a salary and allowed them to travel in carriages. This irritated the Wei generals, who asked, 'Since the cranes are so highly esteemed, why not let them do the fighting?'

For Westerners, traditional Chinese medicine is invariably associated with acupuncture, but acupuncture is only one of several applications, all of which are based on the precepts of Taoism.

A Yunnan herbalist passes on his knowledge to his son

SLOW BUT SURE
Chinese medicine usually comes in the form of a variety of pills and potions with a plethora of bewildering instructions. Tempting though it is to ignore them, patience and careful observance of the directions often leads to good results. Chinese medicine does not act as quickly as its Western counterpart.

In the pharmacy of the Hospital of Traditional Chinese Medicine, Tianjin

126

Vital essence Chinese medicine is considered un-scientific and imprecise by some Western doctors. But a Chinese doctor might well argue that its imprecision—or flexibility—is in fact its strength. The Chinese refer to organs, but when they do so it is not the organs themselves that are important but their func-tion in the distribution of vital essence (or *qi*) through-out the body. The 11 'organs' by which health is judged are the bladder, circulation, gall bladder, heart, kidney, large intestine, liver, pancreas, small intestine, stomach and something called the 'triple burner', which has no material existence but is a driving force. Over the cen-turies, hundreds of points were located on the body, linked to these organs. By joining them together, meridi-an paths were drawn that traced the flow of *qi*.

Harmony There are 12 meridians, each corresponding to one of the five Chinese elements (metal, earth, fire, water, wood) and each best treated at a certain time of day. A further eight meridians are important in Taoism but of less importance to clinical medical treatment. What concerns Chinese medicine is not the state of the heart itself but the invisible motor that drives the heart to beat. Illness results from a disharmony between mind and body, which can arise when emotional strain, for example, distorts nature's balance.

Diagnosis The Chinese doctor examines the state of the flow of *qi* through the body's meridians by checking the pulse. He or she uses three fingers to read the six different pulses in each wrist that correspond to the 12 meridians. By applying different levels of pressure with the fingers, he or she will notice irregularities. Having read the pulse, the doctor will ask questions of the patient to decide upon the appropriate treatment.

Treatment The aim is to stimulate the flow of *qi* in the blocked meridian using acupuncture (*zhenjiu*), acupressure (similar to acupuncture), heat treatment with needles in conjunction with the burning leaves of mugwort (moxibustion), or massage (*anmou*). The most precise and efficacious of these is acupuncture, which is particularly good for relieving pain.

Diet is considered vital to health and partly explains the Chinese obsession with food. Taoist teaching recommends abstinence from a variety of foods and stimulants, although a less rigorous version of the diet suffices for most. Only food that relates to the organs and the elements associated with them is eaten, so, for example, hot foods are recommended for the lungs.

Much of this, although not scientifically expressed according to Western terminology, does correspond to Western ideas, and there is no doubt that Chinese medicine, even if based on amorphous theories, is extremely effective for some diseases. Some aspects, like the use of talismans and incantations, are less likely to win over sceptics, but Chinese medicine in general deserves serious consideration.

Above: acupuncture
Top: medicinal gourds

127

SKIN TONIC
Taoists believe that following a strict diet for three years will result in the regeneration of skin tissue throughout the body; after 10 years the teeth and bones will be renewed.

A medicine market

Map

RUS

KZ

MGL

4374m
Youyi Feng
Altay
Burqin   Fuyun
(Köktokay)
Tacheng
Karamay
Junggar
Pendi
Sayram
Hu
Ebinur
Hu   Kuytun   Ürümqi
Huocheng   (Urumchi)
Yining   Shihezi   Tianchi
(Gulja)
KS   Bezeklik
7439m   T i a n   S h a n
Aksu   Kuqa   Yanqi   (Turpan)   Hami
Kashi   Kizil   Korla   Bosten Hu   (Turfan)   (Kumul)
(Kashgar)   Tarim He   Kuruktag Shan   Ejin
TJ   XINJIANG UYGUR ZIZHIQU   GANSU   NE
7719m   Tarim Pendi   Lop Nur
AF   Kongur   Shache (Yarkant)   Qarqan He   Ruoqiang   Dunhuang   Mogao   Yumen
Shan   Yecheng (Kargilik)   Taklamakan   Shamo   (Qarkilik)   Caves   Jiayuguan
Taxkorgan   Zhangye
(Tashkurgan)   Hotan   Altun   Shan   Lenghu   Qilian   Shan   Jincha
PAK   8611m   Hotan He   Qiemo   Qaidam   Tianjun   Xinin
Qogir Feng   Yutian   (Qarqan)   Pendi   Qinghai Hu   Bingl
(Keriya)   7723m   Da Qaidam   Gonghe   Huang He
IND   K u n l u n   S h a n   Hoh Xil Shan   Golmud   Xiahe
5442m   (Labrang)
XIZANG ZIZHIQU   Q I N G H A I
(TIBET)   Bayan Har Shan
Tanggula Shan   Tongtian He   S I C

0   200   400   600 km
0   200   400 miles

Inner Mongolia and the Silk Road

Inner Mongolia and the Silk Road

MINORITIES AND NOMADS

The Xinjiang province is usually associated with the Uyghurs, but there are also the nomadic Kazaks of the mountains, fine horsemen who live in yurts; and the Kirgiz, also nomadic, who keep herds of camels. The Xibo Manchus, who live near the Russian border, are descended from Qing dynasty garrison troops.

Wrestlers in the grasslands outside Hohhot. Mongolian wrestling expresses joy in manhood

INNER MONGOLIA (NEI MENGGU) AND XINJIANG
Although these vast areas have separate histories, there is a tendency to place them together, along with the province of Gansu, gateway to the Silk Road oases, and the autonomous region of Ningxia. Perhaps this is because of their location on either side of the Gansu corridor; or because both, like Tibet, are outside the mainstream of Chinese life (much as Beijing would like to believe otherwise); or perhaps because there is a tendency for tour companies to combine the two as a package.

As far as the peripheral regions of the Chinese empire are concerned, the world's attention has been focused on Tibet. But the peoples of the Mongolian grasslands and the Muslims of the northwest chafe at Chinese rule from time to time as well (several protestors were killed in Yining in 1997 as the authorities quelled riots). The former Mongolian People's Republic (known in the past as Outer Mongolia and now simply as Mongolia) is a sovereign state that may yet yearn for reunification with Chinese Inner Mongolia. The Muslims of the northwest have plenty of close relatives across the border in the former Soviet republics—the growing Islamic movement may strengthen ties with the old oasis towns of the Silk Road.

CHINESE RULE Both areas are comparatively recent acquisitions by China. After the fall of the Mongolian empire at the end of the 14th century, the Mongol tribes returned to their nomadic, tribal ways, but under the Qing dynasty the Mongol homelands were absorbed into the Chinese empire, the Chinese at last allaying their fear of the barbarians across the Wall. This huge area was difficult to subjugate, and the Russian empire lopped off the northern, 'outer' part of Mongolia as a protectorate. Inner Mongolia remained part of China until 1911 and the fall of

130

NEW SILK ROAD?
China and Tajikistan celebrated the opening of a
new road between the two
countries on 25 May
2004. The road opens up
Central Asia through to
the Caspian Sea to China,
rebuilding former trade
routes and links.

*Struggling up the
'singing sands'—dunes
near the oasis town of
Dunhuang, Gansu
province*

*Hui Muslim from
Ningxia*

the last dynasty. The two Mongolias were reunified for
eight years. China then reclaimed Inner Mongolia, while
Outer Mongolia declared itself the Mongolian People's
Republic in 1924. The Japanese occupied much of the area
during the 1930s, but after World War II the Chinese
declared Inner Mongolia an autonomous region within
China. China recognized Outer Mongolia as a separate
state in 1946. Inner Mongolia has a population of 20
million, of which a mere 2 million are ethnic Mongolians.

Xinjiang ('New Territory') was brought under Chinese
rule at various times during the Han and Tang dynasties,
but it was the acquisitive Qing dynasty that brought the
region to heel in the 18th century. The Muslims never
accepted Chinese rule and, with the fall of the dynasty in
1911, the region came under the control of a succession of
warlords. An attempt in 1945 to form an independent
Turkestan Republic failed, and the communists absorbed
the area into China with little difficulty in 1949. Now,
more than half its population of 13 million is Han Chinese.

In both regions, although some concessions have been
granted to cultural differences, on the whole Chinese rule
is paramount. None the less, daily life for many of the
natives of these areas is quite different from that of their
compatriots behind the Great Wall, a fact that is still very
much in evidence, particularly in the towns of the Silk
Road or at the annual Naadam Fair in Mongolia.

OVER THE BORDER
In the mid-1980s a little-
reported phenomenon
was taking place in the
remote border regions of
the Mongolian People's
Republic and China, for
many years a sensitive
area because of their
traditional enmity. The
infrequent trains between
the two were crammed
with Chinese men and
women who had been
living in Mongolia and
who, as a result of ten-
sion between the two
countries, were being
sent back to China.
Belongings and food were
piled high in the compartments, only to be confis-
cated at the frontier.

Buddhist dancers depicted in the Mogao caves (Cave 112)

▶ ▶ ▶ Dunhuang   *128C2*

A small oasis town in Gansu province, Dunhuang (which means 'blazing beacon') is the most important site on the Silk Road itinerary because of the magnificent array of early Chinese Buddhist paintings in the **Mogao caves** ▶ ▶ ▶ (25km/15 miles away). Dunhuang was made a prefecture in 117BC by Emperor Han Wudi, and some of the beacons made of yellow earth that were part of the Han extension of the Great Wall are visible between the town and the railway station at Liuyuan, the nearest point of arrival.

The cave paintings, accumulated over several centuries, were the legacy of the pilgrim monks on their way to India and of merchants and nobles who made their own artistic contributions as a blessing for their caravans and salvation for their souls. The painters were sometimes locals, sometimes masters brought in for the purpose. The cave temples were excavated by monks from AD366; their walls were covered in mud and then layers of dung, plaster and animal hair, and kaolin was added to provide a suitable surface on which to paint. As the Silk Road declined, the caves became less important, and in the 10th century they were sealed. In 1900, they were rediscovered by a monk who made it his life's work to return them to their former glory. Soon after, the Anglo-Hungarian explorer Sir Aurel Stein persuaded the monk to part with a remarkable collection of manuscripts and silk paintings, now displayed in the British Museum and the Bibliothèque Nationale, Paris.

The caves (*Open* daily 8–5.30. *Admission: expensive*) were made a national monument in 1961. Of the 1,000 caves, about 40 are thought worth visiting. A morning and afternoon visit is necessary to fully appreciate the caves, while a torch (flashlight) is an essential accessory.

The earliest caves date back to the fourth century (Northern Wei dynasty). A good example is Cave 257, famous for paintings on the west wall depicting the story of the Buddha who, as Deer King, was betrayed by a man whose life he had saved. It also features a very early landscape. The later Western Wei is represented in Cave 249, with some beautiful landscape paintings.

SUTRAS AND DOCUMENTS
Sir Aurel Stein's finds at Dunhuang consist mainly of manuscripts written out as acts of devotion, as well as the Diamond Sutra (now in the British Museum), claimed to be the world's earliest known printed book (AD866); some of the documents were of a secular nature—tax and census returns, and bills of sale, for example—which appear to have been sealed in the caves for safe-keeping, and there is also a manuscript fragment containing musical notation for the lute.

Cave 428 was decorated during the Northern Zhou with portraits of figures who had sponsored sacred paintings—these are beneath the story from the life of Buddha on the east wall.

The finest caves of the Sui dynasty are 150, 244, 410, 420 (with a spectacular temple painted on the ceiling) and 427. By this time foreign influence (Indian, Central Asian) had been replaced with a purer Chinese style.

Dunhuang's art peaked during the Tang dynasty, when religious traditions were combined with observations of real life. Murals vary from scenes from the sutras to portraits of individuals. The finest examples are in Caves 1, 16, 17, 51, 70, 96, 130, 139, 148, 172, 202, 209, 320, 321, 323, 328, 329, 332, 365 and 387.

The **Crescent Lake▶▶** (6km/4 miles south) is a spring-fed pool (*Open* daily 8–6. *Admission: expensive*) surrounded by giant sand dunes (called 'the singing sands') that can, with difficulty, be climbed. Camels and drivers are available to take you, for a fee, to the dunes.

The 'old city movie set', a Song-dynasty-style town constructed for the Sino-Japanese film *Dunhuang*, is in the desert to the southwest.

Dunhuang Museum▶ (*Open* daily 8–6.30. *Admission: inexpensive*) on Yangguan Donglu, has exhibits from some of the caves at Mogao and also from the old fortresses at Yangguan and Yumen.

133

A Tang dynasty 'Apsara', celestial angel, in Cave 44

Perfect statuesque calm at Dunhuang: seated Tang Buddha in Cave 328

Inner Mongolia (Nei Menggu) was absorbed into the Chinese empire in the 18th century. The history of the Mongolian people before that is long and occasionally illustrious.

Above: the tomb of Genghis Khan

BENEATH THE GRASSLANDS
The attractions of Mongolia for the Chinese are concealed below the earth's surface. It is the best place in the country for rare earth minerals, and there are at least 60 verifiable mineral ores in 500 different locations, including coal, iron, chromium, copper, lead, zinc, gold, mica, salt and mirabilite.

The Lamaist Wudangzhao Monastery, north of Baotou

Nomads For centuries, the Mongols were a loose confederation of nomadic tribesmen based on the banks of the Onon River, and a constant threat to the Chinese, who constructed the Great Wall to keep them out. In the early 13th century, the various tribes united under Genghis Khan and conquered most of Eurasia. The Mongols ruled China (the Yuan dynasty) for over 100 years, but with Kublai Khan's death in 1294 the empire disintegrated. Although major khanates remained in western parts of the former empire, the Mongols returned to their homeland and their nomadic ways.

Grasslands Something of the traditional Mongol way of life is still evident on the grasslands. Round felt tents, or 'ghers', and herdsmen on horseback can sometimes be seen but visitors are discouraged from discovering the grasslands for themselves other than through organized tours by CITS or foreign travel companies.

Highlights Inner Mongolia has its own atmosphere, and there are a number of places worth visiting, particularly in summer. The capital is **Hohhot** (**Huhehaote**) where the main attractions are the **Inner Mongolia Museum▶▶** (*Open* daily 9–6. *Admission: inexpensive*), which displays objects of traditional Mongolian life and a locally discovered mammoth; the **Old Town▶▶**, with its low houses and markets and temples and mosques; and the **Five Pagoda Temple▶** (*Open* daily 8–6. *Admission: inexpensive*), unique in China for its Classical Indian style. Tours can be arranged to the grasslands.

Xilinhot has little to recommend it but is a good base from which to arrange a visit to the grasslands.

Baotou is the largest city of Inner Mongolia. Its main attraction, apart from the steel mill and a small locomotive museum, is the 13th-century **Wudangzhao Monastery▶▶** (*Open* daily 8.30–6.30. *Admission: moderate*), 72km (45 miles) to the north and the best example of a Tibetan-style monastery in the region. Set on the side of a hill, it consists of temples, houses, a hostel and lamas' living quarters. It is well worth the drive from Baotou.

135

About 64km (40 miles) south of Baotou you can visit **Yimeng Xiang Shawan**, or the resonant sand gorge, filled with dunes up to 82m (270ft) high.

Hailar, on the banks of the Heilong Jiang (Amur River), is another good starting point from which to visit the grasslands. **Manzhouli** is even better; from here you can also visit Dalai Lake, one of the largest lakes in China.

From Dongsheng, south of Baotou, you can reach **Genghis Khan's Mausoleum** (*Open* daily 7–7. *Admission: expensive*) via Ejin Qi. The mausoleum dates from 1954, when the Khan's ashes were returned from Qinghai. He remains an object of veneration to Mongolians.

Perhaps the best time to visit Inner Mongolia is in the summer, usually the month of August, during *Naadam* (the word means exhibition or game or joke). In recent years it has come to mean the national festival, a celebration of archery, wrestling and horsemanship.

The Five Pagoda Temple, Hohhot

A harsh climate makes for tough people: Mongolian wrestlers at the annual Naadam *fair*

Traditional Kashi cloth in vibrant hues

▶▶ Jiayuguan   *128C2*

This small town is at the far end and narrowest point of the Gansu Corridor, marking the western extremity of the Great Wall and the traditional boundary of Han China. 'One more cup of wine for our remaining happiness. There will be chilling parting dreams tonight,' wrote a ninth-century poet of a parting at Jiayuguan. Just outside the town is an imposing **Ming fort▶▶▶** (*Open* daily 8.30–5. *Admission: moderate*), built in 1372 in a dramatic setting between two ranges of mountains that crowd in on the pass. It rises in spectacular fashion—crenellated walls 10m (33ft) high surmounted by towers with elegant roofs—from an area of flat-stone desert. The **Heishan rock carvings▶**, reputedly made by the Huns about 1,500 years ago, are 19km (12 miles) northwest. Some 6km (4 miles) north of the fort is a reconstructed section of the Great Wall, with fabulous views of the Valla mountains.

▶▶▶ The Karakorum Highway   *128A2*

The route between Pakistan and China was opened in the mid-1980s using what was once a branch of the Silk Road. It is a magnificent way of leaving or entering China. From Kashi, a day's drive through awesome mountain scenery, passing rippleless lakes and crumbling caravanserai, takes you to Tashkurgan (an uncomfortable overnight stop). From Tashkurgan, the road winds up to a height of nearly 4,900m (16,077ft) before it crosses the border into the mountain valleys of Pakistan.

▶▶▶ Kashi (Kashgar)   *128A2*

Conjuring up a host of magical images, Kashi, or Kashgar as it is more widely known, manages to meet expectations in many ways, despite steady historical decline, Chinese indifference to local culture and creeping modernization. Its importance grew from its location as an oasis at the point where the northern and southern arms of the Silk Road converged, forming a natural gateway to the mountain passes leading to India and Russia. Kashi was held by the Chinese periodically from AD78, but by the 10th century it was firmly in the Islamic world, where it remained until the Chinese reconquered the area in the 18th century. Kashgar became a focal point for the rivalry between Russia and Britain, a tussle for hegemony in Central Asia known as 'the Great Game'. Kashgar became a haven for spies of these empires, both of which opened consulates (the former British one stood at the back of the Chini Bagh Hotel grounds, the former Russian one is the Seman Hotel).

There are several places to see. The **Id Kah Mosque▶** (*Open* daily. *Admission: inexpensive*) is the largest in Xinjiang, with room for at least 6,000 people. Founded in 1442, its present appearance dates from 1838. The **Abakh Hoja Tomb▶▶**, in the eastern suburbs, contains 72 tombs of the family members of Abakh Hoja, a saintly man of the 18th century whose daughter was the legendary 'fragrant concubine' (so-called because she was supposed to have naturally secreted perfume) who was abducted by the Emperor Qian Long. She defied the emperor and was forced to commit suicide by the emperor's mother.

The **market▶▶** in the middle of town is a vibrant daily event and worth lingering in for a couple of hours. Try to be in Kashi for the **Sunday Bazaar▶▶▶**, a meeting point for all the farmers in the area who come, much as they have done for centuries, to sell their wares, from melons to horseflesh. Hot and dusty, it provides a fascinating glimpse into local life.

Since 1999, there has been a railway link with Ürümqi which, some fear, marks the beginning of the end for 'old' Kashi.

THE FINAL FRONTIER
The Inner City of Jiayuguan town, the last Chinese outpost on the Silk Road, with its 10m (33ft)-high wall, was a citadel that housed the Chinese military commander. Beyond were the 'barbarian' tribes. Outside the west gate is a stele inscribed with the characters: 'The Greatest Barrier Under Heaven'.

Preparing for the weekly bazaar, Sunday in Kashi, where Uyghur merchants gather from all over the area

137

*The Tang dynasty
Future Buddha in
Bingling Buddhist caves,
Gansu province*

▶▶▶ Kuqa   128B2

Kuqa is the second largest town in the central part of
Xinjiang and was once the capital of an ancient feudal state,
the Kingdom of Qiuci. The ruins consist mostly of sand-
brick walls, but convey a little of the region's past glories.
Taken by the Chinese in the seventh century, it was an
important focal point for Buddhism and the home of
Kumarajiva, one of the greatest translators of Sanskrit
works into Chinese. Kuqa had its own Indo-European language, lost for more than 1,000 years until the script was
discovered by the sinologists Paul Pelliot and Albert Von le
Coq on items in the caves at Kizil at the turn of the 20th century. The manuscripts found here, on palm leaves, paper,
bark and wood, were removed and deciphered in Paris.
Modern Kuqa is rather dull, although there is an interesting bazaar held each Friday.

Kizil ▶▶▶ (*Open* daily 9–8. *Admission: expensive*) is just
over an hour's drive away from Kuqa. The caves in cliffs
above the Muzart River were decorated between AD500
and 700, before Chinese stylistic devices had reached this
far, and the paintings are both Indian and Iranian in
style. Of the 236 caves, about 70 are reasonably well preserved. Many of the best frescoes were removed by
Albert Von le Coq to Berlin, where some were destroyed
during World War II. Others can still be seen in Berlin's
Museum of Indian Art. The remains of two other ancient
cities, Gucheng and Tonggusibashi, can also be visited
from Kuqa.

▶▶ Lanzhou   129D1

The capital of Gansu province lies on the upper reaches of
the Yellow River. A former staging post on the Silk Road, it
has become an industrial city of remarkable ugliness. The
city has a few items of note. The **Gansu Provincial
Museum** ▶▶ (currently being rebuilt) contains the finest

display of Yangshao (early neolithic) pottery in China, and bronzes from the Han-dynasty tomb of General Zhang, including the famous 'flying horse', its hoof poised on a swallow's wing. It is now a widely used symbol of the area.

The **Five Springs Mountain (Wuquanshan) Park▶** attempts to reconcile concrete with traditional Chinese architecture, with some success. In the park (*Open* daily 6.30–6. *Admission: inexpensive*) is the Chongqingsi, a 14th-century temple with a 13th-century iron bell. From here there is a chairlift (*Open* 8–8. *Admission: inexpensive*) to **Lanshan Park**, high up in the Lanshan mountains.

The **White Pagoda Mountain Park▶** (*Open* daily 6.30am–8pm. *Admission: inexpensive*) consists of several temples including the Yuan-dynasty **White Pagoda**.

The main reason for a stop in Lanzhou is to visit the **Buddhist caves at Bingling▶▶▶** (*Open* daily 8–6, except during low-water periods, usually in winter. *Admission: moderate*), 97km (60 miles) from the city. Organized tours are recommended, as trips to the caves are dependent upon the unpredictable river-water level and involve a two-hour bus journey and a further two hours by boat. *En route* you may visit the **Liujia Gorge Dam**, one of the largest in China.

The 34 caves at Bingling contain several hundred statues (the largest of which, in Cave 172, is a Tang Future Buddha, about 27m/89ft high) and many paintings. The earliest caves date back to the Northern Wei period, but painting continued through the Tang, the period of greatest activity, to the Qing. Some of the best work is in Caves 4, 10, 11, 82, 114 and 169.

It is also possible to visit **Xiahe** and the **Labrang Monastery** (described on pages 146–147) from Lanzhou, although the journey will take seven hours. Xinglongshan, 50km (31 miles) from Lanzhou, is a mountain covered in Han-dynasty temples.

TREACHEROUS WATERS
The Yellow River carries heavy deposits of silt down from the loess region of the northern steppe. For centuries the silt has caused severe flooding and drainage problems. Construction of the dam at Sanmenxia in Gansu province began after 1949, but later the reservoir became clogged with the river's sediment and had to be rebuilt.

View across the Yellow River over the city of Lanzhou from White Pagoda Mountain

Ningxia Huizu Zizhiqu is the Autonomous Hui Region of Ningxia and is very similar to Gansu province, of which it was once a part. Its landscape varies from the arid and mountainous south to the northern desert region (the Tengger Desert, part of the Gobi), bisected by the Yellow River.

NORTHWESTERN FRONTIER TROUBLE

The Western Xia (Xixia) were a northern Tibetan (Tangut) tribe who became the dominant force in their homelands. They invaded the Chinese northwest in 1040, at first with considerable success, but the sheer size of the Chinese army and its sophisticated hardware, which included early hand grenades, in the end was too much for the Xia. The Song dynasty, none the less, was compelled to pay tribute to the Xia, as well as to the Khitan (another tribal state threatening Chinese stability) as the price of peace. The Xia were finally vanquished by Genghis Khan in 1227.

140

Discussing religion at a Ningxia mosque. The Hui, whose ancestors came from the Middle East, are an Islamic people

The Hui Ningxia is one of the poorest and most underdeveloped areas of China; even now, perhaps half the population earns less than the equivalent of 20 US dollars per year. In this region of parched soil, everything depends on rainfall and there is even a relocation scheme to move people who can no longer make a living from the land.

Ningxia has a population of 4 million, of whom about one third are Hui people. The Hui are Muslims. With Chinese features, and darker skin, they are descended from Arab and Iranian traders who came to China along the Silk Road during the Tang dynasty and intermarried with the local population. Their numbers swelled further during the Yuan (Mongol) dynasty, when more arrived from Central Asia. During the Muslim Uprisings of 1862–78, the Hui played a major role, but they were mercilessly punished by the imperial troops. Ningxia was created as a separate administrative region in 1928, was absorbed into Gansu in 1954, and re-emerged as an autonomous region in 1958.

Highlights Ningxia is not a major area for tourism, but it is not without interest. The provincial capital, once the

capital of the 11th-century Western Xia dynasty, is
Yinchuan▶▶. Set amid irrigation canals used since the
Han dynasty, the city has little to offer, except in the old
town, which houses the 400-year-old Yuhuang Pavilion,
the Drum Tower, several mosques, the West Pagoda, the
North Pagoda (rebuilt in 1771), the South Gate, a
Catholic church and Ningxia Museum.

More enticing is **Gunzhongkou**▶▶, west of Yinchuan,
among the Helanshan mountains, which reach more than
3,350m (10,990ft) in height. Here are the Twin Pagodas
and the Western Xia Mausoleum, constructed by the

*Below: sheepskin coracle
on the Yellow River
Below and top, opposite:
details from Gao Temple,
Zhongwei*

founder of the Western Xia dynasty, Li Yuanhao.

About 97km (60 miles) from Yinchuan, near
Qingtongxia▶▶, are 108 white Dagobas built during the
Yuan dynasty, mysteriously in the shape of a triangle.

Zhongwei▶ is a small but ancient town which has the
Gao Temple (*Open* daily 7–6.30. *Admission: inexpensive*), an unusual edifice in wood constructed for use by
Buddhists, Confucianists and Taoists. East of the town
are remains of the Great Wall and, on the edge of the
Tengger Desert at Shapotou, the **Desert Research
Centre** (*Open* daily. *Admission: inexpensive*). Its original
aim in 1956 was to find ways of preventing the desert
sands from encroaching onto the railways, and it seems
to have met with some success. Like Yinchuan,
Zhongwei is watered by ancient irrigation canals. Rafts
made of sheep leather, a traditional method of
transportation on the Yellow River, can sometimes still
be seen at work.

Guyuan, in southern Ningxia, has more than 130 caves
cut into the mountains. The caves contain fine Buddhist
work up to 1,400 years old.

Maijishan: the name means 'Corn Rick Mountain'

Clay sculptures outside the spectacular Maijishan Buddhist caves

▶ **Linxia** *129D1*

Another former Silk Road town in Gansu province, which is interesting because of its minority inhabitants: the Hui, Dongxiang and Uyghur peoples.

▶▶ **Maijishan** *129D1*

The Buddhist caves (*Open* daily 8.30–5. *Admission: expensive*) on Maijishan, a mountain 32km (20 miles) southeast of Tianshui in the south of Gansu, rank with those at Datong, Dunhuang and Luoyang as the most important in China. Joining a group with a guide is advisable, and a torch (flashlight) is useful. The caves are reached by a network of precipitous stairways.

The earliest date back to the fourth century. Some 200 remain, many of those on the west side untouched since the Song dynasty—notable are Caves 100, 133 and 165. On the less well-preserved east side, the most interesting caves are 4, 7, 13, 72a, 102, 133 and 191. At **Gangu**, west of Tianshui, is a Tang-dynasty Buddha overlooking the Wei River.

▶▶▶ **Turpan (Turfan)** *128B2*

Turpan, which is served by train from Daheyan, is perhaps the most delightful town along the Chinese Silk Road, in part for its interesting sights, but chiefly because it still exudes, with its trees and traditional Uyghur mud-brick houses, a tranquil, old-world atmosphere rare in China. Although most of the inhabitants are Uyghur, much of Turpan's historical importance is pre-Islamic. The Uyghurs, originally nomads from Siberia and Central Asia, settled in the area after the ninth century, when they were converted to Islam. They still retain much of their way of life, wearing traditional clothes, building trellised courtyards and small kilns for drying the famous grapes from the area, and following a diet—mutton, flat bread, dried fruit, pilau rice— quite distinct from that of Han China.

Most of the places of interest lie just outside the town, but there are a few things of worth within its walls. Turpan's **market**▶▶, with its dried fruit, exotic medicines and gleaming rolls of cloth, is endlessly fascinating. The **Imin**

Minaret▶▶, part of a former mosque, was built in 1778 and is made of beautifully decorated brick in the tapering Iranian style. It is no longer open to the public.

Outside the town are some remarkable ruins, graves and caves, many of which were disturbed by turn-of-the-20th-century archaeologist adventurers. The **Cave Temples at Bezeklik▶▶**, 50km (31 miles) northeast, (*Open* daily 8.30–8. *Admission: inexpensive*), are part of a monastery that existed between the 6th and 14th centuries, carved out of the cliff face above the Murtuk River in a desert setting. There are some fine paintings remaining (in an Indo-Iranian style with Chinese influence), but many were removed by Von le Coq to museums in Berlin, and some were subsequently destroyed by Allied bombs.

To the west of Turpan is the abandoned town of **Jiaohe▶▶**, and to the southeast the ruined city of **Gaochang▶▶▶** (*Open* daily 8–8. *Admission: moderate*) and the ancient graveyard of **Astana▶▶** (*Open* daily 8–8. *Admission: inexpensive*). Jiaohe was originally a Han garrison town, taken by the Uyghurs and abandoned in the Yuan dynasty perhaps because of a lack of water or Muslim iconoclasm. It is poignant and spectacular in its clifftop setting, as is Gaochang, another Han garrison town, which was the Uyghur capital from 840 to 1209. It was abandoned at the beginning of the Ming dynasty.

Astana is a graveyard used between the third and eighth centuries. Well-preserved bodies have been discovered here, as well as documents, coins and pottery, now displayed in Turpan and Ürümqi museums. Three of the graves are open, one showing two of the occupants, the others with charming Tang wall paintings.

Also near by are the **Flaming Mountains▶**, which glow at sunset, and **Grape Valley▶**, heart of grape production.

Every evening the Flaming Mountains outside Turpan reflect the desert heat

143

LOW LAND
Turpan lies in the Turpan depression (Turpan is a Uyghur word meaning 'lowland'), one of the lowest landfalls on earth, descending to 152m (500ft) below sea-level at its deepest point. Depressions such as this are a characteristic feature of the northern part of western China. Encircled by mountains, the oases high up are fed by melting snow in summer, while the middles remain true desert.

WELL-WATERED DESERT
Turpan is noted for its underground water channels, which are known as *karez*. These carry water formed by the melting snow from the nearby mountains and prevent it from evaporating in the intense heat of the summer. The system is thought to have been imported from Persia 2,000 years ago.

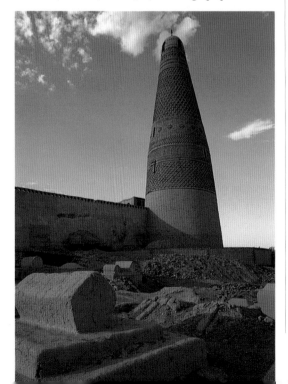

The Imin Minaret, Turpan, built in 18th-century Iranian style

The Silk Road is the collective name given to a number of trade routes linking the Chinese and Roman empires. Many commodities passed along it, but silk was for centuries one of its mainstays because silk production remained a mystery outside China (see pages 182–183).

Detail from a mural in Mogao Caves, Dunhuang

144

FLYING HORSES
General Zhang Qian's mission west took 13 years, during which time he was taken prisoner twice by the Xiongnu tribe. One of his most significant discoveries was the existence of the so-called 'flying horses' of Ferghana, in Uzbekistan, which were altogether more powerful than the horses familiar to the Chinese and which were taken in large numbers to build up the Chinese cavalry.

Exploration The Silk Road opened up during the reign of Emperor Han Wudi, who in 138 BC dispatched General Zhang Qian on a mission to seek an alliance with peoples west of China against the northern tribes. The information he brought back about Central Asia led to the westward extension of the Great Wall along the oasis towns of the Gobi and Taklimakan deserts, which were to become vital links in Silk Road trade. Beyond China, much of what was to be dubbed the Silk Road had been in use for centuries, since communication between the fringes of the great civilizations of Egypt, Mesopotamia and northern India was already possible, if not commonplace. When Alexander the Great marched east, many Western ideas found their way east as well, and vice versa. Zhang Qian's mission formed the final link in the chain. The Romans unified the Mediterranean area, which was linked to Central Asia by means of the imperial highways of the Persian empire. The Silk Road was to remain in constant use until about the mid-14th century.

Merchants The traffic went in both directions—China imported grapes, glass, amber, saffron and, during the cosmopolitan Tang dynasty, a variety of faiths including Manichaeism and Nestorianism, as well as Buddhism from India and, later, Islam. The starting point for Chinese exports was the imperial capital of Xi'an (or Chang'an as it was then). Very few merchants would have accompanied their stock all the way to its final destination. Goods were transported by camel through Gansu and Xinjiang from oasis to oasis, through many middlemen, notably in the Middle East. In Xinjiang the route went north or south of the Taklimakan, meeting at Kashi, from where it went west via either Balkh or Samarkand and Bukhara.

Kashi market: trade still flourishes along the Silk Road

Tea shop selling tea and traditional snacks, on the road between Turpan and Kashi

Foreign influence The centuries passed, and governments, rulers and dynasties changed—the Parthians and the Sassanians succeeded the Persian empire; the Roman empire fragmented and Byzantium emerged in its place, along with the kingdoms of western Europe—but the Silk Road continued as a commercial artery. The greatest upheaval was the gradual expansion from the seventh century of Islam throughout Central Asia to the borders of the Chinese heartlands, a movement that had the effect of binding a vast area together in faith. The Silk Road was probably most open to trade between China and the West under the Mongols during the 13th century, the period when Marco Polo's great journey to China was made.

Decline By the 16th century, the Silk Road had lost its significance, as the great empires declined and as maritime trade replaced caravans. The desert swallowed some towns; political instability made travel difficult; and the Chinese became more inward-looking after the Tang. Oasis towns whose existence had depended on trade were left to bask in the desert sun until their rediscovery by 19th-century adventurers and current visitors.

JUST DESERTS
The Taklamakan ('go in, not come out') Desert in Xinjiang province, which separates the northern and southern arms of the Silk Road, was explored by the archaeologist-explorers Sir Aurel Stein and Sven Hedin in the late 19th century. A hundred years later, the Taklamakan was again further explored, this time by an Anglo-Chinese expedition led by Charles Blackmore in 1993–94. The expedition discovered many lost towns previously hidden under the sands.

Modern-day tourist caravan at the Singing Sands, Dunhuang

INFAMOUS WARLORD
After 1911, Xinjiang was ruled for several decades by a succession of war-lords. The most infamous of these was Yang Zhengxin. His legendary ferocity led him to behead his enemies at banquets to which he had cordially invited them in a spirit of reconciliation. In the end he was shot at a banquet in 1928.

▶ **Ürümqi (Wulumuqi)**   *128B2*

The capital of Xinjiang, with a population of about 1 million inhabitants, is rather uninspiring in appearance, but there are good reasons for going there. Its position as capital and transportation hub make a visit almost inevitable. Despite an unprepossessing exterior and a lack of any precise hub, the city is of interest for its 'minor-ity' quarters, where Hui and Uyghur peoples live with their own markets and restaurants. The excellent **Minority Peoples' Museum▶▶** (*Open* Mon–Fri 10–6, Sat–Sun 10.30–4. *Admission: moderate*), on Xibei Lu, imaginatively explains the ways of life of the various nationalities in the area and is well worth a visit. There is also **Hongshan Hill** with its Qing pagoda and view; factories that produce car-pets, jade and musical instruments; and the Eighth Route Army Office Museum.

Ürümqi's main attraction lies outside the city—**Tianchi (Heaven's Lake)▶▶▶** (*Open* summer, daily. *Admission: expensive*) is 100km (62 miles) away at an altitude of 2,000m (6,560ft) among the Tian Shan (Heavenly Mountains), which rise to nearly 6,000m (19,680ft). It is a magnificent (and popular) sight, well worth the journey; if you have the time and the inclination, you can go on horseback with a Kazakh guide to the snowfields above and spend the night in a yurt. From Ürümqi, it is also possible to visit the beautiful **Nanshan grasslands** (Baiyanggou), where it is also possible to stay overnight.

▶▶▶ **Xiahe and the Labrang Monastery**   *128C1*

Xiahe is almost 3,000m (9,840ft) above sea-level in eastern Gansu, some 160km (100 miles) from Lanzhou and within striking distance of the old Tibetan northeastern province

Kazakhs in the summer meadows of the Heavenly Mountains, Baiyanggou

of Amdo. It is a place of exceptional interest, home to one of the six major Tibetan monasteries, the **Labrang Tashi Khyil** (**Labulengsi**)▶▶▶ (*Open* daily 8–6. *Admission: moderate*), an important place of pilgrimage for Tibetans who flood here in their distinctive finery.

The monastery was built in 1709 by Jamyang Zhepa (a renowned abbot of Drepung Monastery in Lhasa). At one time there were 4,000 monks (reduced to 1,700 now) filling the six institutes of Esoteric Buddhism, Medicine, Law, Astrology and Higher and Lower Institutes of Theology, and the various halls and residences. On religious holidays, followers of Tibetan Buddhism pour in to mix with the monks in religious celebrations. The Great Prayer Festival (Monlam) takes place just after the Tibetan New Year (based on the lunar calendar and therefore variable) either in February or March, and there are some fascinating celebrations on the 13th, 14th, 15th and 16th days of the relevant month. In the vicinity of Xiahe there are beautiful areas of grassland, at Ganjia and Sangke, where yaks are grazed.

▶ **Yining** 128A2

Yining, heart of the Ili Kazakh Autonomous Prefecture, and the scene in recent years of clashes between the authorities and Uyghur separatists, is a town near the Russian border that has only recently opened to foreign tourists. Near by, in the Ili Valley, is **Almalik**, thought to have been the capital of the empire (today's Xinjiang) inherited by Chaghatai, the second son of Genghis Khan, in 1227. The northern arm of the Silk Road ran through here on the way to the great oasis towns of Central Asia.

There is little to see in Yining unless you are lucky enough to witness a **traditional celebration by Kazakh horsemen**▶▶▶ in the nearby pastures, a performance of high-spirited horsemanship that includes competitive games and a peculiar chase on horseback with a dead goat.

The countryside is beautiful though, particularly in the region of the **Sayram Lake**▶▶▶, on the road to Ürümqi, where the waters are sapphire blue.

Monks at Labrang Monastery, Xiahe

147

BORDER PARTY
The border of Kazakhstan is very close to Yining. Since the 1950s, Westerners had been forbidden to cross it, but in 1985 an international group of tourists was allowed across in celebration of 2,000 years of the Silk Road. A bar was set up on the Soviet side of the frontier (after customs) and Beatles music was broadcast across the wilderness. The tourists were met by a prancing dragon on the Chinese side. Travel across the frontier by train is now commonplace.

Jade (yu) is the stone most often associated with China. Usually thought of as deep green, in fact it has an unexpectedly wide range of hues, from creamy white to almost black.

TOAD GREASE
The oily substance that blends the abrasive mixture used in jade cutting is called 'toad grease', and, according to Chinese texts, was produced from toads killed in a special way. In fact, the grease is tallow from mutton or lard from pork.

A jade craftsman in Yangzhou, Jiangsu

148

History The point just outside Dunhuang, where the northern and southern arms of the Silk Road divided, was known as Yumenguan or 'the Jade Gate', and jade has long been associated with both imperial and magic powers and known for curative properties, particularly for kidney diseases. It was one of the principal items of tribute payable by tribal princelings to the emperor.

Nature Just what is jade? And how do you tell good from bad, or even good from less good? The oldest jade is a calcium-magnesium-aluminium silicate with a hardness of 6.5 on the Mohs' Scale. It is classical nephrite, found most particularly in Hotan, the old Silk Road town of

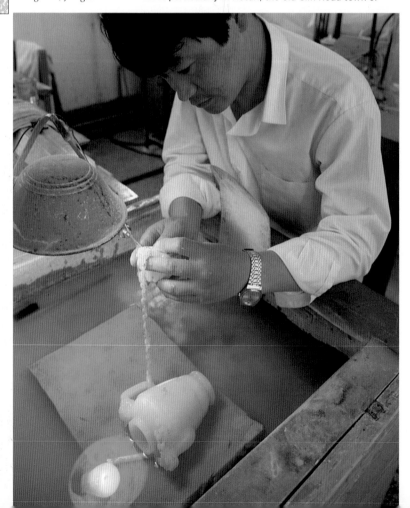

Khotan. In the 18th century, the brilliant green jadeite from Burma became popular. Other stones, particularly serpentine, are sometimes also called jade. What passes for jade in shops in Hong Kong is often no more than fluorite, a soft stone that, compared with jade, is of little value. Jade's hardness is one of its distinguishing features and what makes it valuable to the Chinese.

Hues Nephritic jade was originally found in the form of pebbles from alluvial deposits in Chinese Turkestan (Xinjiang) and was first mined from rock in the 12th century. Curiously, for a mineral so treasured by the Chinese, it is not found in China proper at all. 'Its fascination derives from its subdued smooth brilliance which can be redolent of the deep waters of a mountain lake or of the mistiness of a distant summit.' White jade, which is slightly opalescent and translucent, is known in China as 'mutton-fat' jade. Nephritic jade occurs in a wide variety of hues because of the presence of metallic oxides or silicates, usually iron, that endow it with shades of grey. Ferrous silicates produce shades of green ranging from pale to almost black, while ferric silicates bring browns and oranges and, most prized of all, yellow. Streaks in the jade are caused by trace elements—manganese, for example, produces pale jade with threads of pink or purple. The most common shade—and widely considered the loveliest—is the pale smoky green, called cabbage jade by the Chinese. Jade can also change with age, giving added depth to the shade.

Hard, dark-green jade, similar to an emerald of the deepest hue, is more likely to be jadeite. Although very similar in appearance to nephritic jade, jadeite has a different chemical composition and was for long considered by the Chinese to be of inferior value. Jadeite can also be a brilliant red, because of the presence of chromium, which is never found in nephritic jade; the presence of manganese produces a lilac tint.

Heaven Jade is still commonly used in the manufacture of jewels and ornaments, but its use for tribal objects goes back to neolithic times—the jade *pi* can be seen in many Chinese museums. This flat disc, with a large central hole, is often said to represent Heaven and is thought to derive from ancient sun cults. The oldest known example dates back to 2000BC. What is most remarkable is its perfectly formed central hole, suggesting that the Chinese already knew how to use a primitive lathe.

APPEASEMENT
The Chinese believed that various earthly spirits remained in the body after death, once the Celestial Spirit had departed. It was feared that such spirits might become angry, leave the body and torment the relatives. To prevent this, the body orifices were plugged with jade, and offerings were made to encourage the spirits to leave peacefully.

A jade pi *with decorated surface. A* pi *was a ritual disc that symbolized heaven*

149

Sichuan and the Tibetan Plateau

Map showing: Shache (Yarkant), Yecheng (Kargilik), Hotan, Taklamakan Shamo, **XINJIANG UYGUR ZIZHIQU**, Qiemo (Qarqan), Yutian (Keriya), *Altun Shan*, Dunhuang, Yumen, *Qil...*, Lenghu, *Har Hu*, *K u n l u n*, *S h a n*, 7723m Muztag, Da Qaidam, Delingha, *Qaidam Pendi*, *Hob Xil Shan*, Golmud, **QINGHAI**, 5442m Gyarin Hu, Wüjang, *Tuotuo He*, *Tongtian He*, *Bayan*, **XIZANG ZIZHIQU**, Gêrzê, *Tanggula Shan*, *Ningling*, Yushu, **(TIBET)**, Kangrinboqê Feng 6714m, Coqên, *Siling Co*, *Gyaring Co*, Amdo, Barga, *Gangdisê Shan*, Nagqu, *Nu Jiang*, Qamdo, Burang, *Maquan He*, *Nam Co*, *Nyainqêntanglha Shan*, Saga, Xigazê, Lhazê, **Sakya**, Gonggar, **Lhasa**, Ganden Monastery, Samye, Nyingchi, 7782m, Rawu, Zetang, Namjagbarwa Feng, Gyangzê, Yarlung Zangbo Jiang, *Yamzho Yumco*, 7538m, *Shan*, **NP**, 8012m Xixabangma Feng, 8848m Qomolangma Feng, Yadong, **BT**, **IND**, **BD**

Scale: 0 200 400 600 km / 0 100 200 300 miles

The terraced rice fields of western Sichuan, gateway to Tibet

Sichuan and the Tibetan Plateau

An endless cycle—the 'wheel of life', often found at the entrance to Tibetan monasteries

152

Writing on the wall: 'Fu', the character for 'happiness' or 'luck', Baoguang Temple, Chengdu

SICHUAN AND THE TIBETAN PLATEAU It may seem odd to place a province (Sichuan) that is part of China proper in the same chapter with Tibet, which, although part of the modern state of China (as the 'autonomous' region of Xizang), remains quite separate as far as way of life, culture and attitudes are concerned. There are two reasons, one practical, the other geographical and historical. First, the majority of visitors to Tibet enter on direct flights from Chengdu in Sichuan. Secondly, Sichuan is situated at the foot of the Tibetan Plateau, and indeed much of the western mountainous area of the province forms part of it. Furthermore, in the distant past some of what is now Sichuan was ruled by Tibetan tribes, and consequently traces of Tibetan culture remain in the area. Chongqing and Dazu, however, are discussed in the Yangtze valley chapter (pages 170–173) since they are usually visited only by those making the journey through the Yangtze Gorges.

Sichuan, the largest and most populous (over 100 million people) of China's provinces, is quite distinctive. The vast Chengdu plain is one of the country's most important rice-producing regions. Sichuanese food—some of the best in China—is hot and spicy. Most famously, Sichuan is associated with the giant panda; a few are found in adjoining provinces, but Sichuan is their preferred home. The cultivated valleys give the province a particular beauty, and there is an astonishing array of flora. Its mountainous nature has allowed it to enjoy a degree of independence during the centuries of Chinese rule. Although linked to China since the fourth century BC, it previously enjoyed an advanced civilization of its own, affiliated to the cultures

THAT OLD GANG OF MINE
The architect of China's recent prosperity and democratic reforms, such as they are, was Deng Xiaoping, who was a Sichuanese. Indeed, so many of the people associated with his period of rule are from Sichuan that they are sometimes referred to as the Sichuan Gang.

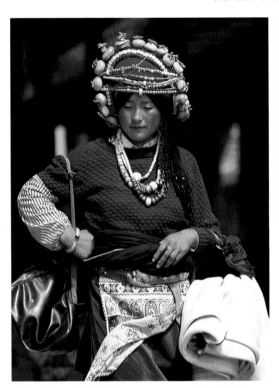

*A Tibetan woman in
Songpan, northern
Sichuan, heavy with
amber, coral and
turquoise ornament*

of Southeast Asia. Sichuan, now one of China's fastest growing areas, continues to retain an independent spirit.

TIBET Dogged by the tag of Shangri-la and shielded by its isolated location among the highest mountains in the world and its determination to exclude outside influence, Tibet, until recently, remained an enigma. Its history before the early seventh century is obscure, but in AD625 Songtsen Gampo became the first king of a unified Tibet, his empire spreading into China and India. The fact that he married Buddhist princesses (as well as Chinese ones) seemed to strike a chord in the Tibetan mind—for within a century, following a debate between an Indian sage and Bon priests, the native Bon religion had been ousted and replaced by Buddhism. After years of internecine struggle, the notion of the reincarnation of religious leaders was introduced, but Tibetan Buddhism remained divided into three rival schools. Finally, in the 14th century unity was established by the Gelukpa (yellow hat) sect, which built the great teaching monasteries.

In 1720, the Chinese took Tibet and, despite British interference, more or less held it until 1911. Tibet then became independent until 1951, when the Chinese re-established control. Repression followed, and the current Dalai Lama fled to India in 1959. The Cultural Revolution saw the destruction of hundreds of monasteries, and although the material existence of Tibetans has now improved, there is still repression. But Tibetan traditions continue, some of the monasteries still function, and Tibet remains one of the most naturally beautiful places on earth.

MONKEY BUSINESS

There is an interesting explanation of the origins of the Tibetans. It is said that the Sakyamuni Buddha, observing that there were no humans in Tibet, elected to confine his work to India. The responsibility for dealing with Tibet was passed to Avalokitesvara, who assumed the form of a monkey and descended on to a mountain in Tsetang. After he mated with a demoness, six offspring were born, half human and half monkey, the first Tibetans.

153

'PURE LAND'

The most popular form of Chinese Buddhism is called *jingtu* (Pure Land), and is unknown in India or Central Asia. It teaches that the Pure Land is a kind of heaven or nirvana that can be achieved by chanting the name 'Amitabha Buddha' (the Buddha of the future). Most of the Buddhist temples still operating in China today are of this type.

Pagoda at Xindu's Monastery of Divine Light, near Chengdu

▶▶ Chengdu

151E1

The capital of Sichuan combines modern tree-lined avenues with narrow streets of traditional half-timbered houses and is one of the fastest growing cities in China. Renowned for its prosperity from silk, lacquer and precious metals, it has always been outside the mainstream of Chinese life, perceived as a place of refuge by poets and rulers alike. Chengdu's main attractions include a sense of well-being unusual in modern Chinese cities, and the streets themselves, which still have much character, although many of the older ones have been demolished. There are also several places to visit outside the city.

Du Fu's Thatched Cottage▶▶ (*Open* daily 8–6.30. *Admission: inexpensive*) is a memorial to one of China's greatest poets, Du Fu, a minor official under the Tang dynasty who was forced to flee from Chang'an (Xi'an) after a rebellion. He spent four years in Chengdu, where he wrote many of his best poems. He is highly regarded because his poetry was compassionate in an age when compassion was rare. The memorial, constructed 200 years after his death, is set in a pretty bamboo garden where there is a museum containing early versions of his poetry.

Of the several temples in Chengdu, the most interesting (and much patronized by locals) is the **Wenshu**▶▶ (*Open* daily 8–6. *Admission: inexpensive*), which has four halls and a tea-house in the garden. The **Provincial Museum**▶ (*Open* daily 10–5. *Admission: inexpensive*), being renovated, is important for its displays of Sichuanese culture. **Chengdu Zoo**▶▶ (*Open* daily 8–5. *Admission: inexpensive*) has a large number of giant pandas. Even better is the **Giant Panda Breeding Research Base**▶▶▶ (*Open* daily 8–5.30. *Admission: moderate*), which opened in 1995.

There are several excursions from Chengdu. About 16km (10miles) away is **Xindu**▶▶ a town associated with multi-hued basketware and the **Monastery of Divine Light** (**Baoguangsi**; *Open* daily 8–5. *Admission: inexpensive*). The monastery dates from the Tang dynasty, but it was reconstructed in the 17th century. It has some pretty gardens and courtyards, a 13-floor leaning pagoda, a fine tablet from AD540 bearing a frieze of 1,000 Buddhas and an Arhat hall with 500 Buddhist statues.

Also of interest is the ancient **Dujiangyan Irrigation Scheme**▶▶ at Guanxian, about a two-hour drive west of Chengdu. Begun in 256BC by the governor of the state of Shu to tame the Min River, it is a remarkable precursor to modern dams. The original stone and bamboo dike divided the river into an 'inner' and 'outer' channel while a second dike was built to divert water in case of flood. The system now irrigates more than 3 million ha (7.5 million acres). The best views are from the nearby Fulong (Subdued Dragon), or the Erwangmiao (Two Kings) Temples, on a hill above the Anlang chain bridge.

Also worth a visit is the **Qingchengshan Taoist Mountain**▶▶ (*Open* daily. *Admission: expensive*), which can be climbed in one day. Shangqinggong, its highest temple, stands at over 1,500m (4,920ft). The going is not too tough, and the Taoist belief in harmony with nature gives a rustic feel to the buildings *en route*. Alternatively, there is a cable-car. Finally there is the **Wolong Nature Reserve**▶▶ (*Open* daily 9–12, 2.30–5.30. *Admission: moderate*), a day's drive from Chengdu, established in the 1970s for panda conservation and now China's largest reserve. More than 50 giant pandas live at the reserve's research and conservation centre, most of them bred in captivity.

155

Bamboo culture: a tea-house at the People's Park, Chengdu

Prayer flags on the summit of Emeishan

FLORA AND FAUNA
Emeishan is attractive not only for pilgrims searching for 'the way' but also for its wide variety of animal and plant life. Aside from the monkeys there are the famous bearded frogs, 200 species of butterfly, silver pheasants, lesser or red pandas, medicinal herbs, tea bushes, rhododendrons and an array of vibrant flowers.

Kumbum stupa at Palkhor Monastery, Gyangzê

▶ **Dêgê**   *151D2*
This town, on the road from Chengdu to Lhasa, is famous for its 250-year-old **Bakong Scripture Printing Lamasery** (*Open* daily. *Admission: inexpensive*), which houses the last surviving copy of a woodblock history of Buddhism in 555 plates.

▶▶▶ **Emeishan**
    ('Lofty Eyebrow Mountain')   *151D1*
Open: 6am–7pm. Admission: expensive
One of the holy mountains of Buddhism, the abode of Samantabhadra the Bodhisattva of pervading goodness, Emeishan, in the southwest of Sichuan province, rises to well over 3,000m (9,840ft). The pair of peaks with a green fir coat, and frequently a topcoat of dense mist at various levels, makes a magnificent sight. From the base to the summit is a distance of some 50km (31 miles) but, although it may require two days to complete the pilgrimage (ascent or descent), no special climbing skills are necessary. A minibus goes from the Baoguo Monastery up to Jieyindian, and from there you can continue either on foot or by cable-car to the summit (or even by sedan chair). You can descend the whole way on foot, spending the night in one of several temples *en route* that offer overnight lodgings. Unfortunately, the inclement weather often obscures the spectacular view, but many like to stay the night here to see the sunrise, others to

enjoy the rainbows and fantastic shadows, called 'Buddha's Glory', which sometimes appear on the clouds below during the late afternoon. Lower down is the famous Xixiangchi (Elephant Bathing Pool), where the elephant belonging to Samantabhadra was believed to have bathed; here the moon is supposed to cast an eerie light. The mountain is famous for its monkeys (especially on Xianfeng, or Fairy Peak), which can be fierce and should not be approached.

It is also possible to combine a visit to Emeishan with one to **Leshan** (see page 160), only a short distance away.

▶▶▶ Ganden Monastery   150C1

East of Lhasa lie the remains of what was once one of the most important monasteries in Tibet. Ganden, 'the Pure Land of Tushita', where Maitreya the Future Buddha resides, was founded by the great 14th-century reformer Tsongkhapa (or Je Rinpoche), who is generally depicted wearing monk's robes and a yellow hat. The main hall of the monastery was not consecrated until 1417, and its founder died here in 1419. The head of the monastery, the Ganden Tripa, is also the head of the Gelukpa order. By 1959 there were 5,000 monks, but the Cultural Revolution reduced the monastery to ruins. Set on the slopes of Mount Drokri, it is being painstakingly reconstructed. Among the most interesting buildings are Tsongkhapa's Golden Tomb and the Amdo Khantsen. A path leads behind the hill, with breathtaking views. Pilgrim buses for Ganden leave early each morning from Lhasa.

▶ Ganzi (Garzê)   151D2

The capital of the Ganzi Tibetan Autonomous Prefecture (as distinct from the Tibetan Autonomous Region), in remote Sichuan, is home to the Ganzi Lama Monastery, from where there are splendid views of the Ganzi Valley.

▶▶ Gyangzê (Gyantse)   150B1

A small Tibetan town (once the hub of the wool trade), at a height of 3,766m (12,356ft) and east of Xigatse, old Gyangzê forms a street of traditional Tibetan houses dominated by the **Palkhor Monastery**▶▶▶, which was built in 1429. Once much larger, the monastery now has only the main temple and a nine-floor stupa, Tibet's largest, decorated with the stern eyes of Buddha outside and fine murals within. It is overlooked by the **old fort** (*Open daily 8–8. Admission: inexpensive*), set astride a pinnacle. In 1904, Gyangzê witnessed one of Britain's lesser military exploits, when Francis Younghusband, sent to enforce a trade agreement, allowed the massacre of 700 Tibetans. The fortress was captured and a trade mission was then established.

▶▶ Jiuzhaigou   151D2

Open: daily 7.30–5.30. Admission: expensive

This little-known scenic area in the Aba Autonomous Prefecture of Sichuan, far north of Chengdu, rivals Guilin for its beauty, with the added attraction of Tibetan and Qiang minority settlements. It is an area of lakes, mountains and waterfalls not yet spoiled by tourism, although more roads and hotels are being built for large numbers of visitors. An important transit point for Jiuzhaigou is Songpan, a pretty town set in dazzling scenery.

IN A STUPA

Stupas (known as chorten in Tibet) probably evolved in India as prehistoric burial chambers for local rulers, but under Buddhism they acquired a sacred status as the symbol of Buddha himself. Subsequently, they became burial places for the ashes of saints or repositories of holy scriptures or relics. In Tibet stupas have square bases (earth), surmounted by a globe (water), a triangle (fire), and a crescent moon (air) and sun (infinite space).

The Five-Colour Pool, Jiuzhaigou

Although the giant panda has received the most publicity over the years, China is also home to a number of other endangered species.

HAIRY MONSTER
Not strictly speaking an endangered species, the yak is found in any numbers only in the Tibetan region. It is so well adapted to high altitudes and the bitter cold that it could not survive in mild, lowland areas. Bulky yet nimble, it needs a daily supply of fresh water, snow being an inadequate substitute.

158

Giant panda Although it is impossible to know just how many pandas remain in the wild, it is thought that the number is no higher than 1,500, insufficient to ensure their survival. They are found mostly in Sichuan, but there are a few in the adjoining provinces of Shaanxi and Gansu; in these provinces, 13 reserves have been established to preserve the panda (no easy task where even the death penalty fails to deter poachers from trapping and skinning them). Live pandas were discovered in 1896, although remains dating back over 600,000 years have been found. The animals prefer altitudes of up to 3,000m (9,840ft), consume 20kg (44lb) of a specific

Above: giant panda, sensitive to its environment
Top: Père David's deer, now found only in captivity

variety of bamboo per day, and are very sensitive to their environment. When bamboo supplies failed in the 1970s, up to 200 pandas were estimated to have died of starvation. Their mating habits are mysterious and the birth rate in the wild is very low, although captive breeding at the Chongdu and Wolong research centres has had some success. The future for the giant panda remains uncertain.

Père David's deer The outlook is more optimistic for some of China's other rare animals, since efforts are now being made to ensure their survival. One of the most intriguing is the Père David's deer (or Milu), first discovered in the imperial hunting parks by the French priest and zoologist Père Armand David in 1865, when they were already extinct in the wild. They are thought to have come from Manchuria and Kokonor. By 1900, there were none left in China, even in the parks, but the species survived at Woburn Abbey in England, where a breeding herd was established by the dukes of Bedford. In 1985, 20 were presented to the Chinese government to live at Chengde, but it is unlikely that they will ever be re-established in the wild.

Tiger China has four subspecies of tiger—the South China tiger, the Manchurian (or Siberian) tiger, the Indo-Chinese tiger and the Bengal tiger. The South China tiger, unique to China, may no longer exist in the wild, because at last count there were only 30–40 left, too few to prevent its seemingly inevitable extinction. The Manchurian tiger's chances of survival are little better, although there are a few more in Siberia. The Indo-Chinese tiger also numbers 40 or less, in Yunnan and Guangxi. The Bengal tiger numbers just 30 and is still found in south Tibet and northeast of Yunnan.

Unfortunately for tigers, some parts of their anatomy are thought to have properties crucial to Chinese virility; trade in these organs is so lucrative that the law banning it is almost impossible to enforce.

Others There are other animals and birds in the same precarious position: the golden monkey, the Yangtze alligator (a smaller cousin of those in the USA), the red-crowned crane and the Yangtze River dolphin. Efforts are being made by the Chinese in co-operation with the Worldwild Fund for Nature and others to ensure their survival, but sadly many Chinese accord them low priority, and the future for many of these creatures is grim.

A Manchurian (or Siberian) tiger. The tiger is a Chinese symbol, yet is almost extinct

MOSQUITO BOAST
Despite its climate, China is relatively free of mosquitoes. This is one of the success stories of the Communist Party, which initiated a determined scheme to eradicate malaria. Similar efforts were made to decrease the sparrow population, which had risen to alarming proportions. It is said that Chairman Mao exhorted citizens regularly to go outside with dustbin lids and make such a racket that the birds would never return. Although sparrows were the target, millions of other birds were, literally, scared to death, too.

ACCLIMATIZING TO TIBET

Since Tibet lies at an average altitude of about 4,000m (13,120ft), you can expect to suffer from shortness of breath because of the thin oxygen supply. This affects everyone to a greater or lesser degree, regardless of age or levels of fitness. To minimize the discomfort, you are advised to rest for a few hours after your arrival, no matter how healthy you feel. This gives your body time to acclimatize gradually. Increase your fluid intake by drinking plenty of water or tea, but avoid alcohol.

RIPPLING WATERS

Lhasa's original name was Rasa, from 'ralasa', the sound made by the wind and the waves ruffling the waters of the lake around which the city was built. The lake was filled up and covered by the Jokhang in the seventh century.

The Buddha's head, of cathedral-like proportions, at Leshan

▶▶ Kangding   *151D1*

Sometimes known as Dardo, Kangding stands at an altitude of 3,000m (9,840ft), but it is dwarfed by mountains of up to 8,000m (26,000ft). Tibetan in style, the town has several working monasteries and some excellent walking. You can also trek along the nearby **Hailuogou Glacier**, said to be the lowest in Asia, or visit the beautiful grasslands at Tagong.

▶▶▶ Leshan   *151D1*

Open: daily 8–6. Admission: expensive

One of the most impressive places in Sichuan (5 hours by road from Chengdu and 90 minutes from Emeishan), this small town has old cobbled streets and considerable charm although tourism and modernization have already made a significant impact on it. Its principal attraction is the colossal **Grand Buddha (Dafo)▶▶▶**, carved out of the cliffs at the confluence of the Min and Dadu rivers. In a sitting posture, the position preferred by Maitreya the Future Buddha, it is the largest Buddha in China, towering to more than 70m (230ft)—one of the toes alone is 8.5m (28ft) long. Narrow, twisting stairs to the right of the figure take you up on to the Buddha's head, and above the right shoulder are the **Grand Buddha Temple▶** and Song-dynasty **Lingbao Pagoda▶**. A boat ride past Dafo is especially recommended (boats operate 7–5). There is a temple at the statue's head from where a staircase takes you to its feet.

The **Wuyou Monastery▶▶**, dating back to the Tang dynasty, is situated on Wuyou Hill and is a short ferry ride away from Leshan dock. Opposite the temple, on the same bank as the Grand Buddha, are several tombs and a crudely fashioned Buddha that dates from AD159, about the time that Buddhism was introduced to China.

The Orient Buddha Park (*Open daily 7–6. Admission moderate*) contains a newly carved reclining Buddha, at 170m (558ft), the longest in the world.

▶▶▶ Lhasa

The Tibetan capital since the unification of the country in the seventh century, dominated by the magnificent Potala, Lhasa has been shabbily treated by the Chinese, but still manages to convey much of its unique character, if only because of its remote, ethereal location—the name Lhasa means 'Ground of the Gods'. For the 600 years, between the end of the first Yarlung dynasty in the ninth century and the beginning of the era of Dalai Lamas in the 15th, Lhasa was capital in name only, as Tibet was torn by civil war and religious schism. Since the arrival of the Chinese in 1951 there have been many more changes, very few aesthetically for the better.

Lhasa has a wealth of things to see, most of them concerned with Tibetan religious life. The first place to visit is the **Barkhor (Intermediate Circuit)**▶▶▶, the oldest part of the city and a quadrangle of streets surrounding the Jokhang Temple, the most revered and ancient of Tibetan temples. The Barkhor teems with religious and commercial activity—pilgrims doing clockwise circuits, frequently on their hands and knees, and street vendors selling their wares. This is the heart of old Tibet and, although about one-third of it has been gutted in order to build shopping malls, it nevertheless still manages to retain something of its old quality.

The **Jokhang (Shrine of Jowo)**▶▶▶ (*Open daily 9–5*), facing the newly built 'plaza', is open from 9 to noon (enter via a side door in the afternoons). Only some woodwork on chapel doorways and the statue of Jowo Sakyamuni, given to King Songtsen Gampo by his Chinese wife and believed by Tibetans to have been made by the celestial artist Vishvakarman, date back to the shrine's founding in the seventh century. The atmosphere here is similar to, but more intense than, that of any other temple in Tibet—the smell from the thousands of flickering candles fills the gloomy air, and pilgrims prostrate themselves before altars. The main chapel, and the most elaborate, is the

The Potala Palace seen from Chokpuri through prayer flags

The endless knot, Tibetan Buddhist symbol of eternity, adorns the roof of Jokhang Temple, Lhasa

Sichuan and the Tibetan Plateau

The Time Wheel dagoba at Taer Monastery, Huangzhong, Qinghai

CHINA'S GULAG
Qinghai is a bleak and, in many ways, forbidding place, a reputation not helped by the fact that the Chinese government has built work camps here for criminals and political dissidents from all over China. Nobody knows for certain how many people are imprisoned in them, but it is alleged that the Chinese undercut most of the world's export prices with the aid of a cheap workforce both in these camps and in many others all over China.

Chapel of Jowo Sakyamuni, whose statue is laden with brocade and jewels. There are dramatic views across the city from the roof.

The beautiful **Potala Palace**▶▶▶ (*Open* daily 9.30–3. *Admission: expensive*), named after a holy mountain in India, was first built on this site in the seventh century, but the current structure dates from 1645. It was the home of successive Dalai Lamas and has been their winter home since the construction of the Summer Palace in the 18th century. Several chapels, part of the living quarters, and the tombs are open to the public.

The **Norbulingka (Summer Palace)**▶▶ (*Open* daily 9.30–5.30. *Admission: expensive*), in the west of Lhasa, has been used as a summer palace since the time of the 8th Dalai Lama. More of a park than an estate, it has a tranquil, bucolic air. Architecturally less imposing than the monasteries and the Potala, the palace's atmosphere allows an insight into the more domestic aspects of theocratic rule. It is from here that the Dalai Lama escaped in 1959.

Other principal monasteries here, are the **Sera**▶▶ (*Open* Mon–Sat 3–5. *Admission: moderate*), north of Lhasa, and the **Drepung**▶▶ (*Open* daily 9–5. *Admission: expensive*) to the west, both of which deserve extended visits.

▶▶ Qinghai Province   150C2

Formerly the Tibetan province of Amdo, Qinghai forms part of the Tibetan Plateau, but has provincial status separate from the Tibetan Autonomous Region. An area of high grassland, mountain ranges and salt marshes in the northwest, it includes the sources of three important rivers: the Yellow River, the Yangtze and the Mekong. The largest town in the province is Xining, interesting only for a 14th-century **mosque**▶, and the excellent **West Gate market**▶▶. Some 25km (15 miles) southwest is one of the most venerable of Tibetan monasteries, the **Taer at**

Huangzhong▶▶▶ (*Open* daily 9–5. *Admission: expensive*), noted for its yak-butter sculptures.

Qinghai's main attractions are the scenery, the peoples and—perhaps most spectacularly—**Kokonor** (**Qinghai Lake**)▶▶▶, China's largest saltwater lake and a bird-lover's paradise. Huge flocks of migrating birds land here, particularly from March to June, the mating season.

▶▶ Sakya 150B1

Southwest of Xigazê is the focal point for the Sakyapa sect, which was founded in the 11th century. There are two monasteries: the northern one was virtually destroyed during the Cultural Revolution, while the southern monastery, an imposing fortress-like building, still stands, complete with assembly hall and fine chapels.

▶▶▶ Samye 150C1

Open: daily 9–6. Admission: moderate
The first monastery built in Tibet (AD770) is in a spectacular position on the north bank of the Brahmaputra River (Yarlung Tsangpo), northwest of Zêtang. An irregular ferry takes 1.5 hours to make the river crossing and a lorry takes you to the monastery. It is worth the effort.

▶▶▶ Xigazê (Xigatse) 150B1

Tibet's second town, and the site of one of its greatest monasteries, the **Tashilhunpo**▶▶▶ (*Open* daily 9.30–5.30. *Admission: moderate*), is the spiritual home of the Panchen Lama (the incarnation of Buddha Amitabha), second to the Dalai Lama. The monastery dates from 1447 and is outstanding architecturally, if not spiritually—the last Panchen Lama, who died in 1989, was widely regarded as a Chinese puppet. Since then, there has been a stand-off between the Chinese government and the Dalai Lama over the election of a successor.

Taking the ferry to Samye across the Yarlung Tsangpo (the Brahmaputra)

163

SUPPRESSION OF A CULTURE
Traditional Tibetan culture may never recover from the damage inflicted by the Chinese after the revolt of 1959. The Cultural Revolution of the 1960s and 1970s saw the brutal suppression of religious life and the destruction of many of Tibet's cultural treasures. During the 1980s, there were demonstrations and violent clashes against Chinese rule. Material aspects of life have improved, however, although the Tibetans' appetite for Western pop music and films further undermines their unique way of life, which can never now be re-established.

Sakya rooftops, excellent for drying crops and yak dung and for hoisting prayer flags

Buddhism took root in India and spread throughout Asia. In Tibet, Buddhism competed with the native shamanistic religion (Bon), which it eventually absorbed, while retaining some Bon symbolism.

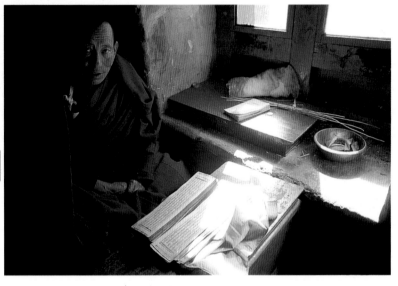

164

Monasteries (above, Ganden) hum with the recitation of sutras

MONK BUSINESS
Monks who choose to follow the full course of philosophical training are required to study a range of subjects over a period of up to 20 years. The basic course lasts two or three years, followed by further study of the five main subjects of Buddhist philosophy, eventually leading to the degree of Geshe, or Doctor of Divinity. The remaining years are devoted to tantric studies.

Devotees prostrating themselves in front of Jokhang Temple, Lhasa

Jewels Buddhism is the following of the path to self-awareness and enlightenment, a way of dissolving the existential confusion within ourselves that is seen as the source of human strife. The Buddhist must commit himself to the 'Three Jewels'—to the Buddha (Sakyamuni, the manifestation of the ideal of enlightenment); to the Dharma (the way revealed by Buddha); and to Sangha (the religious community). And in Tibet there is a fourth 'jewel', devotion to a spiritual teacher, or lama.

Vehicles There are three types of Buddhism. The first is known as Theravada ('Way of the Elders'), which presents the basic teachings of the Buddha himself; it requires a high degree of moral discipline combined with meditation. As the number of devotees grew, so the monasteries expanded, requiring more complex administration on the part of the monks, which in turn had political implications. Gradually Tibetan government became theocratic, a process reinforced by the custom whereby families made a contribution to the Buddhist order by offering a son as a monk.

Mahayana ('the greater vehicle') is based on Theravada but asserts that enlightenment (nirvana) cannot be attained on one's own but instead necessitates the liberation of all humanity. Compassion is one of the central themes of Tibetan Buddhism, embodied in the 'bodhisattva', the disciple who refrains from entering nirvana in order to save others. In Tibet, the most important bodhisattva is Chenrezi, manifested in human form as the Dalai Lama. You can see Chenrezi in many temples, sometimes with four arms, sometimes a thousand, and as many faces. The vocal expression of compassion is 'Om mani padme hum', which you hear murmured everywhere you go. Sometimes the chanting is accompanied by the beating of a drum to ward off the supplicant's ego, for his quest is to know emptiness, to be free of all prejudice in his interpretation of himself and of the world around him.

The third type is Vajrayana ('the diamond'), also based on the twin objectives of compassion and enlightenment, but through the teaching of Buddhist tantras. Sutras are the words spoken by Buddha for all, but tantras are vouchsafed only to a select few. Tantric Buddhism sees the human condition as more than making moral choices. Internal energy, if misdirected, adds to the store of human misery, but, by focusing it in the correct way, you achieve nirvana. Studying the tantras helps speed up the way to enlightenment.

A devotee rotates a prayer wheel at the foot of the Potala, Lhasa

Temples Tibetan temples are filled with images. Mandalas are a series of vivid squares within a circle and are used as an instrument of meditation. You must shed all preconceptions about reality, and imagine you are a deity and that the mandala is your world. The wheel of life, often seen at temple entrances, represents the eternal universe, seen by Tibetan Buddhists as an infinity of systems inhabited by humans, animals, giants, ghosts, devils and celestials. Existence without enlightenment is a meaningless cycle of reincarnation from one to the other. Liberation is achieved by breaking out of this cycle.

The size of the Tashilhunpo Monastery reflects the significance of monasteries in Buddhist culture

TANTRAS AND TANGKAS
Buddhist terminology can be confusing for the uninitiated. It is easy, for example, to confuse tantras with tangkas, although they are very dissimilar. While tantras are prayers and teachings, tangkas are painted scrolls, usually depicting lamas and deities and various events from their lives, that serve as an aid to meditation.

LAMAS AND MONKS
Lamas and monks are not necessarily one and the same. A lama does not need to be a monk, for a lama is someone spiritually qualified to lead others on the path to enlightenment.

The Yangtze Region

The Yangtze Region

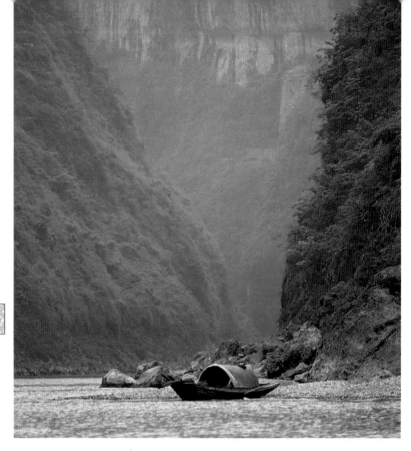

The Yangtze River, the heart of China: one of the three lesser gorges along the Daning River

MARCO'S MISCHIEF
It has always been assumed that Marco Polo, the Venetian explorer, actually went to China. Yet, although he was allegedly the governor of Yangzhou, there is no mention of him in any Chinese records. This is surprising given that few Westerners would have had contact with China in the 13th century. Also, there are certain aspects of Chinese culture that would have made an impact on a Westerner—calligraphy, for example—of which Polo makes no mention. Some scholars believe that his book was a fictionalized autobiography based on the medieval conception of the Orient.

THE YANGTZE REGION In a sense, this region does not exist. The course of the Yangtze River neatly divides China into north and south, passing through eight very separate provinces, but the reason for creating this artificial region and for classing so many heterogeneous places together is simple: they are all destinations that are likely to be visited on the same trip, their common link being the Yangtze River.

The Yangtze (Yangtze is a corruption of a local, Yangzhou-area pronunciation of Chang Jiang, which means 'the long river'), 6,340km (3,940 miles) in length, is the third-longest river in the world after the Nile and the Amazon. It rises in Qinghai province, part of the Tibetan Plateau, and disgorges into the Yellow Sea. It is joined by some 700 tributaries along its course and is divided into three sections. The Upper Reaches, possibly the most spectacular part, run from its source across the Sichuan Basin, through the Three Gorges (see pages 194–195), to Yichang in Hubei province. The Middle Reaches are between Yichang and Hukou, at the mouth of Boyang Lake in Jiangxi province, where the river, wide and sluggish, flows through flat, low land, fed by waters from the Dongting as well as Boyang Lake. The Lower Reaches run from Hukou to the estuary, a landscape characterized not only by its flatness, but also by the network of canals that criss-cross it. Known as the 'Land of Fish and Rice', it is home to a third of China's population, producing some

40 per cent of national grain output (including 70 per cent of paddy rice), 33 per cent of cotton, 50 per cent of fresh-water fish and 40 per cent of industrial output.

NAVIGATION Although the river was once a vital naviga-tion artery of the Chinese empire, the arrival of the rail-ways almost emptied the Yangtze of the traditional sampans ('three planks'), wupans ('five planks') and junks that used to throng its length as far as Chongqing. Nowadays, ocean-going vessels penetrate upriver as far as Wuhan, and local traffic is much in evidence. Not so long ago boats had to be pulled by trackers through the treacherous rapids, exhausting toil that was little better than slavery. Instructions were relayed to the harnessed trackers, heaving on ropes, by means of a beating drum. Some craft could require as many as 400 trackers to pull them. Isabella Bird, the indefatigable Victorian English globetrotter who, at 64, made a journey along the Yangtze in 1896, observed 300 trackers dragging a junk without making perceptible progress in two hours. 'Suddenly the junk shivered, both tow ropes snapped, the lines of track-ers went down on their faces, and in a moment the craft was spinning down the rapid; and she flew up into the air as if she had exploded.' The tow-paths carved into the rocks are still visible here and there. The main obstacles to safe navigation were blown up after 1949.

After 1861 annual tea races were held on the Yangtze, when competing clippers from foreign companies raced to bring the freshest tea from China to Britain, the United States and Russia. After the China tea trade collapsed, the Yangtze impinged on Western consciousness only in 1949, the year of the Yangtze incident. The *Amethyst*, a British frigate, was fired on by the communists, who were about to launch a final offensive on the nationalists. The ship's daring nocturnal escape is now part of British naval folklore.

The Yangtze, the greatest river in China, remains a powerful symbol of Chinese civilization, and much that is most fascinating about the country is still to be seen in this region.

DONGTING LAKE
Dongting Lake was once China's largest freshwa-ter lake. Now, because of the accumulation of silt from the four rivers that feed it, it is only the sec-ond largest. Flood-preven-tion schemes (over 6,000 irrigation or drainage channels and 15,000 sluices) mean that the surrounding area is pro-ductive year-round, and the lake acts as a reser-voir for flood-water in the summer. In the middle is an island where Junshan Silver Needle Tea is grown. The tea was once presented as tribute to the emperors.

The Yangtze demands careful navigation

Cable-car across the Yangtze at Chongqing

THE HAN RIVER
The Yangtze's longest tributary is the Han (1,540km/957 miles), which rises in the Qingling mountains in Shaanxi province. Like the Yellow River, it is temperamental and prone to flooding. In 1488, it changed its course, separating Hanyang from Hankou (two of the cities that make up modern Wuhan).

Red Plum Pavilion at Changzhou, one of the less-visited towns on the Grand Canal

▶▶ **Changzhou**   167E2

The old heart of Changzhou has much to commend it. On the Grand Canal, with a network of smaller canals spanned by little stone bridges and a labyrinth of narrow streets and alleyways, it has an atmosphere of its own. The restored **Temple of Heavenly Tranquillity (Tianningsi)** ▶▶, founded 1,300 years ago, is a beautiful example of temple art, with its elegantly curving eaves and shining plum-hued lacquer. Behind the temple is the **Red Plum Park (Hongmei Gongyuan)** ▶, which has two pagodas and a tea-house. The **Ma Garden (Mayuan)** ▶ is worthy of a visit, and the **Mooring Pavilion (Yizhouting)** has literary associations with the Song-dynasty poet Su Dongpo. An exploration of the main streets, Dong Dajie and Nan Dajie, will be rewarded. Tours around Changzhou's ornamental comb factory are also possible.

▶▶ **Chongqing**   166A1

Most people who journey through the Yangtze Gorges usually start or finish at Chongqing. It is perched high on the cliffs overlooking the confluence of the Yangtze and

Map labels:
Bus Station, Martyrs' Cemetery & SACO Prisons
JINSHA ST
Jialing
Chaotianmen Dock
Cable Car
Guiyuan
ZHONGSHAN SI RD
ROAD
BEIQU ROAD
CANGBAI RD
XINHUA RD
SHAANXI ROAD
JIALING RIVER BRIDGE
RENMIN
Renmin Hotel
LINJIANG RD
ZOURONG RD
MINZU RD
Luohan Temple
LIZIBA ROAD
ZHONGSHAN SAN RD
Cultural Palace of the Labouring People
ZHONGSHAN ER RD
ZHONGSHAN YI RD
MINQUAN RD
Liberation Monument Clocktower
Red Cliff Village
Loquat Hill
JIEFANG ROAD
Chongqing Museum
Wanglongmen Cableway
Eling Park
Railway Station
NANQU ROAD
CHANG JIANG BRIDGE
Chongqing Zoo, Northern Hot Springs Park; Dazu Stone Carvings & Artists Village
Southern Hot Springs Park
Yangtze
0 ½ 1 km
0 ½ mile

the Jialing rivers and although it is not a beautiful city, its position lends it an air of grandeur. Now an important industrial and mineral hub (which gained special municipality status in 1997), it has always been Sichuan's trade outlet with the rest of China. One of the farthest flung of treaty ports (opened to foreign trade in 1890), Chongqing came to prominence as the nationalist capital in 1938, after the Japanese took Nanjing. Filled with spies, it was the object of continuous bombing missions by the Japanese during World War II.

Chongqing has few specific attractions, but plenty to enjoy. The best park, and the city's highest point, is on **Pipashan** (**Loquat Hill**)▶▶, entrance on Zhongshan Erlu, (*Open* daily 8.30am–11pm. *Admission: inexpensive*), with panoramic views across the city. **Chongqing Museum**▶ (*Open* daily 9–4.30. *Admission: inexpensive*) is in the park—Han-carved tomb bricks, dinosaur remains and some excellent paintings are on display. Farther down, at the end of Xinhua Lu, Shaanxi Lu and Minzu Lu, by the docks, is **Chaotianmen**▶▶, the meeting point of the two rivers and a hub of activity. Overhead, to the left, is the cable-car, which gives spectacular views over Chongqing's rocky promontory (Cangbai Lu and Jinsha Jie are the two stations). Another cable-car, at Wanglongmen, spans the Yangtze to the south.

South of Minzu Lu, near the junction with Cangbai Lu, is **Luohan Temple**▶ (*Open* daily 8–5. *Admission: inexpensive*), founded in the Song dynasty and well known for its hall of 500 lifelike arhats. The main shopping streets are at the corner of Zourong Lu, Minquan Lu and Minzu Lu, around the Liberation Monument Clock Tower.

Just north of the Renmin Hotel, on the south bank of the Jialing River, is **50 Z engjiayan** where Zhou Enlai (China's Foreign Minister during the Maoist era) lived and worked.

The **Red Cliff Village** (**Hongyan cun**) (*Open* daily 8.30–5. *Admission: inexpensive*) to the west of the city illustrates China's modern history. This was the residential area for the representatives of the Communist party during the Guomindang Communist alliance of World War II. There is a good museum of revolutionary history here.

171

AIR RAIDS AND FLOWERS
The writer Emily Hahn was in Chongqing during World War II. 'Chungking. What does the name evoke in my mind? Air raids. Oranges. Szechuan food, good, full of strong pepper, probably to warm up the blood on the cold, wet, muddy days...Yet Chungking is a place of flowers. You can have roses in your garden all the year round. I am not kind in my description... but I liked it.'

Taking home a new washing machine, Chongqing docks

Vision of Hell, a Buddhist carving at Baodingshan, Dazu, bears remarkable similarities to contemporary Christian visions of hell

Classic Purple Sand teaware from Yixing. The teapots, it is claimed, retain both the tint and the taste of the tea

▶▶▶ **Dazu** *166A1*

Dazu is famous for its Buddhist **stone carvings**▶▶▶. Set in lush, picturesque countryside, and less formal than the other major groups at Datong and Luoyang, thousands of the sculptures and reliefs exhibit a vibrant liveliness peculiar to Sichuan, in which the storytelling element is as important as orthodox religious iconography. The carvings are in two principal areas—Beishan (North Hill), and the more interesting Baodingshan (Precious Summit), where the carvings were completed according to a plan and follow the area's contours. Mostly Buddhist, the carvings also carry elements of Taoism and Confucianism.

The carvings at **Beishan** (*Open* daily 8.30–5.30. *Admission: expensive*), 2km (1 mile) north of Dazu, were begun in the ninth century. The work continued for about 250 years, and some 10,000 statues were made. The earliest caves are numbers 2, 3, 5, 9 and 10. Cave 245 contains more than 600 figures and scenes of everyday Tang life. In Cave 113, a divine Avalokitésvara (who became Guanyin in Chinese Buddhism) gazes in rapture at the moon's reflection. In 136, the largest cave, Samantabhadra (Bodhisattva of pervading goodness) rides an elephant, with Manjusri (Bodhisattva of wisdom) on a lion, while Sakyamuni is surrounded by representations of Guanyin, goddess of mercy and bringer of sons.

Baodingshan (*Open* daily 8.30–5.30. *Admission: expensive*) lies northeast of Dazu. There are two groups of carvings here: Xiaofowan and Dafowan. The latter is the more vivid, with lively scenes from Buddhist scriptures. The carvings were completed between 1179 and 1249 and are in a horseshoe-shaped gully reached down a flight of stairs by some reconstructed temple buildings. 'A fierce tiger coming down the mountain' greets you at the bottom right. Niche 3 reveals the Wheel of Life with the founder of the site,

Zhao Zhifeng, as its focus; above him is the Pavilion of the Western Paradise, flanked by the animals that represent stages of rebirth. Niche 8, the Dabei Pavilion, contains the figure of the 1,000-arm Avalokitésvara, the largest ever carved in China. In niche 11 is the famous reclining Buddha, 30m (98ft) long, whose posture symbolizes entry into nirvana. Try to make time to see niches 14 (Buddha Teaching), 15 (Requital of Parental Kindness), 21 (Eighteen Layers of Hell) and 30 (Cowherds with Oxen, a symbolic story of taming the passions).

▶▶ Dingshu 167D2

To the west of Wuxi is Yixing county, dotted with tea plantations, bamboo groves and miniature lakes. The area is famous for its pottery and underground caverns. Although the hotels are in Yixing town, the place of greatest interest is **Dingshu (or Dingshan)**▶▶▶, which has specialized in the production of glazed ceramics since the Han dynasty. Its Purple Sand pottery is seen all over China, particularly as teapots. The stores are filled with modern pottery at very low prices, and a stroll around the streets is well worthwhile. Factory tours are usually possible, while the **Exhibition Centre** displays older and more sophisticated examples of Dingshu ware. The Ceramic Research Institute is worth visiting, and the Ceramic Museum, on the road to Yixing, has examples of Yixing pottery from 6,000 years ago to the present day.

Excursions are also offered to the three groups of **caves**▶▶: Shanjuan (*Open* daily 7.30–5. *Admission: expensive*); Zhanggong (*Open* daily 8–5. *Admission: moderate*; Linggu (*Open* daily 7.30–5. *Admission: moderate*). Wear shoes with a good grip and take waterproof coats and flashlights. The **Shanjuan** group is 26km (16 miles) southwest of Yixing. You leave the caves by boat along a subterranean stream. The **Linggu**, south of Yixing, is the largest group. **Zhanggong Cave** is 18km (11 miles) south of Yixing.

LOST ART
Despite claims to the contrary, it seems that the Chinese have almost lost the art of making beautiful porcelain. Cheap, practical, occasionally interesting porcelain is produced in vast quantities, but little has any true beauty. It is possible to find exact replicas of famous museum pieces in shops aimed at the foreign tourist and in museum shops, and these are bargain purchases.

TANTRIST SCULPTURE
Zhao Zhifeng, who founded the Buddhist site at Baoding (Dazu), was from the nearby village of Miliang. Between 1179 and 1249, he supervised the carving of thousands of images in the mountain face representing the teachings of Buddhism, making Baoding one of the most important sites of Tantric Buddhism in China.

173

Wheel of Life, Dazu, with Zhao Zhifeng at its hub

*West Lake, Hangzhou,
an 'earthly paradise', is a
traditional destination
for honeymooners*

▶▶ Hangzhou 167E1

The capital of Zhejiang province, Hangzhou lies on the
banks of Qiantang River, about 97km (60 miles) from the
sea. Famous above all for the West Lake, it is also the
southern terminus of the Grand Canal (see pages 176–177),
which reached Hangzhou during the Sui dynasty and is a
testament to the former importance of this now comparatively provincial town. Renowned for its scenic beauty,
Hangzhou is a popular destination for newlyweds. Its reputation as a place for leisure and sensual pleasures goes
back to the Song dynasty, when it succeeded Kaifeng as
capital of the Southern Song. Marco Polo wrote about its
captivating women and the loveliness of its temples and
gardens. Under the Qing, Hangzhou remained one of the
richest towns in China, but in the mid-19th century,
during the Taiping Rebellion, much of it was razed.
Although many historic buildings have been destroyed,
parts of the town have not changed for centuries, and the
lake and surrounding hills retain their reputation as one of
China's best-known beauty spots.

West Lake (Xihu) ▶▶▶ was originally a shallow inlet
off Hangzhou Bay. In the fourth century, silt deposits
from the Qiantang River built up, creating a barrier, and
the present lake was formed behind it. Two sections of
the lake are enclosed by two causeways, the result of
water-control work undertaken during the Tang and Song
dynasties.

The Bai Causeway encloses Beili Lake and runs from near the Hangzhou Hotel on the north bank to Gushan Island, and then back to the north bank farther east. This makes a good walk with fine views from the Duanqiao (Broken Bridge, so called because snow melts first at the bridge's hump, giving the impression of a gap) and from the top of Gushan. **Zhejiang Provincial Museum**▶▶ (*Open* Mon 12–4, Tue–Sun 9–4. *Admission: inexpensive*) is housed in a Qing pavilion, which includes a hollow brick from the collapsed Leifeng Pagoda (rebuilt in 2002), the oldest finds associated with rice and silk culture in China, and ancient maps of the city. At the eastern end, the Pavilion of the Autumn Moon on a Calm Lake is perfect for watching the moon, and doubles as a tea-house.

The Su Causeway links the north shore with the south (at the Huagang Park, filled with fish pools) and encloses the Xili. Near the north end is the **Tomb and Temple of Yue Fei**▶, a much venerated Song general.

Detail from the Lingyin Temple

No visit to Hangzhou is complete without a boat excursion around the lake. Steamers depart from Gushan, the east shore (Hubin Lu), and Huagang Park for tours of the islands, including **Three Pagodas Reflecting the Moon** (**Santanyinyue**) island, which contains four miniature lotus-covered lakes.

The **Lingyin Temple**▶▶ is a celebrated Chan (Zen) Buddhist temple, founded in AD326. The current structure dates from the late Qing dynasty. Its highlights are the Great Hall, with camphor-wood statue of the Buddha, and the Feilaifeng (Peak Flying From Afar), a hill opposite the temple covered with inscriptions and reliefs carved into the rock dating from the 10th to the 14th centuries, the most important such site in south China. A cable-car rides to the top of the nearby northern peak.

Other places worthy of attention are the **Six Harmonies Pagoda**▶, the **Dragon Well Tea Plantation**▶ and the **Silk Spinning Factories**▶ as well as the China National Silk Museum on Yuhuangshan Lu (*Open* daily 8.30–4.30. *Admission: free*).

HEAVENLY WALK
Hangzhou is a delightful town in which to stroll. Aside from the obvious walk around the lake, you can explore the hills by following a path behind the Yue Fei Temple, or wander along the canals on the eastern side of town.

A carved laughing Buddha, here with entourage, on the 'Peak Flying From Afar'

The Grand Canal (above and opposite) has been in constant use for more than a thousand years

WATER-BORNE
One of the features of the Grand Canal is the string of barges following each other nose to tail. In the past, entire families lived aboard, but apparently nowadays factories own most of the boats and allocate apartments to the boatmen they employ. However, judging by the family atmosphere on some of the barges—children, pets and cooking all in evidence—it is more than likely that the new liberal approach to the economy is encouraging the re-emergence of old habits.

▶▶▶ **The Grand Canal (Da Yunhe)**   *167E2*

A cruise along the Grand Canal is one of the easiest and best ways of seeing what makes China tick. In half a day you can travel between Wuxi and Suzhou (or vice versa), through a jostling floating hubbub that has barely changed in over a thousand years.

The Grand Canal, which in parts dates back to 400BC, is still the world's largest artificial waterway. The early sections were built in the north for the movement of troops, but it was the Sui Emperor Yangdi who undertook the construction of the main canal in the seventh century, with a workforce of 5.5 million conscripted men—in some places this meant all the commoners between the ages of 15 and 55. They worked under the supervision of 50,000 police, and those unable to finish their work quotas were flogged or forced to wear neck weights. The Sui emperor celebrated the completion of the canal by arriving amid a flotilla of beautifully decorated dragonboats pulled by teams of the loveliest girls in the empire.

The emperor's original aim in building the canal was to link his two capitals, Xi'an and Luoyang, but he decided to extend the canal as far as Hangzhou, so as to connect the four major trading rivers: the Yangtze (which it crosses by means of locks), the Yellow, the Qiantang and the Huai—thus linking the rich area of the Yangtze valley, the rice-bowl of China, with the more heavily populated north. Normal trade was not its only function, it was also used to convey tribute to the imperial court: 'nine thousand barques conveying tribute to

The Grand Canal

The Grand Canal

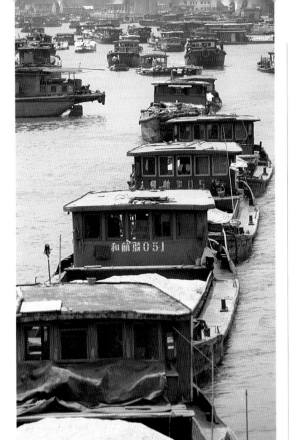

177

One of the commodities commonly carried along the Grand Canal is bamboo. China's culture is sometimes said to have been founded on bamboo, a sentiment illustrated by the following remark by the poet Su Dongpo (1036–1101): 'I would rather eat a meal without meat than live in a place with no bamboos. Without meat one may become thin: without bamboos one becomes vulgar.'

the emperor', as a contemporary wrote to convey the frenetic activity on the canal.

During the 12th century, China's economic focus moved to this region, and the towns bordering the canal grew in status. During the Mongol dynasty, the canal's importance was such that it was extended to the new capital, Beijing. Although the decadent Qing dynasty liked to allow passage to imperial pleasure barges in preference to shipments of grain, the canal did not lose its supremacy until the beginning of the 20th century, when the course of the Yellow River altered, the railways proved more efficient, and coastal shipping began to be used more widely. In 1793–94, the first British embassy to China, under Lord Macartney, returned to Macau from Beijing by way of the Grand Canal (and several rivers), a journey of 3,200km (2,000 miles) of which a mere 80km (50 miles) had to be negotiated over land. In 1896, the globetrotter Isabella Bird described the canal as 'wonderful even in its dilapidation'; after arriving at Tianjin (Tientsin) from Tungchow 'her boat took two days and a half to make its way through the closely jammed mass of cargo and passage boats at the terminus'.

Since the 1950s, the Grand Canal has undergone a renaissance. The southern stretch between Zhenjiang and Hangzhou is navigable year-round, and cruise boats, some equipped in imperial livery, ply the waters. An overnight service also operates between Suzhou and Hangzhou.

LOOKING TO THE FUTURE
There are plans afoot to improve the northern stretches of the Grand Canal, which have been silted up for centuries, by diverting water from the Yangtze to the more arid regions of the north and dredging some sections to enable navigation by vessels of up to 2,032 tonnes.

MOON MAN
A famous drunk, the poet Li Bai met a most romantic end, or at least one in keeping with his philosophy ('With three cups I penetrate the Great Tao. Take a whole jugful—I and the world are one'). He drowned while drunkenly leaning overboard trying to embrace a reflection of the moon.

178

Huangshan, featured in innumerable paintings and even on stamps

▶ Hefei 167D2

Hefei is the capital of Anhui, a comparatively poor province created in 1662. The **museum▶▶** (*Open* Tue–Sun 9–11.30, 2.30–5.30. *Admission: inexpensive*) is due to reopen at the end of 2006 after renovations. Its highlight is a Han-dynasty jade burial suit. It is the nearest point of departure for a visit to the tomb of China's most eminent poet, Li Bai (701–762), who is buried near the place where he drowned. Some 97km (60 miles) northeast of Hefei, near Fengyang, are the **remains of the capital built by the first Ming emperor▶** close to his birthplace before he realized that Nanjing was a better site. The foundations and, near by, the impressive 'spirit' (or royal) way to the tomb of the emperor's parents are visible.

▶▶▶ Huangshan (Yellow Mountain) 167D1

Open: **daily 7–6.** *Admission: expensive*
One of a range of 72 peaks in south Anhui, the highest reaching 1,800m (5,905ft), Huangshan is considered the most beautiful mountain in China. It is set amid gorgeous rural landscapes and its slopes are covered with pine trees and swathed in cloud. It is a strenuous but not difficult climb to the summit. There are several routes, but the best way is to take the eastern, shorter route up and the longer,

more spectacular western route down (just possible in 10 hours). A bus takes visitors to the main path, which starts from the lower cable-car terminal, the quickest way to the summit (cable-car service operates 7.30–4). Nearby are the preserved villages of Xidi and Hongcun, where scenes from *Crouching Tiger, Hidden Dragon* were filmed.

▶▶ Jiuhuashan   167D1

Jiuhuashan, the southern holy Buddhist mountain in Anhui province, is revered as a place of pilgrimage for the bereaved. Not as stunning as Huangshan, but still a splendid sight, the climb can easily be accomplished in a day, or ride the cable-car which takes visitors up part of the way. You can get to Jiuhuashan from Nanjing by bus (7 hours), from Wuhu (4 hours) or from Huangshan (6 hours).

▶▶▶ Nanjing (Nanking)   167D2

The capital of Jiangsu province lies on the south bank of the Yangtze and is one of the most delightful Chinese cities, despite the sprawl of modern buildings. The heart of the city retains its Ming street plan, the old city wall is largely intact, and an air of dignified calm, absent elsewhere in China, pervades the city's tree-lined streets.

179

It has been a capital at various times during the last 2,000 years—of the kingdom of Wu after the collapse of the Han, of local dynasties when China later fragmented, of imperial China under the early Ming and of Republican China under the nationalists between 1911 and 1949.

Nanjing is an even mix of imperial and revolutionary China. The heart of the city is around Zhongshan Lu and Hanzhong Lu. But start with the **Ming city wall▶▶▶**, which ignores the usually rigid rectangle, by necessity following instead the natural contour of the land for 32km (20 miles), making it the longest city wall in the world. Much of it is still complete and can be seen from the park surrounding the **Xuanwu Lake▶**, or in detail on the road to the **Purple and Gold Mountains Observatory▶** (*Open* daily 8.30–4.30. *Admission: inexpensive*), the largest in China. The **Zhonghua City Gate▶▶**, made of stone and clay bricks (each stamped with the name of its maker), has three inner gates designed to trap would-be attackers who breached the first gate in a compound. Steps lead up to the ramparts, which command fine views over the city. The local polished stones (particular to Nanjing) are often on sale around the foot of the gate.

Just back into the city from Zhonghua Gate, along Zhonghua Lu, are the **Taiping Museum▶** (*Open* daily 8am–10pm. *Admission: inexpensive*) and the **Confucian Temple** (*Open* 8am–10pm. *Admission: moderate*). The museum is in the residence and garden of one of the leaders of the Taiping Heavenly Kingdom Rebellion (1851–64) (see page 42),

Astronomical instrument at the Purple and Gold Mountains Observatory, Nanjing

The Yangtze River Bridge, Nanjing, a feat of engineering that took eight years to complete. A second bridge opened in 2001 and a third in October 2006. A fourth is also planned

TOMB OF THE KING OF BORNEO
In 1408, the king of Borneo arrived in Nanjing, along with his extensive family, to pay tribute to the Ming court. His mission was evidently not entirely successful, because he died there the same year and is buried just to the south of the city walls.

and exhibits maps, coins, weapons, documents and other artefacts relating to the Taiping movement. Taiping wall paintings have recently been found at 74 Tangzi Jie. The area around the Confucian temple, called **Fuzimiao**, has become a lively area of restaurants, sideshows and shops.

The **Nanjing Museum**▶▶ (*Open* daily 9–4. *Admission: inexpensive*), at 321 Zhongshan Donglu, in an attractive building constructed in traditional style, is noted for its Han jade burial suit—jade squares linked by silver thread. Other display items include ceramics and bronzes from prehistoric times to the Qing dynasty.

The ruins of the **Ming Palace**▶ (*Open* daily. *Admission: free*), a model for Beijing's Forbidden City, rest under the trees near the Provincial Museum, a little farther west along Zhongshan Donglu. Two sets of five marble bridges, part of the old Meridian gate and a crop of carved pillar bases remain. On the other side of the road there are a few scale-version buildings, which give an idea of what the original palace would have been like.

With the exceptions of the **Ming Bell** and **Drum Towers**▶ (on Beijing Xilu), Nanjing's other attractions lie on the outskirts of the city. The magnificent **Yangtze River Bridge** (**Nanjing Changjiang Daqiao**)▶▶▶ (*Open* daily 8–5. *Admission: inexpensive*), always cited as an example of what the Chinese could do when the Russians said it was impossible, is to the northwest of the city and links south with north China. Before its opening in 1968, trains crossed the river on a special ferry, taking two hours for each journey. The bridge is for both rail and road, and, at over 2km (1 mile) long between its extreme points, it is one of the longest bridges in China. A lift takes you up to a viewing tower on the south side.

To the east of the city, a road weaves through bamboo groves to the **Tomb of Zhu Yuanzhang**▶▶ (*Open* daily 8–5. *Admission: expensive*), the first Ming emperor. The tomb is not open, but you can walk down the spirit (or royal) way lined with statues, less grand than its counterpart in Beijing, but also less spoilt by commercialism. At the end farthest from the tomb the road curves to the right, but walk straight ahead to see the large brick arch, part of the wall that used to surround the tomb.

Farther on, east of the Ming tomb and embedded in the slopes of the Purple and Gold Mountains (Zijin Shan) is **Sun Yatsen's Mausoleum**►►► (*Open* daily 8–5. *Admission: moderate*). Founder of Republican China, he died in 1925 in Beijing, where he was laid out in the Biyun Temple. The competition for the design of his mausoleum was won by Y. C. Lu, who was influenced by the shape of the Liberty Bell in Philadelphia. The tomb itself is in the uppermost pavilion, reached by several flights of steps. Sun Yatsen's remains are covered by a marble effigy.

East of the Mausoleum is the **Linggu Pagoda**►, built by an American in 1929. Near by is the fine **Beamless Hall**►► (*Open* daily 8–5. *Admission: inexpensive*), made entirely of brick without any wooden beams. It was part of a temple that existed on the site of the first Ming emperor's tomb.

THE RAPE OF NANJING
Between 13 December 1937 and the end of January 1938, during the Japanese occupation, it is estimated that at least 400,000 civilian residents of Nanjing were murdered or raped with appalling brutality. In the 1980s, a school history textbook was published in Japan that gave only a passing mention to this massacre. The Chinese government protested until changes were made.

or cycle ride—Nanjing

Start from the pretty, old wooden-fronted houses outside Zhonghua City Gate and head north along Zhonghua Road. Turning right along Changle Road to Bailuzhou Park leads you to an area of alleys and old houses. Return to Zhonghua Road, go past the Taiping Museum and ornamental gardens and then turn left along Jianye Road to Chaotiangong, one of the oldest parts of the city and home to the Municipal Museum. Return to Zhonghua Road, go to the Xinjiekou circular road and up Zhongshan Road to the Drum Tower. East from the Xinjiekou circular takes you to the Ming Palace site and the Nanjing Provincial Museum. You can continue on to the Purple and Gold Mountains (Zijin Shan) by bicycle.

Nobody knows the precise date of the discovery of silk, but Chinese tradition ascribes it to the Empress Xi Ling, who apparently harnessed the natural skills of the silkworm for the benefit of humanity in the year 2640BC.

182

Sericulture The Chinese kept the secret of silk for 3,000 years until, it is said, perfidious princesses and cunning missionaries exported it to the West and throughout the Orient. The word 'sericulture' derives from the Greek word for silk, *serikos*, and refers to the raising of silkworms and the production of raw silk. Farmers breed the silkworms and then deliver the cocoons to spinning factories, where raw silk is drawn on to bobbins, ready for commercial use.

The silkworm is the caterpillar of the moth *Bombyx mori*, a native of China. One moth may lay 500 eggs, which are hatched in incubators or open trays at about 22°C (70°F). The caterpillars are black or grey, later turning creamy white, and eat mulberry leaves, supplied to them every three to four hours. After five weeks, the caterpillars are 8cm (3in) long and extremely sensitive to smells or noise; when full-grown they reject food and become restless, a sign that they are ready to make their cocoons. Small straw frames are then placed on the trays for this purpose.

The silk is produced by a pair of tubular spinning glands, each of which secretes a single strand. One strand is joined together with the other by muscular contraction, producing a thread up to 90m (295ft) long. A gummy secretion holds it all together in its cocoon shape. This process takes about 10 days, after which 90 per cent of the cocoons are sent to the factory, while the farmer keeps 10 per cent for breeding.

The factory Once at the factory the cocoons are sorted to reject any that are flawed, and the remainder are then steamed to kill the live chrysalis. The threads from six or seven cocoons are needed to produce a yarn strong enough for weaving. The cocoons are immersed in hot water to loosen the threads, which are then extracted from the water and reeled together as one by machine. The cocoon case left behind is used as an ingredient in traditional medicine.

Top: silkworms and cocoons
Above: a silk-embroidered double-sided peony, on display in Suzhou Silk Museum

Old fabric, new style

The newly created thread is then transformed into a yarn suitable for weaving by a process of doubling and twisting, known as 'throwing', which gives it durability and strength. The amount of throwing varies according to the use to which the yarn will be put. After a certain point, silk loses its sleekness and is left with a granular surface, known as crêpe.

The twisting is done mechanically—rows of machines transfer the yarn from one bobbin to another, with each bobbin moving at a different speed in order to achieve the amount of twist required.

From here the silk goes to dyeing factories and then to weaving factories to be made into cloth or carpets, or perhaps to institutes that specialize in the production of silk embroidery. The most famous of these is in Suzhou, and there are others in Guangdong and Sichuan.

SILK MARKETS
Much of China's 46,000-tonne silk production is exported. China has 90 per cent of the world market for raw silk and is attempting to increase its 40 per cent share of the finished silk market.

183

Separating the silken strands from cocoons at a factory in Suzhou

Temple of Confucius, Jiading & Guyi Garden, Nanxiang

ZHENNAN ROAD

Zhabei Park

Shanghai West Railway Station

JIAOTONG ROAD

BEI ROAD

HENGFENG ROAD

Bus Station

Shanghai Railway Station

CAO'AN ROAD

ZHONGSHAN ROAD

Jiaotong Park

WUNING ROAD

TIANMU

XIZANG BEI RD

CHANGSHOU ROAD

Wusong River (Suzhou Creek)

CHENGDU

Jade Buddha Temple

SHIMEN RD

BEIJING

4

3

Wusong River

Changfeng Park

Zhongshan Park

WANHANGDU RD

Shanghai Acrobatic Theatre

No 1 Dept Store

BEIJING XI ROAD

XIZANG ZHONG RD

NANJING

BEIZHAI ROAD

Changning Railway Station

Jing'an Temple

Art Gallery

Exhibition Centre

NANJING XI RD

People's Square

CHANGNING ROAD

Children's Palace

Shanghai Library

Shanghai Museum

YAN AN

Jing'an Park

Renmin (People's) Park

YAN AN ROAD

YAN AN XI ROAD

ZHONG ROAD

Great World Entertainment Centre (Shanghai Youth Palace)

HUASHAN ROAD

Shanghai Art Theatre

ZHONG ROAD

Shanghai Zoo

Shanghai Arts & Crafts Research Centre

HUAIHAI

Fuxing Park

Site of the 1st National Congress of the Communist Party of China

2

Hongqiao Airport

HONGQIAO ROAD

XI ROAD

HUAIHAI

XI ROAD

Former Residence of Sun Yatsen

Residence of Zhou Enlai

NAN XIZANG NAN RD

EXPWY

Songjiang

ZHONGSHAN XI

Xujiahui Railway Station

HENGSHAN ROAD

XUJIAHUI RD

LUJIABANG

ZHILOU RD

ZHAOJIABANG ROAD

St Ignatius' Catholic Cathedral

Guangqi Park

Shanghai Indoor Stadium

CAOXI ROAD

NAN ROAD

ZHONGSHAN

LUPU BRIDGE

1

Longhua Park

Longhua Temple Pagoda

Huangpu

Hangzhou

Shanghai Botanical Garden

A   B   C

CITY SLICKERS

In pre-1949 Shanghai, stockbrokers dashed between offices in the financial districts as the rates fluctuated, in low-slung, four-wheel carriages, drawn by little Mongolian ponies. Each sported a coachman dressed in all his finery.

▶▶▶ **Shanghai**   *167E2*

Shanghai, with a population of more than 13 million, is one of China's largest cities and, as one of China's four munici-palities (along with Tianjin, Beijing and Chongqing), is under direct central government control. It was a town of reasonable importance from the 13th century, when it became a county seat and was located in the area now known as the old town, which until the early part of the 20th century had its own wall. In the 19th century, the foreign powers recognized Shanghai's potential as a port, situated as it is on the banks of the Huangpu, only 27km (17 miles) from the mouth of the Yangtze. The Treaty of Nanjing in 1842 (which concluded the Opium Wars) ceded areas of Shanghai first to the British and then to the French

Early morning dance lessons in Shanghai

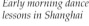
THE GREAT WORLD

On the corner of Yan'an Road and Xizang Road is an extraordinary building resembling a wedding cake. The building was formerly called the Great World. Inaugurated in 1917, it was a cross between bazaar and freak show. Open from noon until late at night, each floor was devoted to different attractions from the burlesque to the vile: sing-song girls (see page 189) and peep-shows, a stuffed whale and imported toilets. It is now open again in the evenings with fairground amusements and live performances of opera, trick-cyclists and other entertainments.

and Americans, forming what was known as the 'Foreign Concessions'. The British and Americans then combined to form the International Settlement, while the French Concession remained separate. The rules governing these enclaves were complicated, but essentially foreign nationals were not bound by Chinese law, but were subject to the jurisdiction of their own consuls. Up until 1949, foreigners dominated commerce and industry, amassing huge fortunes, as did a number of Chinese.

The colonial legacy is a bizarre one. Although Shanghai is a vital part of Chinese industry, and despite a rapidly changing skyline, it looks like a European city in a Chinese setting. A walk around the Bund and its nearby streets is a good way to soak up its atmosphere.

THE GREAT HORSE ROAD

The Nanjing Road was originally cobbled and is named after the Nanjing treaty of 1842, which ceded areas of Shanghai to foreign control. For the Chinese it was always the *Da Malu*, or Great Horse Road, since it was built for horsemen. It was noted by the writer John Steinbeck as one of the most interesting streets in the world.

For superb views, go to the **Oriental Pearl TV Tower►** (*Open daily 8am–9.30pm. Admission: expensive*), or the Jinmao Tower, at 421m (1,380ft), currently the world's fourth tallest building. Both stand opposite the Bund in the Pudong area. The Shanghai History Museum is at the Oriental Pearl.

The **Jade Buddha Temple** (**Yufosi**)**►►** (*Open daily 8–4.30. Admission: inexpensive*), on Anyuan Road, has a restored main hall and the remarkable Jade Buddha, brought back from Burma by a local abbot. The temple is lively on the first and fifth days of the lunar month. Shanghai's two other active temples are the **Jing'an►**, on Nanjing Xi Road, and the **Longhua►**, Longhua Road. The **Shanghai Museum►►►** (*Open daily 9–5. Admission: inexpensive*), has a fine collection of Chinese art and porcelain. Of the many parks, the most interesting are the Renmin, the Hongkou and the Jing'an.

The Shanghai Bund and its surroundings

See highlighted map, pages 184–185.

The **Bund►►►** (derived from the Anglo-Indian word meaning waterfront), about 2km (1 mile) long, is the city's fulcrum. Ideally, devote a half day to a walk through the area, the Bund and the nearby streets, and the Friendship Store (China's largest), or a day, if you combine the walk with a cruise to the Yangtze mouth (boats leave near the Peace Hotel). At the far end of the Bund, just the other side of Suzhou Creek, is **Shanghai Mansions Hotel,** a 22-floor brick ziggurat, in what would have been the American Concession.

Opposite, on the other side of Zhongshan Dong Road, is the **Pujiang Hotel,** formerly the Astor House, and opposite that the **Russian Consulate.**

Cross the Waibaidu Bridge back to the Bund. The former **British Consulate** (1870) at No. 33, set in manicured lawns, now has commercial offices. The Bund proper, now known as Waitan, consists almost entirely of pre-1949 buildings in grandiose style. No. 29 was originally the Banque de l'Indochine and No. 31 the former offices of Jardine, Matheson & Co, upon whose opium deals the prosperity of Shanghai was founded.

The outstanding buildings this side of the Nanjing Road are the **Bank of China**, with its New

Huxinting tea-house

York façade and Chinese roof, and the **Peace Hotel**. The Peace Hotel was originally the Cathay, built by Sir Victor Sassoon as the finest in Asia. Redolent of the 1930s, it sounds like the 1940s, courtesy of an old jazz band that thumps out period tunes in the bar at night.

Nanjing Road▶▶ is one of the busiest streets in China, with a huge variety of items for sale, though it is now somewhat upstaged by **Huaihai Road**, the main street of the old French Concession. It leads through the heart of the city to the old **Race Course** (now **Renmin Park**), the department stores, Jing'an Temple and the opulent villas of former foreign residents. The easternmost section of the road is now pedestrianized.

Continuing along the Bund you pass the old **Customs House** at No. 14, with some fine mosaics in the lobby ceiling and surmounted by **Big Ching**, a clock that used to chime like Big Ben in London. Number 12 is the former premises of the **Hong Kong and Shanghai Banking Corporation**, built in 1921, now the Pudong Development Bank. Number 3, the Dong Feng Hotel, was originally the famously snobbish **Shanghai Club** (the British Club), watering hole of the taipans (bosses of the foreign trading companies) and home to the longest bar in the world.

Yan'an Road was formerly Avenue Edward VII, the boundary between the International Settlement and the French Concession. The waterfront strip (Zhongshan Er Road) was the Quai de France. Walking along here will bring you to the former Chinese Bund, which runs in front of the **Old Town▶▶▶**. Turn right along Dongmen Road past Waixiang Guajie on the left, site of a local **food market**. Continue on to Fanbang Zhong Road until, on the right, you meet the Ming gateway to the **Temple of the City God** (**Chenghuangmiao**), and beyond it the Yu Garden, with its lake and tea-house.

Pass through the gateway and into the heart of the old town, a maze of quaint shops and restaurants reminiscent of old China. In the middle is a small lake. The zigzag bridge leads to the 18th-century **Huxinting tea house▶▶**, a mid-lake pavilion and an excellent place for a pot of green tea.

The Ming-dynasty **Yu Garden▶▶** (*Open* daily 8.30–4.30. *Admission: moderate*) nearby is a fine example of miniature landscaping, built in 1559. The first pavilion is the ceremonial Three Ears of Corn Hall, followed by the Hall for Viewing the Grand Rockery. Turn right as you come out of here, follow the pond shore, then keep right past pavilions, halls and gardens to re-emerge in the old town behind the tea-house.

187

The skyline of the Shanghai Bund

Shanghai is a legend. A generation after the last 'Shanghailanders' relinquished their privileges, the name continues to evoke nostalgia for a way of life that can never be the same again.

The Peace Hotel Jazz Band, still thumping out 1940s classic tunes

FOX-HUNTING MEMORIES
Part of the charm of pre-1949 Shanghai was its absurdity. It was an oasis of unreality in a world that was all too real beyond the boundaries of the Foreign Concessions. For the British, memories of home were reinforced by such events as the paper hunt. A pack of foxhounds would set off in pursuit of a chemical trail with the odoriferous qualities of a fox. Horses and huntsmen galloped across the coun-tryside not far behind, with the last man in the field being responsible for mollifying any outraged farmers.

The old Cathay Hotel, now the Peace Hotel, where Noël Coward wrote Private Lives

A unique city The European man's pre-1949 Shanghai seemed to be 'life itself'. It was an extraordinary mix of the seedy and the decadent, immense wealth and terri-ble poverty. It has even given its name to a verb—according to the dictionary, to be shanghaied is to 'be drugged and shipped as a sailor, when unconscious'.

The city's oddities were due to the peculiar circum-stances of the city's existence. Written into the Treaty of Nanjing was the notion of extraterritoriality, which meant that foreign nationals in Shanghai were outside Chinese law, which was of medieval severity. Of course, each of the concessions had its own laws, but in reality almost anything went. Shanghai became a magnet for the dispossessed, seekers of wealth and adventurers.

Shanghailanders Most of what is left of concession Shanghai dates from between 1920 and 1949. The character of the two concessions (the French and the International Settlement) was quite different—not only did you change buses at Edward VII Avenue but also electricity systems. The International Settlement was a combination of the British and the American Settlement. Each concession reflected different national personas and attracted different characters. And Shanghai was full of characters: wealthy Baghdad Sephardic Jews like Sir Victor Sassoon, owner of the Cathay Hotel (today's Peace Hotel), with his stable of greyhounds—greyhound racing was a passion among expatriates—whose names coincided with his initials ('Very Slippy', 'Veiled Secret', 'Very Soon'); Silas Hardoon, the wealthiest man in Shanghai, who owned an estate (now covered by the old Soviet-style Exhibition Centre) in the city where he kept his Eurasian wife and adopted children; and underworld criminals, such as the notorious Pockmarked Huang and Big-Eared Du, who ran the city from the French Concession. The mixture of propriety and duplicity that was Shanghai is exemplified by the careers of these two: Huang was the Chief Detective of the French Sûreté, and Du would threaten those who spurned his offers of protection by delivering a coffin to their door.

Nightlife Above all, Shanghai was a nocturnal city. Night started with the tea-cocktail hour, 'tea for propriety and cocktails for pep', and perhaps finished at dawn at Blood Alley (Xikou Lu). Taxi-dancing was an institution—hostesses were for hire in vast dance halls, but required that a drink be bought, invariably cold tea but billed as champagne or whatever the lady requested. Then there were the sing-song girls, who provided entertainment at restaurant dinner parties. Although they were not above prostitution, their main accomplishment was seductive singing, accompanied by a man playing the *erhu*, a two-string Chinese violin. The sing-song girl was easy to identify in her highly polished lacquer rickshaw; a bell announced her presence, while a lamp at her feet was angled to highlight her face and the lotus in her hair.

After years of darkness, Shanghai's famous night-life has returned

AFTER DARK
White Russian refugees arrived in the wake of the 1917 Revolution and were an important and volatile element in the make-up of pre-1949 Shanghai. They are credited with the development of the cabaret. Young Russian women teamed up with Filipino dance bands to perform in Chinese-owned cabarets and were frequently cited in scandalous divorce cases. As a contemporary guide-book pointed out, 'There are three classes of cabaret—high class, low class, and no class.'

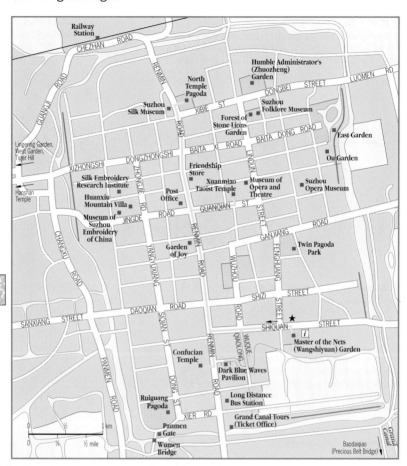

Walk

Suzhou's gardens and temples

A short walk introduces you to some of Suzhou's principal sights. In Wangshi Xiang, an alley off Shijin Street close to the Suzhou Hotel, is the **Master of the Nets Garden (Wangshiyuan)**▶▶▶, a miniature garden built around a pool and first laid out in 1140. It has several small halls carved in lattice and fretwork on the principle of 'framing a view'.

From Wangshiyuan, turn left to Shiquan Street and then take the first left into Wuqueqiaolong until you reach the **Dark Blue Waves Pavilion (Canglangting)**▶▶, which dates back to the 10th century.

Back on Shiquan Street, turn left and walk until you reach the junction with Renmin Road, then turn left again and continue to the **Confucian Temple**▶ where you will find a street plan of Suzhou, the earliest such map extant in China.

Return to Renmin Road, retrace your steps northwards and turn right into Guanqian Street, to reach the Song-dynasty **Xuanmiao Taoist Temple**▶ (*Open 7.30–5. Admission: inexpensive*). Continuing north along Renmin Road will take you past the Friendship Store (No. 504) to the impressive **North Temple Pagoda**▶▶ (*Open 7.45–5.30. Admission: inexpensive*), set in a pretty garden.

▶▶▶ Suzhou

167E2

A comparatively small town in Jiangsu province, Suzhou is one of China's most charming cities, recognized for centuries for its loveliness. Its fame rests on its silk and its gardens, and the pretty houses overlooking narrow canals spanned by traditional bridges—once a standard feature in this area—are now attractions in their own right.

Suzhou's history dates back to the sixth century BC when it was founded on a network of canals built to control the Yangtze flood-waters. Its subsequent prosperity was due to the construction of the Grand Canal and the growth of the silk industry, which flourished under the Tang and became even more important under the Song, with the establishment of the capital at Hangzhou. Later it was known as a great cultural city, but it has remained relatively unaffected by the convulsions of Chinese politics.

The wealth of Suzhou's officials, scholars and traders was invested in their **gardens** (all *Open* daily 7.30–5.30. *Admission: moderate*). The greatest, the 10th-century **Humble Administrator's Garden (Zhuozheng-yuan)▶▶▶**, is also the largest, occupying a 4ha (10-acre) site; the poetically named 19th-century **Lingering Garden (Liuyuan)▶▶▶** is small with delightful rockeries. The **Forest of Stone Lions Garden (Shizilin)▶▶▶**, about 0.5ha (1 acre) in size, has four lakes, rocks, bridges and hills and is considered one of Suzhou's finest gardens. The **Yi Yuan (Harmony Garden)**, on Renmin Road, is a Qing-dynasty garden featuring distinctive pebbles and rockeries.

At the **Silk Embroidery Research Institute▶▶▶** you can watch craftspeople creating their painstaking masterpieces (sometimes embroidering with a strand that is a mere one-fortieth of a silk thread) as well as buy samples of their work. **Suzhou Silk Museum▶▶** (*Open* 9–4.30. *Admission: inexpensive*), near North Pagoda on Renmin Lu, offers a fascinating insight into the story of silk, with live silkworms and a collection of silk looms.

Outside the city is **Tiger Hill (Huqiushan)▶▶▶** (*Open* daily 7.30–5.30. *Admission: moderate*), a scenic spot, with a Song-dynasty leaning pagoda with some Tang features and built in brick to imitate wood architecture. In 1957, workers discovered sutras there and a record of its construction date (959–961). The low, long **Precious Belt Bridge▶▶** affords excellent views of life on the canals.

BRIDGES OVER CANALS
Handsome bridges spanning the canals are a feature of Suzhou. One of the most impressive is the Maple Bridge, near the Hanshan Temple, the subject of a poem by the Tang poet Zhang Ji entitled 'Anchored by night at the Maple Bridge'. Another, offering a classically picturesque view, arches across the old moat near the Panmen Gate.

191

Wangshiyuan, the Master of the Nets Garden

Luohan Hall in the 'Temple of the Return to the Fundamental Principle', Guiyuan Temple, Wuhan

REBEL HEADQUARTERS
Between 1926 and 1927, Wuhan was the head-quarters of a faction of the Guomindang that opposed Chiang Kaishek. The faction commander was Wang Jingwei, who at the time allied himself to the communists. In 1927, in an abrupt *volte-face*, Chiang Kaishek turned on them, murdering 100,000 of their supporters in the Wuhan district. Wang was eventually to lead a Japanese puppet government in Nanjing in 1940 and to die in Tokyo in 1944.

▶▶ **Wuhan**   *166C1*

Wuhan, capital of Hubei province, is an iron and steel city on the Yangtze made up of the three former cities of Wuchang, on the south bank, Hanyang and the former treaty port of Hankou on the north. Wuchang was briefly capital of the state of Wu in the third century, and Hanyang was founded during the Sui dynasty. Hankou was little more than a fishing village until the Western powers established concessions there from 1861. Wuhan was the focus for the revolutionary activity that culminated in the 1911 uprising and overthrow of the Manchu dynasty.

Wuhan tends to be seen merely as an embarkation or disembarkation point for the Yangtze River cruises, but the old city has some attractions. The most striking of these is the **Yellow Crane Pavilion (Huanghelou)**▶ on Sheshan (Snake Hill) in Wuchang, by the river bridge. It was originally built in the third century. Commemorated in many poems, it gets its name from the story of a Taoist priest, Wang Zian, who alighted here on a yellow crane on his journey to become one of the Immortals. If you have time to explore Sheshan a little farther, you will find the **Shengxiang Baota** lama stupa, embossed with interesting carvings, and the **tomb of Chen Youjing**, who declared an independent state at the end of the Yuan dynasty, both worth a visit.

Farther east is the **East Lake (Donghu)**▶, a spacious, pleasant place for a boat trip or stroll. Nearby is the remarkable **Provincial Museum**▶▶▶ (*Open* daily 8.30–noon, 1.30–5. *Admission: moderate*), mostly devoted to the finds excavated from the tomb of Marquis Yi of the state of Zeng, who died in 433BC, and important because it demonstrates the extraordinary richness of Chinese cultural life well before China became a single, unified state. The highlight is a set of 64 bronze bells on racks, supported by bronze soldiers, which are used daily in concerts of ancient music. The crawling dragon motif is repeated on many of the ritual lacquerware vessels that were also discovered in the tomb. There is a fine collection of ritual bronzes, as well as other ancient musical instruments.

In Hanyang, the **Guiyuan Buddhist Temple**▶▶ (*Open daily 8–5. Admission: inexpensive*) on Cuihui Jie, built in the Qing dynasty on the site of a Ming garden, is celebrated for the 500 figures sculpted by two artists between 1822 and 1831. **Guishan (Tortoise Hill)**▶ was once covered in temples and pavilions, some of which have been reconstructed, including the Song-dynasty **Guqin Terrace (Guqintai)**. It was built to commemorate two Han-dynasty musicians, Yu Baiya and Zhong Ziqi, who used to play together here. One year Yu arrived to find that his friend had died; after playing a farewell tune on his lute, he broke the strings, vowing never to play again.

Hankou▶▶, like Shanghai, is interesting for its European atmosphere, a legacy dating from 1861 to 1949 when the foreign powers were established here. The British Concession went from Jianghan Dadao to the train station; then, in sequence, were the smaller Russian, French, German and Japanese concessions. The old waterfront along Yanjiang Lu evokes a sense of nostalgia with its former European trading houses, Butterfield and Swire, Litvinoff, British-American, as well as the major consulates and the Customs House. **Zhongshan Dadao** is the main shopping area of Hankou (and Wuhan), while there are markets in the Jiefang Dadao area. Jiefang Park and **Zhongshan Park** were the former racecourses.

Wuhan is a major carpet producer, and the factory can be visited by appointment.

The Yangtze River Bridge was completed in 1957. More than 2km (1 mile) long, it carries both rail and road traffic. A second bridge was completed in 1995.

The Yellow Crane Pavilion, overlooking the Yangtze, Wuhan

193

Although the river itself and the life along its banks are fascinating in themselves, the focal point of the cruise along the Yangtze is the dramatic journey through the Three Gorges.

YANGTZE GORGES
The Three Gorges were formed about 70 million years ago when earth movements caused a vast inland sea draining east to cut into limestone faults in zigzag fashion, creating the perpendicular cliffs and sharp curves of the gorges.

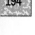
194

Transportation For most people the journey along the Yangtze begins or ends either at Wuhan or Chongqing (downstream takes 3 days and 2 nights, upstream 5 days). Between the two cities are the gorges themselves and a host of small towns and villages. As well as the luxury ships run by CITS and those chartered by foreign tour companies, there are local steamers that have basic passenger facilities, ranging from fairly unpleasant dormitories to two-berth cabins of an acceptable standard with a small lounge. They have restaurants that serve, on the whole, execrable food. Some of them have upgraded cabins with private bathrooms and air-conditioning. If you can secure a cabin, eat the food, and tolerate the booming whistle, a trip on one of these ships is a worthwhile experience.

Sights The Yangtze is lined with evocatively named rocks and hills. East of Chongqing is the **Stone Treasure Stronghold** (**Shibaozhai**), a 30m (98ft) rock said to resemble a jade seal, with a brilliant red pagoda against the side. At its summit is an early 18th-century temple. About 50km (31 miles) beyond, **Wanxian** is a typical settlement, high on the banks and reached by a long flight of steps. An established trading hub, it has a market piled high with fruit, nuts and traditional basketware. There is also a silk-weaving factory. At **Yunyang**, the Zhang Fei Temple is dedicated to a Three Kingdoms general renowned for his honesty. Next is **Fengjie** with its Ming walls, then **Baidi Cheng**, followed by the Gorges.

The Gorges The Gorges are a spectacular sight. The first is the 8km (5-mile) **Qutangxia** (**Bellows Gorge**). As you

Shooting the rapids in one of the Yangtze's three 'Lesser Gorges' along the Daning River

enter it, **Red Shoulder Mountain** appears on the north side, pockmarked with square holes, ancient burial places said to have been used as bellows by the god of carpenters, Lu Ban. On **White Salt Mountain**, on the south bank, are the remains of a sixth-century city. High up on the north side of the gorge is the old towpath. The gorge ends at the town of **Daixi**.

Boats often moor at **Wushan** in order to visit the three beautiful small gorges along the Daning River. A fee is charged for this extra boat excursion.

Next comes the 45km (27-mile) **Wuxia (Witches Gorge)** lined by 12 peaks, 6 on either side, each with a poetic name based on the legend of Yao Ji, daughter of the Queen of the West, and her 11 sisters. **Zigui** was the home of the third-century BC statesman Qu Yuan of the state of Chu, whose suicide, when his advice to resist the rise of the state of Qin was ignored, is commemorated in annual dragonboat races. Finally comes the 76km (47 mile) **Xiling Gorge**, comprising seven smaller gorges. The main ones are the **Gorge of the Sword and the Manual on the Art of War** (named after Zhuge Liang, a third-century minister said to have hidden his treatise on military strategy here); the **Ox Liver and Horse's Blood Gorge** and the **Shadowplay Gorge**, named after rock hues and shapes.

A former treaty port, Yichang is now famous for its **Gezhouba Dam**, completed in 1986 (see panel).

Though the waters are rising, the gorges remain a most spectacular sight

SUNKEN GORGES
The topping-off of the Three Gorges Dam in May 2006 was a key moment for the world's largest hydroelectric project. Despite funding scandals and warnings of an ecological disaster, the project is on course for completion by 2009, creating a vast reservoir and submerging the gorges under 175m (575ft) of water. The project, which involves relocating about 2 million people, aims to prevent flooding, ease shipping and provide power to China's interior.

The dam is already a tourist attraction. Visits can be arranged to its precursor, the Gezhouba Dam, and the White Horse and Three Visitors caves.

Traditional Huishan clay figurine 'fatties', still made in Wuxi

FIGURES OF CLAY
Wuxi is not only known for its rocks and silk, it also produces the famous Huishan figurines made of local clay. Depicting characters from traditional fairy-tales, operas and plays, they may not be to everyone's taste, but even if they do not appeal to you, a visit to the factory to watch them being made is worthwhile.

ATTRACTION OF OPPOSITES
In *Behind the Wall*, Colin Thubron describes the rocks of Lake Tai as 'a frozen turmoil' that 'concentrated the wild energy of nature'. In traditional gardens, rocks represented the hard, masculine 'yang' principle, in contrast to the water, next to which they were usually placed, which was soft, feminine 'yin'. 'Water was stone's antithesis. It was the blood of the earth, drunk by the kings of old legend in search of immortality.'

▶▶ **Wulingyuan**

This mountainous, lush area in northwestern Hunan is home to several minority peoples and is the site of China's largest cave. Trails provide some excellent hiking and it is possible to go rafting. An airport has been built to serve the area.

▶▶ **Wuxi and Lake Tai**   *167E2*

Wuxi town is a convenient access point for **Lake Tai (Taihu)**▶▶, one of the largest freshwater lakes in China. It is famous for its ornamental limestone rocks pierced with holes by the action of the waters, which were highly prized and often adorn traditional Chinese gardens.

Wuxi, one of the principal ports on the Grand Canal, has one of the fastest growing economies in the country. Although an old town (it got its name, which means 'no tin', during the Han dynasty when the tin mine on Xishan dried up), its economic expansion dates only to the turn of the 20th century when wealthy Shanghai entrepreneurs established new factories and developed the silk industry. A visit to the **Number 1 Spinning Mill**▶▶ is worthwhile.

There are hotels at the lakeside (some distance out of town) and in the heart of the city, which has a lively port atmosphere. The city is dominated by Xihui Hill and Park, where one of the most noted gardens in China, the **Jichangyuan (Attachment to Freedom Garden)**▶▶ (*Open daily. Admission: inexpensive*), stands on the site of an ancient monastery. Such was its fame that the Emperor Qianlong replicated it as the Garden of Harmonious Interest in the Summer Palace in Beijing. Xihui Park was created in 1958 by linking the Hui Mountain, with its nine dragon peaks and spring water, its temple and its Song-dynasty bridge, with Xi Mountain and its 16th-century Longguang Pagoda and Temple. There is another garden, the **Liyuan** (Wormy Garden), near the lakeside Hubin and Shuixu hotels. The **Meiyuan (Plum Garden)**▶, on the road to the Taihu Hotel, is particularly pretty in the early spring, when its thousands of plum trees are in blossom (*Open daily. Admission: inexpensive*).

Opposite the Taihu Hotel is **Yuantouzhu (Tortoise Head Promontory)**▶ (*Open daily 7.30–5. Admission: expensive*), a beauty spot dotted with tea-houses in a lakeside setting. From here, boat trips to Sanshan Island are sometimes possible. There are infrequent boat services across the lake and by canal to Yixing (Dingshu), Hangzhou, Changzhou, Suzhou and Xidongtingshan, where the ornamental rocks are prepared. In Wuxi town on the main streets of Renmin

Zhonglu, Jiefang Xilu and Zhongshan Lu, some older houses or restaurants (serving the delicious local dishes, whitebait or Wuxi spare ribs) still survive.

►► Yangzhou 167D2

Yangzhou, Jiangsu province, has a cultured past that has bequeathed many poets and painters, gardens, a local opera style and the still-live tradition of recitation of novels in the street.

The Xu Garden (Xuyuan)►►, on the west side of the Narrow West Lake, is noted for the beautiful carved woodwork inside the pavilions. Three other **traditional gardens (Xiyuan, Yechunyuan and Hongyuan)►►** cluster around the moat to the west of the Xiyuan Hotel.

The **Geyuan►►** (*Open* daily 7.15–5.45. *Admission: moderate*), on Dongguan Jie, was the 19th-century home of a salt merchant, one of several merchant houses in this area.

DESIGN DIFFERENCES
Yangzhou gardens tend to be smaller than those of Suzhou—sometimes indeed the residential area is larger than the garden area. The gardens, furthermore, seem to have absorbed a mixture of influences, ranging from southern architectural motifs like curved gable end walls to the more restrained northern style.

197

Eternal China: view through a moon gate, 'Five Pavilion Bridge', Yangzhou

Another attractive garden is the **Heyuan►►** (*Open* daily 7.30–6. *Admission: moderate*) on Xuningmen Jie, small but ingeniously contrived. The **Museum►** (*Open* Tue–Sun 9–5. *Admission: moderate*) is on Yanfu Xilu in a Qing temple. To the northwest are traces of the Tang city walls and the **Fajingsi Temple**. The **Slender West Lake (Shouxi Hu)►►** has the famous Five Pavilion Bridge (Wutingqiao). Another unusual point of interest is the **Tomb of Puhaddin** (a Yuan-dynasty Muslim preacher and descendant of Mohammed), which overlooks the Grand Canal.

The current **Daming Monastery (Monastery of Great Brightness)►** (*Open* daily 7.45–5. *Admission: moderate*) was built in 1934 on the foundations of a much older monastery. The original temple, established more than a 1,000 years ago, was founded by the Tang-dynasty monk Jianzhen, who spent many years in Japan as a missionary. The temple's Jianzhen Memorial Hall is based on the great hall of the Toshodai Temple in Nara, Japan.

YANGZHOU ECCENTRICS
Europeans associate Yangzhou with Marco Polo, who is supposed to have been governor here, but for the Chinese it brings to mind the 'eccentrics of Yangzhou', a group of painters who incurred imperial disapproval. Also known as the Eight Eccentrics, they specialized in simple, dramatic works and one, Gao Qipei (1672–1734), is especially remembered for painting with his finger and fingernail.

▶ **Zhenjiang** *167D2*

Zhenjiang's prosperity was founded on silk and the Grand Canal. Industrial now, in the 19th century it was a treaty port, and the **museum**▶ (*Open* daily 9–4.30. *Admission: inexpensive*) is housed in the former British Consulate in an area which leads down to the river. Jinshan is dominated by the **Jinshan Temple**▶▶ (*Open* daily 6–6. *Admission: moderate*), with its stunning, renovated Main Hall of Golden Buddhas and the **Cishou Pagoda**▶. **Jiaoshan**▶ is bamboo-forested and home to the **Dinghui Temple** and remains of the gun batteries. On **Beigushan**▶ are the 11th-century **Iron Pagoda** (**Tieta**), the **Sweet Dew Temple** (**Ganlusi**) and the **Soaring Clouds Pavilion** (**Lingyunting**).

Hall of the Golden Buddhas at the Jinshan Temple, Zhenjiang, one of the oldest temples in this region

198

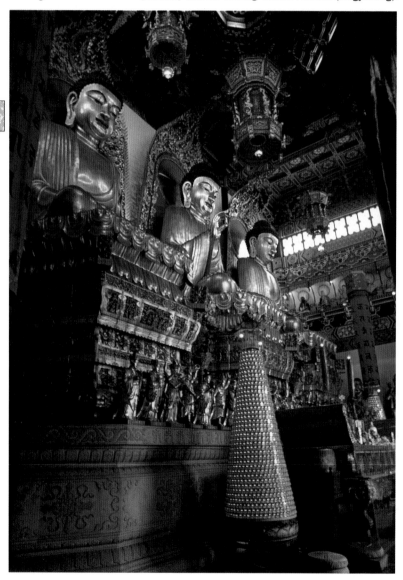

Chinese gardens are works of art that mirror the Taoist principle of harmony with nature. Imperial parks aside, wealth could not buy the large country estates that it did in Europe, so the Chinese garden was a city retreat for the cultivated scholar-official whose yearnings for rural peace and quiet were sublimated in the gentle art of gardenscaping.

Balance The most famous Chinese gardens are the miniature gardens of southern China, where ponds become lakes, rockeries mountains, and where bridges and pavilions provide the human element. But not all gardens need be small—to the Chinese, the Summer Palace in Beijing is a garden where the pond really is a lake, the pavilions are palaces and the rockeries are dwarfed by hills. It is the natural world in microcosm, an expression of both the wealth and majesty of the emperor and the variety of the world at large.

Top: Taihu rock in the Forbidden City

Below: The zigzag pathway in the Master of the Fishing Nets Garden, Suzhou, illustrates the concept of never revealing the whole garden at once

199

Harmony In a Chinese garden all the emotions experienced in the natural landscape should be aroused. Lofty mountains are evoked by rocks and stones piled up together; ponds reflect clouds and shadows, mirroring the sky; sunlight gives way to shade; and paths lead from high to low. The garden expresses the physical Taoist precepts of balance and harmony and the coexistence of the natural and the artificial.

Bamboo, pine and plum-blossom, pots of flowers, scented shrubs and intricately cut gateways giving tantalizing glimpses of what is to come complete the tranquil scene. The cultivation of the garden was an accomplishment for the cultured scholar-official equal to painting and poetry-writing. It was a place for recreation, contemplation and philosophizing, to be enjoyed in all weathers.

NATURE AND NURTURE Although the Chinese garden intends to imitate, if miniaturize, nature, the human touch is considered an integral part of a garden landscape. Calligraphy is frequently inscribed on rocks or over doorways, and the fanciful names that are given to pavilions are usually taken from literary sources and supposed to enhance enjoyment of the garden.

South China

SICHUAN

Daxian
Wanxian
Yunyang Fengjie Wushan
Badong
Yichang
Enshi
Qianjiang
Dayong
Daozhen

Chang Jiang (Yangtze)

HUBEI

Han Shui
Suizhou
Antu
Jingmen Tianmen
Jingling
Shashi
Jinshi
Shishou
Datong Hu
Hong Hu
Xiantao
WUHAN
Ezhou
Puqi

Changde

Dongting Hu

Yueyang

Machang
Tongcheng
Luan

Dabie Shan

Taihu

Huangshi
Wuxue
Guling Jiujiang
Lushan Hukou
Poyang Hu
Boyang

Muru Shan

Nanchang

Jiuling Shan

Gan Jiang

Wuling Shan
Yuan Jiang

Jishou

2942m

Tongren
Huaihua

HUNAN

Yiyang

Changsha
Shaoshan
Xiangtan
Zhuzhou
Loudi
Liling

Yichun
Linchuan
Nancheng

JIANGXI

Lengshuijiang
Shaoyang

Hengyang
Xiang Jiang

Pingxiang
Ji'an

Guangchang

GUIZHOU

Zhenyuan
Hongjiang
Jingxian

Dong'an
Leiyang
Yongzhou

Suichuan

Wuyi

Duyun Kaili
Miao Ling
Rongjiang
Dushan

Xiang Jiang
Chenzhou
Ganzhou
Ruijin

2142m

Quanzhou
Daoxian

Dayu

Hechi

Rongshui

2081m

Guilin
Yangshuo
Pingle
Jianghua
Lianxian
Lechang
Shaoguan
Longnan
Meizhou

Liuzhou

Li Jiang

Nan Ling

Lianping

**GUANGXI
ZHUANGZU ZIZHIQU**
Heshan
Pingnan
Wuzhou

Huaji
Qingyuan
Conghua

Bei Jiang

GUANGDONG

Heyuan
Lianhua
Lufeng

Binyang
Guigang
Rongxian
Zhaoqing
**GUANGZHOU
(CANTON)**
Huizhou

Nanning
Yulin
Luoding
Jiangmen
Foshan
Zhongshan
Macau
Shenzhen

Xi Jiang

Qinzhou
Kaiping
Yangjiang
HONG KONG

Yunkai Dashan
Yunwu Shan

Beihai
Maoming

VN

Leizhou
Zhanjiang
Haikang
Bandao

Beibu Wan

Xuwen

Qiongzhou Haixia

Nan Hai

Haikou
Wenchang

HAINAN Hainan Dao

Changjiang
Qiongzhong
Xinglong
1867m
Wuzhi Shan
Dongfang
Tongshi
Sanya Xincun
Luhuitou

A B C

200

▶▶▶ REGION HIGHLIGHTS

BIG WIND

Typhoons (from the Chinese 'da feng', or 'big wind') strike China more frequently than any other country, at a rate of about seven a year. By Chinese standards, a gale of force 8 to 11 is regarded as a typhoon. Generally speaking, they arrive between July and September and can, though rarely, penetrate as far as 400km (250 miles) inland and last several days. On the whole, however, they fizzle out after a few hours.

A traditional sampan, an increasingly rare sight in modern China

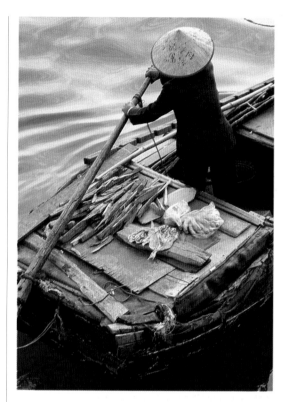

CRUDE CONFLICT

One area not mentioned in this section are the Spratly Islands. This group of islands in the South China Sea are claimed by China, Brunei, Malaysia, the Philippines and Vietnam, but would be of little importance were it not for their possible oil reserves. Though the existence of oil is unproven, the lure of its potential wealth is enough to make all the countries concerned unusually protective. In November 1998, the Philippines warned off a pair of Chinese naval ships from the area, accusing China of creeping colonialism.

SOUTH CHINA Broadly speaking, south China is the area south of the Yangtze, excluding southwest China, as well as a number of towns and cities already included in the Yangtze region, for demographic, historical or geopolitical reasons. What is left is a relatively homogeneous area quite different from the north. The provinces included are Hunan, Guangdong, Hainan Island, Fujian, parts of Jiangxi and Zhejiang, as well as Hong Kong and Macau.

Two thousand years ago, the south was populated by indigenous tribes that were only incorporated into a larger China when the first Qin emperor unified the country in 221BC. Even then, the area remained marginal: Chinese settlements were sparse and uprisings frequent. It was only in the 12th century, as the threat from northern tribes became more urgent, that the Chinese headed south in greater numbers, slaughtering the native tribes or driving them into mountain strongholds, or forcing them still farther south on to Hainan Island or into Indo-China. The merchant classes, formerly despised, began to prosper in the bountiful south, and the entrepreneurial spirit, often associated with the Chinese, became very much a southern characteristic. By the early 13th century, with the Southern Song capital at Hangzhou, the focus of Chinese life shifted south, albeit temporarily since under the Mongols the north was preferred once again, and the Ming dynasty that followed established its capital at Beijing. The south, therefore, although quite obviously part of China, has maintained a separateness that is still evident today.

The major visual differences between south and north are hues and topography. The north is brown and yellow (the tints of earth, sand, dust and silt), the landscape is generally flat, and any hills or mountains are dry and arid. The south is green, with a wet, steamy climate. Its rolling hills are layered with terraces. Like the north, the south has hot summers, with July averages between 25°C (77°F) and 30°C (85°F). Winters are mild, with frost a rarity in many areas and in some parts unknown. Rainfall is between 100cm (40in) and 250cm (100in) per year, and although summer is the wettest season, rain is spread more evenly throughout the year than in the north. Along the coast the summer is also the season of typhoons. The south's most important crop is rice, except in the mountainous province of Fujian where fishing and forestry traditionally take priority. As in the north, the pig is the main meat source and fish are also widely eaten; the water buffalo, not seen in the north, is used as a draft animal everywhere. Architecture differs, too—courtyards are less popular and houses with two floors are more common, often with the upturned eaves and roof decoration that typify traditional Chinese architecture.

Most important are the cultural dissimilarities between north and south. Although the dialects of the more northerly parts of the region are based on Mandarin, and although Chinese characters are universal, the dialects of the south are compounded of many distinctive words, a plethora of tones and implosive consonants. Finally, unlike the insular north, the indented coastlines of Fujian and Guangdong, with their excellent natural ports, have a tradition of foreign trade that dates back to the arrival of Arab merchants during the Tang dynasty.

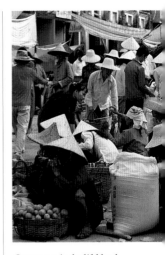

Commerce is the lifeblood of the south

Sanya Harbour, Hainan Island: China's 'Water People' have lived on boats for generations

YOUNG MAO
It is difficult to reconcile the Mao of later years with the young man in Shaoshan who threatened to commit suicide when faced with an arranged marriage, or the student who failed his art examination by drawing a circle and calling it an egg. However, while a student in Changsha in 1917, he became 'student of the year', simultaneously organizing student societies, an experience that would stand him in good stead in later life.

Fuzhou is one of the foremost cities for attracting Taiwanese investment in China

▶▶ Canton

See Guangzhou, pages 206–209.

▶ Changsha
200B4

The capital of Hunan province, Changsha is of interest for its provincial museum and its relative proximity to Mao's birthplace at Shaoshan (see page 224). The **museum**▶▶ (*Open* daily Apr–Sep 8–6, Oct–Mar 8.30–5.30. *Admission: inexpensive*) has a fine collection of neolithic pottery and bronzes from the Shang and Zhou dynasties. But its most famous attraction is the mummified body of the wife of the Marquis of Dai, prime minister to the king of Changsha in 193BC. The body was remarkably well-preserved when unearthed, its skin still supple. There are several links with Mao, including the **Hunan No. 1 Teacher Training College** (*Open* daily 8.15–5.30. *Admission: inexpensive*).

▶ Foshan
200B2

Foshan, famous for its Shiwan ceramic ware since the Han dynasty, is 25km (16 miles) from Canton (Guangzhou). The **ceramic factory** may be visited by appointment. In the south of the town is the **Zumiao (Ancestral Temple)**▶▶ (*Open* daily 8.30–6.30. *Admission: inexpensive*), founded in the Northern Song dynasty, a Taoist temple devoted to the worship of the demon-slaying Emperor of the North, with complex wooden carving and ceramic roof decoration.

▶ Fuzhou
201D4

Fuzhou's importance as a trading port goes back to the Tang dynasty, although its heyday was from the 10th

OLD HABITS
Lin Zexu's efforts to deal with the opium trade in the 1830s by confiscating smokers' equipment, forcing addicts to enlist for cures and severely punishing dealers, have present-day parallels. Liberalization of the economy has resulted in increased drug trafficking, and a government crackdown on those involved. Dealers are shot, and suspected addicts are sent on compulsory three-month rehabilitation courses.

A lantern maker in Fuzhou. Although much of old China has disappeared, the traditional skills are still alive and well

century onwards. Its cosmopolitan nature attracted foreign settlers, and it became known as a focus for Nestorian Christianity. Under the Treaty of Nanjing in 1842, it was one of the first cities opened to Western residents. Marco Polo described Fuzhou as 'a veritable marvel', and reminders of its trading past still remain here and there.

Fuzhou sits astride the scenic Min River. Its heart is the streets of Wuyi Lu, Gutian Lu and Dong Dalu.

The **Fujian Provincial Museum**▶▶ is in Xihu Park, site of an artificial lake dug in AD282 for irrigation purposes. The museum includes ceramic figures from a tomb dating to the 10th century, a full-size boat-coffin 3,500 years old, a collection of Nestorian crosses and examples of the locally produced Song-dynasty black ceramics.

The most noteworthy of Fuzhou's temples is the **White Pagoda**▶ on Yushan, first constructed in AD904, although its brick exterior dates from 1548. Nearby is the **Dashi Hall**, once a shrine where city officials prayed for good fortune and now the **city museum**▶▶. The main exhibit is a Song-dynasty tomb, with its male and female occupants on view in a tank of formaldehyde.

West of Dashi Hall is the **Black Pagoda**, a little way off Bayiqi Beilu. Built in AD799, it bears some fine carvings.

Other sights include the **Lin Zexu Memorial Hall**, on Xiamen Lu, devoted to the memory of a minister who protested, vainly, to Queen Victoria about the opium trade. The former **Foreign Concession area**▶▶ is on the south bank, in the Nantai area across the ancient stone bridge. Halfway up Gushan, a mountain some 8km (5 miles) from Fuzhou, **Yongquan Temple**▶ has two ceramic pagodas.

Map labels:

Guangzhou Railway Station
Baiyun Airport
Long Distance Bus Station
HUANSHI
RENMIN BEI RD
Tomb of Mohammed's Uncle
JIEFANG BEI RD
Orchid Garden
Yuexiu Park
HUANSHI XI ROAD
LIUHUA ROAD
Tomb of the King of Southern Yue
Zhenhai Tower
Statue of the Five Goats
DONGFENG XI ROAD
Liuhua Park
Sun Yatsen Monument
HIGHWAY
Sun Yatsen Memorial Hall
DONGFENG ZHONG ROAD
Glorious Filial Piety Temple
JIEFANG ZHONG ROAD
NANAN
LIWAN ROAD
Chen Family Temple
Renmin Park
Six Banyan Tree Temple
PEARL RIVER BRIDGE
ZHONGSHAN BA RD
ZHONGSHAN QI RD
ZHONGSHAN LIU RD
ZHONGSHAN
Liwan Lake Park
QINGJIN XI ROAD
LONGJIN DONG RD
ZHONG RD
Huaisheng Mosque
JIEFANG NAN ROAD
GUANGZHOU RD
HUAGU ROAD
RENMIN ZHONG RD
Five Celestial Shrine
HUIFU
CHANGSHOU ROAD
DADE ROAD
HUANGSHA ROAD
DUOBAO RD
SHANGJIU RD
LINKAN RD
ENNING RD
BAOHUA RD
XIAJIU RD
RENMIN NAN RD
Roman Catholic Cathedral
HAIZHU BRIDGE
DATONG RD
YIDE ROAD
Qingping Market
YANJIANG ROAD
Pearl
LIU'ERSAN ROAD
Cultural Park
BINJIANG XI ROAD
RENMIN BRIDGE
Shamian Island
White Swan Hotel
Haichuang Park
FANGCUN RD
TONGFU
A
B
C

CANTON OR GUANGZHOU
The origin of the name given to Guangzhou (the Mandarin Chinese name for the city) by foreigners from the 17th century is unclear. It may derive from the English meaning of 'cantonment' as a lodging assigned to troops. A more likely explanation is that it is a corruption of Guangdong, which is the name of the province, not the city.

►► Guangzhou (Canton)   200B2

Guangzhou, or Canton, the capital of Guangdong province, is a major city and port situated on China's fifth river, Zhu Jiang (the Pearl). It is also the city most used to dealing with Europeans, because they have been trading here for over 400 years. Colonized by the Qin in 221BC, Guangzhou came under Chinese control during the Tang dynasty and became a major port, attracting foreign traders from as far afield as the Middle East and Central Asia. The Portuguese were the first Europeans to trade here (from 1516), followed by the Dutch and the British.

Perversely, Guangzhou is a city that does not receive its fair share of appreciation from contemporary foreign visitors, since for many it is merely a transit stop. As a Special Economic Zone aided by foreign and Chinese investment, it is vibrant and lively. Famous for its

SOUTHERN APPETITE
Although Cantonese cooking is admired throughout China, many northern Chinese are contemptuous of the Cantonese people, perhaps a legacy of the Confucianist disdain for trade. The attitude is neatly summed up by a Chinese saying: 'The Cantonese will eat anything that flies except an aeroplane and anything with four legs except a table.'

Snake, it is said, warms you in winter. Try some at Jianglan Lu Snake Restaurant, in Guangzhou

cooking, its restaurants and shops spill out on to its old colonnaded streets, shaded beneath banyan trees with their distinctive hanging, stringy roots. Furthermore, there are several points of interest.

Canton's heart is the area along the riverfront (Yanjiang Road) and the main shopping streets behind—Jiefang, Zhongshan and Beijing. Also on the waterfront, behind the unmistakable White Swan Hotel, is the former foreign enclave of **Shamian Island**▶▶. Before its acquisition by the British as a concession area following the Second Opium War, foreign traders were restricted to the city shoreline, their families compelled to live in Macau. Shamian, which was shared by the French and the British, remains a small village, with European buildings in grandiose colonial style that are gradually being restored, and which once housed the French and British consulates,

Colonial architecture on Guangzhou's Shamian Island

FAIR CANTON
Although present-day China is comparatively open, from the early 1960s, and particularly during the Cultural Revolution when China's borders were effectively sealed, the Canton Trade Fair was the only conduit available to Western traders, journ-alists and intelligence agencies through which to glean an idea of what was going on in the country.

CHINESE HOROSCOPE
The horoscope is repre-sented by 12 animals, with one animal governing each year in a 12-year cycle. Each animal represents one of the Twelve Earthly Branches in Chinese astrology. Traditionally the Chinese remember their ages by the animal sign to which the person belongs and calculate their date of birth from there. The 12 animals are: rat, ox, tiger, rabbit, dragon, snake, horse, sheep, monkey, rooster, dog, pig. In 2005 it was the year of the rooster, 2006 the year of the monkey and 2007 the year of the pig.

banks, and Protestant and Catholic churches. Walk across the island directly from the White Swan, cross the bridge to Liu'ersan Road, turn right, and you will see on your left the narrow entrance to **Qingping Market**▶▶▶, one of the most fascinating in China. It sells everything imaginable in the way of foodstuffs, spices and animal parts. Considering the Cantonese reputation as omnivores, this market is not for the squeamish, but it is the purest Guangzhou, quintessential southern China.

The **Pearl River**▶▶ is the city's pulse. To enjoy a simple and brief encounter with it, take a ferry to the other shore, or take a cruise on one of the pleasure boats that regularly leave from near the Renmin Bridge. You can also take an evening dinner cruise, passing illuminated bridges and key buildings.

Sun Yatsen, born in Zhongshan county, was a Cantonese, and his **Memorial Hall**▶ on Dongfeng Road is in the form of an octagonal playhouse, built in a garden that was the site of the residence of the Qing governors of Guangdong and Guangxi.

Parks and gardens are one of the charms of Guangzhou. If you are here in February, before the humid season, visit the **Orchid Garden (Lanpu)**▶▶ (built on the site of the Muslim burial ground) when the orchids are in flower. A haven of peace with its bamboo groves, pools and pavil-ions, it can be enjoyed at any time. Just behind the garden is the tomb of Muhammad's uncle (Abu Waqqas), who is supposed to have founded the Huaisheng Mosque on Guangta Road, said to be the oldest mosque in China.

To see something of the south bank, go to **Haichuang Park**▶, with its remains of the Ocean Banner Monastery. Guangzhou's largest park is the Yuexiu, which includes the **Zhenhai Tower**▶, built in 1380, the only part of the city wall to remain and now housing the city museum. Nearby to the south is the **Sun Yatsen Monument**, with his bequest to the nation engraved on its side, and to the west the **Statue of the Five Goats**, the city's symbol. The **Cultural Park (Wenhua Gongyuan)**▶, on Liu'ersan Lu, was con-structed in 1956 with mass entertainment in mind. Here you can watch rollerskating, carousels, open-air theatre and opera. Another attractive park with revolutionary connotations is the **Memorial Garden to the Martyrs (Lieshi Lingyuan)▶** on Zhongshan Lu, commemorating a massacre of communists by the Guomindang in 1927.

Guangzhou also has its fair share of temples. The most interesting exemplifying local architectural styles is the **Chen Family Temple (Chenjiaci)▶▶**, which now houses an exhibition of the best of local craftwork. Built in 1890–94 with monies collected among the Chen clan, it has a long front hall behind which extend several other halls, separated by courtyards. The façade and roof of the entrance hall are crowded with figures of deities and with vibrant and fanciful interpretations of operatic tales. The **Six Banyan Tree Temple (Liurongsi)▶▶** (*Open* daily 8–5. *Admission: inexpensive*) is a working temple on Liurong Road and was founded as a home for the Buddha's ashes in AD537. Its name was conferred on it by the Song-dynasty poet Su Dongpo, who was enchanted by the banyan trees (no longer there) in the courtyard. There are panoramic views from the pagoda, the tallest in the city, parts of which date to the 11th century, while in the Hall of the Sixth Patriarch (of the Chan Buddhist sect) is an AD989 bronze figure of the patriarch. **Glorious Filial Piety Temple (Guangxiaosi)▶**, on Guangxiao Road, was founded in the fourth century, though most of the buildings date from 1832. It has a fine main hall and a pair of ancient pagodas, one reputed to be built over a hair of the Sixth Patriarch.

The **Roman Catholic Cathedral (Shishi Jiaotang, or 'stone church')▶**, on Yide Road, is a reminder of the 19th-century European presence in Canton. Begun in 1860 by a French architect, it is built of granite on the site of the office of the Chinese governor of Guangdong, which had been destroyed by the French and British during the Opium War. Its four bronze bells were cast in France.

One of Canton's highlights is the **Tomb of the King of Southern Yue (Nanyuewang Hanwu)▶▶▶** (*Open* daily 9–5.30. *Admission: inexpensive*). Before unification under the first Qin Emperor in 221BC, southern China was a loose confederation of the 'Hundred Yue' nationalities known as Lingnan. After the fall of the Qin empire, a breakaway general established the independent kingdom of Yue with its capital in Canton. It lasted until 111BC, spawning five kings before the Han re-established dynastic control over southern China. This is the tomb of the second king, Chao Mei. The chief attractions are the seven-chamber tomb's burial goods, including swords, jade ornaments, *pi* discs, gold seals, musical instruments, cooking utensils, bronze mirrors and silver boxes.

Guangzhou's Qingping market—freshness is everything

209

GOAT CITY
The symbol of Guangzhou, a herd of five goats, is based on the myth of the city's foundation, a myth that itself aptly reflects the fertility of the surrounding countryside. The legend relates that five celestial beings arrived in the area riding five goats. The goats were bearing bundles of rice, symbols of a promise that the region would never suffer famine.

Guangzhou's founders, in Yuexiu Park

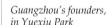

▶▶ Hainan Island

A large tropical island off the south coast, Hainan has several minority tribes, beautiful scenery and reasonably good beaches, but it has traditionally been regarded by the Chinese as a pit of disease and poverty. Since 1978, Hainan has been an important military hub, but nowadays its main industry is tourism.

Hainan was made a province in 1988. The rather run-down capital, **Haikou▶**, has a bustling atmosphere that compensates for its lack of cultural attractions. The liveliest street is Jiefang Lu, criss-crossed by alleys and lanes. Xinhua Nanlu is lined with buildings in Portuguese colonial style. Outside the town is the **Tomb of Hai Rui▶**, a Qing official, or the **Five Officials Memorial Temple** (*Open daily 8–6. Admission: inexpensive*), while the best beach is Shuiying. Also noted for its beaches (and coconut groves) is **Wenchang**, about 72km (45 miles) from Haikou.

However, the finest beaches are on the south coast, where the main town is **Sanya▶▶**. East of Sanya is the resort of Luhuitou, and nearby is the lovely but crowded **Dadonghai Beach**, and **Yalong Wan** (**Asian Dragon Bay**).

There are good bus services along Hainan's two principal roads: around the east coast and across the mountainous central area via Tongshi, the capital of the Li and Miao autonomous prefecture. The hill villages here are home to the Li and Miao minority peoples, who still follow a traditional way of life, although this is increasingly under threat. Farther north is **Qiongzhong▶▶**, with a lively market and nearby 300m (984ft) waterfall.

Xincun, on the southeast coast, populated by Danjia people, is the focus of the pearl industry and departure point for **Monkey Island▶** (*Open daily 8–6. Admission: expensive*), a reserve for Guangxi monkeys. **Xinglong** is famous for its fruit, hot springs and especially its coffee.

THE EDGE OF THE WORLD
Just as Jiayuguan was 'The Last Barrier under Heaven' and Shanhaiguan the 'First Pass under Heaven', so Sanya was known as 'Heaven's Limit'. Mountains in the middle of Hainan Island rise to 1,800m (5,900ft), and the subtropical climate allows coconuts, palm oil, rubber and pepper to be produced.

A beach on China's tropical island, Hainan

▶▶▶ Hong Kong   *200C2*

A few years ago the contrast between Hong Kong and the rest of the People's Republic of China was remarkable. The differences are now no longer so marked, largely because parts of mainland China are becoming more like Hong Kong in the wake of the 1997 hand-over of sovereignty (see pages 214–215).

There is almost nothing old in Hong Kong. Its pull is its frantic, relentless modernity. Its nature is perfectly illustrated by the fate of the charming old colonial-style Repulse Bay Hotel, with an upstairs veranda open to the sea: it was demolished only to be replaced by an exact replica a couple of years later.

Hong Kong is a powerful magnet that continues to exert a fascination. Now linked to the mainland by a modern metro system (MTR), it is still worth taking the venerable **Star Ferry▶▶▶** to or from Kowloon at least once to take in the magnificent skyline of gleaming skyscrapers.

The name Hong Kong ('Fragrant Harbour') originally referred only to the main island, but now also covers Kowloon, the New Territories and the 260-plus Outlying Islands. Standard tours include the main sights: **Aberdeen▶▶**, a port area crowded with junks and sampans; **Stanley▶▶**, with its market specializing in factory outlet clothes; the less well-known **Tin Hau Temple** on Stanley Main Street, the island's oldest, founded in 1770 by pirate Chang Po Chai; and **Victoria Peak▶▶▶**, the island's highest point, which has spectacular views on a clear day and can be reached either by road or by the old funicular railway, the lower station of which is served by minibus from the Star Ferry.

The firing of the midday gun, an event immortalized in Noel Coward's song *Mad Dogs and Englishmen*, can still be

Hong Kong is home to more than 7 million people

ECCENTRIC VIEW
In 1847, Robert Fortune wrote a book entitled *Three Years Wandering in the Northern Provinces of China*. His journey enabled him to form an opinion of Hong Kong. In light of its subsequent history, his verdict is ironic: 'Viewed as a place of trade, I fear Hong Kong will be a failure.'

SUZIE WONG
Hong Kong is invariably associated with Suzie Wong, the entrancing prostitute made famous in Richard Mason's book, *The World of Suzie Wong*. Her world no longer really exists, for many of the bars of Wanchai have closed and those that remain deal mostly in overpriced drinks.

South China

212 *The Bank of China building, Hong Kong. Devotees of modern architecture will find much to interest them in Hong Kong, where a building is old almost as soon as it is built*

witnessed in front of the Excelsior Hotel in Causeway Bay, one of the main shopping areas. Going west by streetcar along the island's north coast takes you through **Wanchai**, the shabby bar and disco district, to **Central**, the main area of multinational companies and designer shops. Tucked among the skyscrapers are small, intimate streets filled with markets and local shops, such as those off Des Voeux Road and Li Yuen, Wing On and Wing Sing streets. The **Man Mo Taoist Temple**▶▶, on Hollywood Road, is one of the oldest in Hong Kong.

Among the museums are **Flagstaff House Museum**▶▶▶ (*Open* Wed–Mon 10–5. *Admission: free*) on Cotton Tree Drive. Housed in a distinctive 160-year-old building, it has a fascinating collection of tea paraphernalia, while the **Fung Ping Shan**▶▶ at the university has fine Chinese art, ceramics and bronzes. The **Botanical Gardens**▶ are a haven of quiet, and nearby is **Government House**, the former residence of Hong Kong governors. On the south side of Hong Kong Island is educational theme park **Ocean Park** (*Open* daily 10–6. *Admission: expensive*), with thrill rides, cable-car, giant pandas and an excellent aquarium.

The **Tsimshatsui area**▶▶ of Kowloon, served by the Star Ferry, is a mecca for those wanting jewels and electronics. **Ocean Terminal** has many shops, but prices are not usually negotiable. If you want to bargain, head to the shops along and off Nathan Road. One of Kowloon's most famous landmarks is the Peninsula Hotel, hidden from the water by more recent constructions but still expensively elegant.

THE STORY OF CHINA TEA
Tea is thought to have been first used in the Chinese southwest. It was known during the Han dynasty, but became popular only during the Tang dynasty, when the creation of the perfect pot of tea became almost an art form. Rituals developed and tea drinking became a cere-mony in itself. While the ceremonial aspect has all but disappeared today, tea-houses remain full. Drivers keep their tin mugs or glass jars on the dashboard all day, half-filled with leaves. Brewed in the cup like this, the second infusion is considered the best, but the leaves can be used again and again.

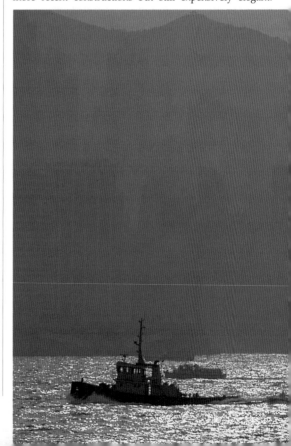

Opposite is the **Hong Kong Cultural Centre**, which contains a Museum of Art and the Space Museum.

North of Tsimshatsui is **Yaumatei** with the dubious jade market on Kansu Street and Temple Street night market. The **Lan Cheung Uk Museum▶** is a Han tomb found in 1954. Farther north are the New Territories bordering China, an area of paddy fields, hills and little walled villages that originally belonged to single clans. Ram Tin is the best place to see these. This rural area is a haven for wildlife, which you can experience at the new **Hong Kong Wetland Park▶▶** (*Open* daily. *Admission: moderate*), a 60ha (150-acre) wetland oasis with over 150 species of birds and 250 other wetland species.

Ferries from Central head to many of the Outlying Islands, where life is generally much quieter. At twice the size of Hong Kong Island, **Lantau▶**, is the largest island and site of the new airport. It is also the home of **Hong Kong Disneyland▶▶** (*Open* daily 10–8. *Admission: expensive*), with four 'lands' and two themed hotels. Another new attraction is **Ngong Ping 360▶▶** (*Open* daily. *Admission: expensive*), which has a cable-car ride into the mountains to a culturally themed village. Nearby are **Po Lin Monastery** and the **Giant Buddha**, the world's tallest outdoor seated bronze Buddha. Lantau has two small towns and an excellent beach at Cheung Sha. Lantau Peak rises to almost 1,000m (3,200ft) and there are scenic walks.

The islands of **Cheung Chau▶▶** and **Lamma▶▶** have pleasant beaches and paths and good seafood restaurants.

STROLL
Although most of old Hong Kong has been destroyed, there are a couple of areas that provide relief from the chromium-plated present—along and around Hollywood Road, for example, or Caine Road and Robinson Road, or the streets off Queens Road East. Another interesting place is the Yaumatei Typhoon Shelter in the New Territories, home to many Tanka and Hokla boat people.

213

Skyscrapers notwithstanding, Hong Kong still exudes a certain exoticism

Since the 1970s, when the issue of Hong Kong's sovereignty arose as China re-emerged from the Cultural Revolution, its future, and by extension the future of Macau and Taiwan, has been of prime concern.

UNREST IN HONG KONG
Considering the controversy engendered by the expiry of Britain's lease in 1997, there has been remarkably little civil unrest in Hong Kong. In 1956, there were riots when communist supporters confronted the Guomindang. In 1966, the year the Cultural Revolution began, mobs rioted in protest at a small increase in the first-class fare of the Star Ferry; and in 1967, a series of disputes among the workforce culminated in a siege of the governor's residence by workers wielding Mao's *Little Red Book*.

Top: Shenzhen, just across the border
Below: Government House, symbolically dwarfed by change

Democracy Hong Kong, which was Britain's last significant colony, remains one of the world's foremost bastions of capitalism. As a European colony on Chinese soil until 1997, Hong Kong was an historical anomaly. It was ceded to the British 'in perpetuity' under the Treaty of Nanjing in 1842; in 1860, Britain acquired the Kowloon peninsula and then, in 1898, the New Territories on a 99-year lease. In 1984, Britain agreed to transfer full sovereignty of the islands and New Territories to China in 1997, subject to Chinese assurances that Hong Kong's economic freedom and capitalist lifestyle would be preserved for at least 50 years—the 'two systems, one China' agreement. Under this agreement, Hong Kong would become a special administrative region within China, with its own laws, budget and tax system, and would retain its free-port status and authority to negotiate international trade agreements. The West feared, however, that once the lease expired, the 6 million citizens of Hong Kong would be unable to withstand undemocratic decisions from Beijing deleterious to Hong Kong's financial standing.

Negotiations between China and Britain were long and difficult. Proper representative democracy had never been accorded to the average Hong Kong citizen, although Britain introduced indirect elections to select a proportion of the new legislative council in 1984, and direct elections

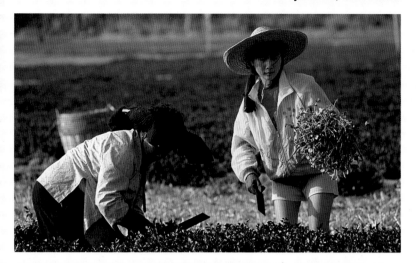

for seats on local councils in 1985. The last British governor, Chris Patten, courted controversy with his attempts to increase democratic representation. Opposition from Beijing culminated in the dissolution of the Legislative Council immediately prior to the hand-over, followed, on 1 July 1997—the first day of Chinese rule—by the establishment of a new legislative council composed of Hong Kong representatives appointed from Beijing.

In the months leading up to the hand-over, the heightened sense of expectation brought a flood of anti-British propaganda from the Chinese government, and much agonizing on the part of the British. On 30 June, the date of the ceremonial hand-over, it rained unrelentingly. The atmosphere was an odd mixture of elation, apprehension and fatalism. Finally, Chris Patten's departure, accompanied by the lowering of the Union Jack, was a dignified and low-key affair. Then, following a fireworks display in the rain, Hong Kong returned to work.

The future Chinese has replaced English as the official language and the Union Jack has been replaced with a red flag emblazoned with a white Bauhinia flower and five red stars, but on the whole not much else has altered, so far. A glimpse into southern China, in particular, where Special Economic Zones such as Shenzhen are almost indistinguishable from Hong Kong, proves that the contradiction between communism and capitalism can be, to some extent, reconciled.

Taiwan and Macau Contact used to be rare, but there are now direct air and sea links between China and Taiwan, and they will inevitably draw closer in many other ways, although Taiwan's free elections in 2000 and 2004 elicited angry threats from Beijing. In 2005, China even declared its right to use non-peaceful means in any secession attempt by Taiwan. Under the 'Macau Pact' of 1987, Portugal agreed to hand over sovereignty of Macau to the People's Republic on 20 December 1999 under similar terms to the 'two systems, one China' agreement. This duly happened and so far there is little sign of change.

Cultivation on an outlying island, where space is still plentiful

215

POISONED BREAD
In 1857, Cheong Ah Lum, the baker who provided bread to the British, thought he could wipe out the British by putting arsenic in the loaves. The attempt failed because his mixture was too strong and the victims vomited the bread up before digesting the poison.

Hong Kong's old trams provide low-cost transport

▶▶ Jingdezhen 201D5

This small town in Jiangxi has excellent local kaolin clay and has been famous since the Han dynasty for its porcelain. The imperial kilns were established here from the Ming dynasty and produced ceramics for the court and the blue-and-white ware exported to Asia and Europe from the 16th century. The town's prosperity is still based on porcelain—there are kilns everywhere and they may be visited by appointment. The **Ceramic Exhibition Hall (Taociguan)**▶ on Lianshe Beilu has a good display (*Open* daily 8–11.30, 2–5. *Admission: inexpensive*). Also interesting is the river area at the west end of Juishan Donglu, the middle of the town around Juishan Donglu, Zhonghua Beilu and Zhongshan Beilu, and the **Ceramic Research Institute**▶ (*Open* Mon–Fri 8–6. *Admission charge*) in a Ming house west of the river. Around the town are artificial hills created by the waste from ancient kilns.

▶▶ Lushan 200C5

Lushan, a beautiful 1,500m (4,920ft) peak in Jiangxi topped by the hill town of Guling, was much preferred by foreign residents during the 19th century, and later by Chiang Kaishek, Mao Zedong and Harry Truman as a refuge from the heat. There is little in particular to see, but plenty to enjoy if you walk around the town made up of European-style villas, and then out to Lulin and Ruqin lakes via the Three Ancient Trees, Dragon Head Cliff and Fairy Cave. At Lulin Lake is a museum commemorating the Politburo meeting here in 1970, when Lin Biao, later to die in mysterious circumstances, clashed with Mao.

Lushan, an 'oriental Switzerland' in the middle of China

▶▶ Macau

The oldest former enclave in Asia, Macau was first established as a missionary trading post in 1537 and was leased to Portugal in 1557. It reverted to China in 1999. About 65km (40 miles) from Hong Kong, Macau comprises the tip of a peninsula and the offshore islands of Taipa and Coloane (which has fine beaches). Most of the population is Chinese with a sprinkling of Portuguese and Macanese, an intermarried group with their own dialect. As Portuguese influence waned so did Macau's importance, but it still possesses considerable old-world charm. It is worth a day trip by jetfoil from Hong Kong to spend a few hours wandering its cobbled streets lined with a distinctive blend of European and Chinese architecture (for example the Largo do Senado and the Rua Central), sampling the excellent Sino-Portuguese restaurants or to bet in the casinos (a forbidden activity in Hong Kong until 1999). It is also possible to enter China from here.

Macau's most famous landmark is the baroque façade of **Sao Paolo**▶▶, built by Japanese Jesuits in 1635 to a design by C. Spinola. Fire destroyed the wooden church in 1835, but many of its fine polychrome wooden figures are now in the Sao Jose Church. Near by is the 17th-century **Monte Fortress**▶ (*Open* Tue–Sun 10–6. *Admission: inexpensive*).

The impressive Ming-dynasty **A-ma Temple**▶▶, near the peninsula's southern tip, is dedicated to A-ma, Goddess of the Sea, who has given her name to Macau. Her feast day is on the 23rd day of the third lunar month.

On Estrada Adolfo Loureiro is the 19th-century classical Lou Lim Yeoc garden, but perhaps more interesting are the **Camoes Gardens**▶, where the great 16th-century Portuguese poet Luis Vaz de Camoes came to relax, and the site of the Casa Villa, a lovely colonial building housing a **museum**▶▶, which has some fine Ming bronzes and Chinese furniture. Near by is the Protestant cemetery where the English painter George Chinnery is buried.

Every November the Macau Grand Prix takes place. **The Grand Prix Museum** (*Open* Wed–Mon 10–6. *Admission: inexpensive*) celebrates the event.

Cobbles add to the old-world ambience of a backstreet in Macau

Ornate Jingdezhen ware

BUILDING BRIDGES
In December 1999, the Lotus Flower Bridge, which connects China with the Macanese islands of Taipa and Coloane, was opened as part of the hand-over ceremonies. There is now a plan being mooted to build a massive bridge linking Macau with the Hong Kong island of Lantau.

Ceramics have a long history in China. During the neolithic period there were two principal types: a red earthenware, often decorated with black animal and geometric designs, from the Yangshao culture (as seen at Banpo in Xi'an), and black ware from the Longshan culture.

A TASTE FOR PORCELAIN
As foreign powers started to take an interest in China from the 16th century, so their desire increased for Chinese ceramics. It is recorded that at least 16 million Chinese porcelain dishes were exported by the Dutch East Indies Company between 1602 and 1682.

There is nothing more Chinese than porcelain or 'china'
Top and below: the celebrated Shiwan porcelain from Foshan

Discoveries During the Bronze Age, Chinese potters discovered that stoneware clays, when fired at high temperatures, fused to form a waterproof surface much tougher than that of earthenware. In the Han period, green lead glazes began to appear on earthenware ceramics used as funerary ornaments.

Decorative porcelain, a finer item than earthenware or stoneware, appeared at about the time of the Sui dynasty (AD581–618). The porcelain was made of a special feldspar clay, found with variations in many areas of China, and fired at a high temperature (the critical feature that distinguishes it from simple pottery) and simultaneously fused with a glaze. Always resonant, the porcelain is sometimes translucent. By the time of the Tang dynasty, porcelain was widely used and exported in enormous quantities, although its method of manufacture remained a mystery outside China until the 18th century. But it was during the Song dynasty that the production of porcelain achieved an artistic elegance that set a precedent not only for subsequent Chinese dynasties, but also for the eventual production of porcelain in Europe.

Specialization During the Song, kilns of different types, both coal-fired and wood-fired, sprang up all over the country and produced both stoneware and porcelain. As production increased, areas began to specialize according to their strengths. In the north, cream porcelain, often with moulded designs, predominated, although olive-green or greyish-toned glaze ware, known as celadon, was also produced; in the south, where the best clays were found, a 'bluish-white' ware was produced. Production overlapped to some extent, not least because Chinese political life was concentrated in the north until the 12th century, and although each kiln tended to specialize in one type of ware, there is evidence to suggest that they would have produced a quantity of the other types as well. Throughout the Song empire, however, all porcelain was distinctive for its simple elegance and monochrome glazes. The only exception was cream Cizhou ware from Hebei, which was decorated either with narrative painting or deep carving.

Technology During the Mongol (Yuan) dynasty the most important advance was the introduction of blue and white underglaze painting. This used cobalt, imported from the Near East, over a white undercoat of clay, a translucent glaze and firing at over 1,280°C (2,335°F).

During the Ming dynasty, considered by many the zenith of Chinese porcelain production, the use of underglaze blue and white painting achieved an unsurpassed elegance. There was also a revival of the three-hued glazes that were popular during the Tang and the beginnings of overglaze tinting. The latter allowed greater variation, since overglazes were added to the finished product and did not have to endure firing at a high temperature. The new technique led to a revival in monochromes at the beginning of the Qing, but using rich pastel hues. By the late 19th century, however, design had become heavy and ornate and, although porcelain is still produced in vast quantities today, the elegance of the great dynasties has yet to reassert itself.

Ceramics from the Ming dynasty, considered by many to have been the greatest period of Chinese porcelain production

EARLY EXPORTS

Porcelain began to be exported in earnest during the Tang dynasty. Chinese ceramics from this period have been discovered in places as far afield as Japan, Korea, Borneo and Egypt. Much was taken by camel along the Silk Road. A ninth-century governor of Khorasan in Persia (modern Iran), offered over 2,000 porcelain vessels as tribute to the Abbasid caliph, and hundreds of shards have been discovered near Cairo. In AD851, an Arab merchant noted: 'The Chinese make pottery clay vessels as translucent as glass. Wine poured into them can be seen from outside.'

Monochromatic porcelain jar of the 18th-century Qing period with animal-head handles

Although Ningbo is fast losing its ancient streets, the Tianyige library is one of the finest examples of extant Chinese architecture

220

AN OVERSEAS VIP
One of Ningbo's most illustrious sons was Sir Y. K. Pao, the shipping magnate who made his fortune in Hong Kong. Among the many companies he owned was the Star Ferry Company, which provides the service around Hong Kong. Like many Chinese-born entrepreneurs living overseas, he invested capital back in China and many of the port improvements at Ningbo are due to him. He died in 1991.

▶ **Nanchang**   *200C4*

The capital of Jiangxi is well known as the temporary home of the 16th-century Jesuit missionary Matteo Ricci and as the site of a communist uprising in 1927. About 10km (6 miles) from here is **Qingyun Pu**, the Taoist retreat of the innovative 17th-century painter Zhu Da (*Open* daily 8.15–5. *Admission: inexpensive*), a descendant of the imperial Ming family also known as Bada Shanren, whose paintings are displayed in the Shanghai Museum. The Buddhist **Youmin Temple**▶ has a bronze bell cast in AD967. Beside the river is the **Tengwang Pavilion** (*Open* daily 7.30–8 in summer; 8–5.30 in winter. *Admission: moderate*), built in 1989 on the site of the original Tang construction, where traditional dances are performed throughout the day.

▶ **Ningbo**   *201E5*

From the Song to the Ming dynasties Ningbo was one of China's most important ports, with a foreign trading presence from the 16th century. Under the Treaty of Nanjing, in 1842, it became a treaty port, but was later eclipsed by Shanghai. It is now a container port, but is famous for the 16th-century **Tianyige**▶▶, on Changchun Lu, the oldest surviving private library building in China. Fire has always been a threat (it is made of wood), as well as theft—in the past all the family members had to be present before the door could be opened. The library is tucked away among merchant houses dating back to the Ming and Qing dynasties, many of which are being torn down.

The area around the Xinjiang Bridge has an exhilarating port atmosphere. To its north is the old foreign concession, filled with crumbling Western-style houses. Ningbo's main thoroughfare is Zhongshan Lu; from there Kaiming Jie leads away to the Tang-dynasty **Tianfeng Pagoda**, currently under restoration. The **Drum Tower** is just north of Zhongshan Lu leading to Congyuan Lu and its old houses. Outside the town is **Baoguo Temple**▶, one of the oldest wooden temples in China dating back to AD1013. **Yuwang Temple**, 25km (16 miles) southeast, is noteworthy for its miniature stupa containing a relic of Buddha.

Off the coast is **Putuoshan**▶▶▶ (*Open* daily. *Admission: expensive*), one of the four sacred Buddhist mountains on a lovely island. A four-hour boat trip from Ningbo, the island is an active site for pilgrims and has lovely walks.

▶ **Qikou (Xikou)**   *201E5*

Qikou or Xikou, south of Ningbo, was the family home of Chiang Kaishek. Several items linked to Chiang's family have been restored and are open to the public.

▶▶ **Quanzhou**   *201D3*

A build-up of silt in the port has contributed to a decline in the economic importance of Quanzhou, once one of the foremost ports in the world, but it remains one of the most fascinating, if neglected places to visit in Fujian province, a town of narrow stone-paved lanes and good seafood. Quanzhou's early importance as a trading city led to the presence here of a large Muslim population, who called the city Zaiton, from which is derived the English word 'satin'. The **Qingjing Mosque**▶▶ on Tumen Jie is one of the oldest in China, dating from AD1009 and intriguing for its absence of Chinese influence.

Women of Xunbo village examine floral hair adornments in Quanzhou market

DELICIOUS DUMPLINGS
Ningbo is well known as the home of a delicious dish called *ningbo* or 'pigeon-egg dumplings'. Rather sweet, looking like small white marbles, they are stuffed with an osmanthous paste and are served in warm water. They are excellent in winter.

The **Kaiyuan Buddhist Temple** ▶ ▶ ▶ on Xi Lu dates back to the seventh century—its main hall, lined with 100 stone columns bearing delicately carved figures, is magnificent. A 13th-century 203,000kg (447,600lb) sailing vessel discovered in 1974 is housed in the grounds, home to the **Quanzhou Museum of Overseas Communication (Haiyun Bowuguan) History** ▶ ▶ (*Open* daily 8.30–5.30. *Admission: inexpensive*), which illustrates the religious diversity and cosmopolitan nature of Quanzhou during the Song dynasty. Tombstones and inscriptions relate to Islam, the Franciscans, Nestorian Christianity and Manichaeism.

Near Quanzhou is Chongwu, a town that retains its Ming-dynasty walls.

Awaiting the faithful, the main Hall of Kaiyuan Temple, Quanzhou

The Chinese restaurant is now a world-wide phenomenon, finding its way into even the smallest village. It is a convenient metaphor for the economic opportunities that have arisen for the Chinese since the expansion of the West into Asia, the Americas and Oceania during the 19th century.

NATIONALS' PRODUCT
Such is the strength of overseas Chinese ties with the homeland that between 1929 and 1941 remittances home averaged between £50 and £62 million ($75–93 million) per year, enough on occasion to offset China's balance of payments deficit.

222

Early traders From the 15th to the 18th century, Chinese colonies grew up in the trading hubs of Southeast Asia in the wake of the extraordinary voyages of the eunuch admiral, Zheng He, undertaken between 1405 and 1433. In the last years of the Ming, overseas trade was banned, and individual traders therefore found it expedient to settle overseas. This pattern continued under the Manchus, whose policy of evacuating coastal regions (to undermine Ming loyalists) forced coastal dwellers to seek a livelihood abroad. Eventually foreign trade restrictions were lifted, but attempts were made by the Qing rulers to control emigration. Emigrants were classed as criminals—an edict of 1712 declared that the Chinese government 'shall request foreign governments to have those Chinese who have been abroad repatriated so that they

CHINESE IN BRITAIN
Most Chinese people in Britain trace their origins back to Hong Kong's New Territories, where Cantonese is the local dialect. For 90 per cent of Chinese in Britain, Cantonese is likely to be the most common dialect in the community, although Hakka, Hokkien and *putonghua* may also be spoken. Since 1979 many Hoa (Chinese) people have settled in Britain from Vietnam, speaking Vietnamese as their first language, rather than any Chinese dialect.

Chinese immigrants have traditionally formed close communities
Right: Chinatown in San Francisco

Chinatown, London. All the ingredients for Chinese cooking are available here, including exotic tropical fruit

ORGANIZED CRIME

Most of the customs that immigrants brought with them from China have enriched the life of their adopted country. One that has not is the Chinese secret society, the Triad, founded originally by Hokkien immigrants to Taiwan. Very hierarchical, the Triad is structured in pyramid fashion, each level given a number or name. For example, the highest authority is Dragon Head or 489, while the lowest recruits are called 49 Boys. The origin of the numbers' symbolism is not certain, but they are accredited with mystical qualities.

may be executed'. This measure was taken partly out of fear of sedition, but it also stemmed from the traditional Confucian contempt for merchants.

Provenance The majority of immigrants came from the two southern maritime provinces of Guangdong and Fujian, which by 1500 had less cultivated land per head than anywhere in China. Once settled, the immigrant sent for a young son or relation to join him, for the family was to be the mainstay of Chinese exiles' success. This can be seen partly as traditional Confucian filial piety and strong identification with ancestors and the native village, but also as simple practicality. With the help of the family, longer opening hours and lower wages are possible, although this attitude was later to become a source of friction with other immigrants. Chinese communities abroad tended to clan together according to dialect or surname, but whoever they were, the desire eventually to return home a success was paramount, and almost the first thing that they did once abroad was to arrange for the return to China of their body in the event of death.

Nineteenth century Large-scale emigration only started in the late 19th century, when more than 2 million Chinese flooded into ports around the world. There were several reasons for this. One was a huge population explosion; another was the Taiping Rebellion that decimated the country; a third was the arrival of the Western powers who needed a reliable workforce to staff their overseas colonies. Most immigrants were unskilled. At first working in the Spanish, Dutch, British and French colonies in the Far East, they soon found their way to African mines and South American sugar plantations or guano fields and then to the goldfields and railways of the USA. Theirs was indentured work of the worst kind—meaningless contracts for years of badly paid, back-breaking work in appalling conditions. Respected companies organized the trade in workers, while Chinese agents in treaty ports press-ganged men. Many died overseas, some returned with pitiful savings, a very few made their fortunes. Thousands died on World War I battlefields. Ultimately, large numbers ended up creating sizeable communities in Britain, France and the USA.

In recent years there has been a new wave of emigration, while many Chinese students do not return home from overseas.

Overseas Chinese money built the Jinling Hotel, Nanjing

224

Old China, alive and well in the old treaty port area around Anping Lu, Shantou

Plenty of fish to fry along South China's coast

▶ Shantou 201D3

Known as Swatow to the Westerners who once traded here, this lively major port on Guangdong province's east coast, is now a Special Economic Zone. The British East India Company was present at Shantou from the 18th century, although formal trading rights were granted only after the 1860 Treaty of Tianjin. The place for a walk is the dock area around Anping Lu, while the main thoroughfares are Jinsha Lu, Shanzhang Lu, Zhongshan Lu and Waima Lu. Boats leave regularly for **Mayu Island** carrying pilgrims who visit the two temples there.

▶ Shaoshan 200B4

Mao Zedong's birthplace is a village in lush countryside southwest of Changsha and was once a place of pilgrimage for millions. Many workaday items have been given the Mao treatment, but the main attraction is Mao's family house (*Open* daily 7.30–5.30. *Admission: free*); with family photographs and domestic chattels. There is a **Museum of Comrade Mao** (*Open* daily 7.30–6. *Admission: inexpensive*), devoted to Mao's life. The surrounding countryside is classic rural China, with well-worn paths leading through bamboo groves to the **Dripping Water Cave**—where Mao spent several days in 1966—and to Shaoshan Peak.

▶▶▶ Shaoxing 201E5

Famous for its yellow rice wine, Shaoxing, in Zhejiang province, was the capital of the State of Yue and important during the Song dynasty, when the court moved to nearby Hangzhou. An unspoiled canal town of traditional houses, narrow alleys and humpback bridges, among them is the **Lu Xun Museum▶** (*Open* daily 8–5. *Admission: moderate*), the childhood home of Lu Xun, the revolutionary writer and philosopher. **Fushan Hill** has good town views. From here you can walk east to Jiefang Lu, surrounded by charming streets, and head for the 13th-century **Bazi Bridge▶**, across a canal lined with pretty houses. In the small alley of Dacheng, near Jiefang Nanlu, is the **Green Vine Study (Qingteng Shuwu)▶▶** (*Open* daily 8–5. *Admission: inexpensive*), the home of the notorious Ming artist Xu Wei and one of the loveliest examples of domestic architecture to survive in China. Outside Shaoxing is the **East Lake (Dong Hu)▶▶**, where boats can be hired to visit the Temple of Yu, dedicated to China's legendary founder.

▶ Tiantaishan   201E5

Tiantaishan mountain, reaching 1,100m (3,610ft), is the home of the Taoist-influenced Tiantai Buddhist sect. A number of monasteries are scattered throughout the area, including the **Bajingtai** at the summit. A bus from the Tiantai Gouqing Monastery at the foot of the mountain goes up to Huadingfeng, a short walk from the monastery.

▶ Wenzhou   201E4

A drab city on the coast of Zhejiang, Wenzhou was a key port servicing Sino-Japanese trade during the Song dynasty, and was famed for its scenery, hot springs and porcelain. Unable to compete with Shanghai in the 19th century because it lacked a deep-water anchorage, Wenzhou drifted into obscurity until 1984, when it was designated one of China's 14 Coastal Open Cities. Since then its development has been rapid, but its attractions for the tourist are somewhat limited. The **city museum▶**, housed in an ancient monastery on an island in the Ou river, displays some fine examples of local porcelain from the 1st to the 14th centuries. In the nearby **Yandang mountains▶** there are Buddhist shrines, scenic cliffs and a 109m (358ft) waterfall.

▶▶ Wuyishan   200C4

This is a mountain reserve in a magnificent setting in the north of Fujian. Raft trips to appreciate its outstanding scenery can be arranged through CITS offices on the spot or in Fuzhou or Xiamen.

COWED BY EAGLES
Wenzhou enjoys the distinction of possessing China's largest dairy. Dairy products are not widely eaten in China, since there is little pasture for cows, but in 1926 a Mr Wu Baiheng decided to compete against the only milk available at the time, 'Flying Eagle' condensed milk. Having started the dairy, he called his own brand of condensed milk 'Snatching Eagle'.

225

The benefits of China's economic miracle have not touched everyone. For some, life is as hard as ever it was

Xiamen University

226

XIAMEN AND ZHU XI
The philosopher Zhu Xi
is supposed to have
preached his neo-
Confucianist ideas in a
cave here at the end of
the 12th century. His
interpretation of the
teachings of Confucius
became the principles on
which the civil service
examinations were based
until early in the 20th
century.

*Colonial architecture on
Gulangyu Island*

▶▶ **Xiamen**   *201D3*

Called 'Amoy' by the foreign traders who settled here at
the turn of the 20th century, Xiamen consists of the island
of the same name and the smaller island of Gulangyu.
Xiamen Island is linked to the Fujian mainland by a causeway built in the early 1950s. The town was founded only
in the Ming dynasty and was the stronghold of the Ming
loyalist Zheng Chenggong (Koxinga). With the advent of
Westerners in 1842, an international concession was
allowed on Gulangyu, while a smaller concession grew
up on Xiamen itself. Xiamen now prospers as a Special
Economic Zone, despite the proximity of the nearby
islands that still belong to Taiwan.

In Xiamen itself, the **Wanshi Botanical Garden**▶ on
Huyuan Lu has an excellent collection of tropical and subtropical flora. On one side of its lake a large grey stone marks
the spot where Koxinga killed his cousin. The **Nanputuo
Temple**▶ (*Open* daily 8–6. *Admission: inexpensive*), against a
mountain backdrop, was originally built during the Tang
dynasty and extensively restored in the 1980s. Gaudily
impressive, its roofs are a vivid confusion of flowers, dragons and mythical figures. Tablets in the pavilions on either
side of the temple's main hall at the rear commemorate
suppression by the Qing secret societies. Steps behind lead
up to inscribed rocks, and in the summer, the lakes in front
are covered with lotus flowers, symbols of purity.

Xiamen University, founded in the early 20th century, is
on Daxue Lu, close to the temple. There is a small
exhibition dedicated to Lu Xun, the eminent writer who
taught here in 1926–27. Nearby are some pleasant beaches.
Southeast along the coast road is the **Huli Cannon**▶, made
in Germany by Krupp and placed here in 1891. The
Overseas Chinese Museum (Huaqiao Bowuguan)▶▶ has
displays showing the lives of Chinese immigrants, many
of whom came from Fujian province (see page 222), as well
as bronzes, ceramics and paintings.

Downtown Xiamen focuses on the waterfront and
Zhongshan Lu. Just opposite, where Zhongshan Lu meets
the port, is the ferry dock to Gulangyu: ferries make the
10-minute crossing regularly, at little cost.

Map:

0 ½ 1 km
0 ¼ ½ mile

Bus Station
XIAHE ROAD
Jimei School Village
People's Stadium
Zhongshan Garden
WENYUAN RD
Railway Station
Worker's Cultural Palace
GONGYUAN NAN ROAD
SIMING BEI RD
Post Office
DATONG RD
Gulangyu Ferry Dock
Overseas Chinese Building
ZHONGSHAN ROAD
Gulangyu Island
Overseas Chinese Department Store
Friendship Store
Lujiang
Hong Kong Ferry Dock
SIMING NAN ROAD
Wanshi Botanical Garden
Channel
MINZU ROAD
Xiamen Museum
Hongshan Park
Koxinga Museum (Zheng Chenggong Memorial Hall)
Post Office
Ferry Dock & Xiamen Seaworld
Musical Hall
Koxinga Statue
Overseas Chinese Museum
Nanputuo Temple
Sunlight Rock
Koxinga (Zheng Chenggong) Park
Shuzhuang Garden
Xiamen Harbour
DAXUE ROAD
Xiamen University
Huli Cannon

227

Walk

Xiamen: Gulangyu Island

This walk will give you a taste of old Xiamen—Sino-European architecture from the earlier part of the 20th century—and one or two key monuments. Disembark from the ferry, near **Xiamen Seaworld** (*Open daily 8.30–7. Admission: expensive*), turn left and follow the waterfront with its extensive views across to Xiamen. Eventually you pass a **statue of Koxinga**, and the road, bearing right, begins to rise and then stretches of beach are visible before the road begins to descend amid the roofs of the **old colonial houses**. Keep to the same road, passing some **fine doorways** with interesting motifs. Emerge before a playing field, with an art gallery on the corner. Turn left here and continue past some shops selling antiques and shark's fin; the path will eventually bring you to the sea. Just before the beach turn right and then go up a flight of steps, coming out onto a small square. Here is the entrance to the **Sunlight Rock**, an array of inscribed rocks, terraces with excellent views across the city and, about half-way up, the porticoed **Koxinga Museum**. Return to the entrance and bear left, which will bring you back to the playing field. Turn left at the corner, left again and then right to the **Risky Cave**. The next left brings you to a large building surmounted by a cross, the former **Protestant Church**. Then turn back and take the first right and then second left, then right and left up to the domed museum. Then return down to the market square and, beyond it, the ferry dock.

The pastel shades of former European influence, Gulangyu Island, Xiamen

Timeless landscape in the Lesser Guilin: Seven Star Crags, Zhaoqing

228

▶ **Zhaoqing**   *200B2*

Noted for its scenery, Zhaoqing, 113km (70 miles) west of Guangzhou, has as its focal point the **Seven Star Crags**▶▶, a group of limestone hills that emerge sharply out of the surrounding countryside. They stand in a park with artificial lakes, concrete walkways and traditional pavilions, so sightseeing can be done either on foot or by boat.

Zhaoqing itself is an attractive town and can easily be explored on foot. The **Plum Monastery** and the **old quarter** lie to the west of the main street, Tianning Lu, which leads north to **Seven Star Crag Park** (*Open* daily 7.30–5.30. *Admission: moderate*) and south to the Xi River and Jiangbin Donglu. Turning left at the river you come to the **Yuejiang Tower (Yuejianglou)** and on Tajiao Lu, amid interesting riverside houses, the **Chongxi (Flowery) Pagoda**. East of Zhaoqing is the scenic area of Dinghushan.

▶ Zhongshan County and Dr Sun Yatsen
200B2

For those visiting China on a day trip from Macau, a popular destination is Zhongshan County and the village of Cuiheng, birthplace of the father of Chinese nationalism, Sun Yatsen (1866–1925). His residence was built in 1892 to his own design; a museum is devoted to the story of his life.

The cult of Mao all but obliterated the part played by Sun in the founding of a united China. He studied medicine in Honolulu and Hong Kong, where he developed his Three Principles: the Principle of Nationalism, which implied the expulsion of foreigners from the treaty ports and the dignity of sovereignty; the Principle of People's Democracy, meaning that the Chinese government must be responsible to the people, who must be educated and taught how to vote; and the Principle of People's Livelihood, which entailed the nationalization of basic industries and utilities and the peasants' right to own the land they worked.

Sun was forced to flee to Hong Kong in 1895 after seeking new recruits in Guangzhou, and later went to Japan where he formed the United League (*Tongmenghui*) dedicated to overthrowing the Qing. He was in the United States fundraising when the successful anti-dynastic uprising in Wuchang occurred in 1911. He became President, but resigned to be succeeded by Yuan Shikai, who had no intention of underwriting a republic. Sun died in Beijing in 1925.

POLITICAL AIDES
Sun Yatsen thought that he stood a better chance of achieving his aims if he could enlist the support of the Chinese secret societies. He therefore joined the Hung Men (Vast Gate) society in Honolulu; when he went to the US in 1904 he went as a society official and was thus able more easily to gain immediate access to Chinese expatriate life.

229

Place of pilgrimage— Sun Yatsen's birthplace, Cuiheng, Zhongshan County

China's economy is one of the fastest growing in the world, although, as commentators are fond of pointing out, it could hardly be otherwise considering its lowly position before the era of reform.

230

CHINA TEES
China's prolific growth has triggered a boom in golf-course building. Since the first course, designed by golf legend Arnold Palmer, opened in 1984, another 200 have sprung up around the country. Many are associated with real estate developments, to cater to China's nouveau riche. But corruption involving some developers and local authorities led to a government crackdown, and approvals for new facilities are now much harder to get.

Growth In a comparatively short period miracles have been worked in the Chinese economy, and the China of today is vastly different from that of only 20 years ago.

In 1992, while the rest of the world still searched for escape routes out of recession, China's economy grew by a staggering 12 per cent. By 2005 it was the world's fourth-largest economy, and growth was still above 10 per cent in the first quarter of 2006. Throughout the 1980s there were hints of dramatic improvements to come, but the legacy of a state-run economy proved too much of a burden and reforms merely highlighted the deficiencies of a still largely 'socialist' economy. Inflation rose as there was nothing to do with earnings except spend them. One woman was reported to have spent all her savings on 2 tonnes of salt. Since then there have been many changes. China once reported a record £130 billion ($234 billion) in personal bank deposits, which can now be sunk into other forms of investment: stocks, bonds and, incredibly, real estate.

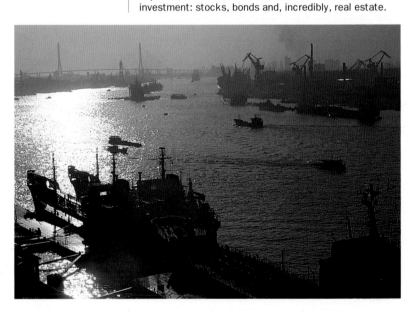

Top: Dalian port
Above: expanding docks on the Huangpu River, Shanghai

Contradictions The principle of state ownership of land was sacrosanct in China, with the landlord cast in the role of wicked villain. But in October 1992 the 14th Communist Party Congress gave its blessing to property speculation, an extraordinary about-face. Local governments were quick to take advantage of this policy change, and it was reported that in Wangfujing, Beijing's commercial hub, for example, land was being sold for

£3,250 per square metre ($6,997 per square yard). In theory, land deeds are valid for only 50 years on average, but this has not prevented continually rising prices. The average price of residential land in major cities in 2004 was £77.50 per square metre ($167 per square yard), an increase of almost 9 per cent on 2003. Prices are forecast to continue rising as demand increases—although average annual per capita income in cities of just £1,000 ($1,800) puts property out of most people's reach.

Optimism While most members of the government now support China's economic reforms to some degree, opinions differ on the speed and methods of implementation. Some who feel that the speed of change is too rapid want to stop reforms now, while others believe that the only way forward is to allow them to be as wide-ranging as possible. The root of the problem is that many institutions are still effectively controlled by the government and so lack credibility to the outside world. At the same time, an element of state control is thought to be necessary to prevent exploitation and a descent into poverty.

Extravagant property deals mean little to the peasant farmers in the poorer provinces, whose income has grown by only 3 per cent, and among whom unemployment may have reached more than 160 million. The gulf between rich and poor is growing, and fear of a reform 'freeze' is almost tangible in prosperous regions. Talk of secession has begun to alarm the mandarins of Beijing.

The Chinese government points to the chaos in the former Soviet Union as an example of what can happen when central control is weak. This view may be popular among the Chinese who crave stability, but it may not be long before state intervention is regarded as an unnecessary burden.

The great majority of China's population still works on the land

231

Inexpensive, high-quality clothing is a mainstay of China's economy

'FLOATING WORKERS'
About 100 million peasants are believed to have moved from rural areas to the fast-growing cities and coastal regions, attracted by the Chinese economic boom. In Beijing, already struggling to meet the demands of its 10 million residents, the additional 'floating population' may be as great as 2 million, overloading essential amenities, posing a serious security threat, and, according to government statistics, accounting for 43 per cent of convicted criminals in the capital. Paradoxically, the population's new mobility is essential to the continuing success of China's economic boom.

The Southwest

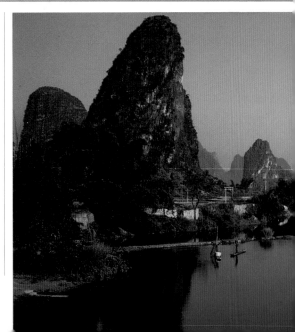

XIZANG ZIZHIQU (TIBET)

Hengduan Shan

Lancang Jiang
Jinsha Jiang

S I C H U A N

7556m
Gongga Shan

3099m Leshan Neijiang
Emeishan **Zigong** Hechuan

Dadu He **Chongqing**

IND

Yuexi
Gongshan

Zhongdian

Yalong Jiang

Daxue Shan

Min Jiang

Luzhou
Suijiang Yibin

Dégên

3

Muli Xichang

Dechang

Jinsha Jiang

Zhaotong Bijie

Qianxi

Daliang Shan

Dalou

Nu Shan (Salween)

5596m
Yulong Xueshan

Jianchuan Lijiang

G U I Z H

Liupanshui **Guiyang**

Panzhihua

3302m

Gaoligong Shan

Shaping
Xizhou Erhai
Dali

Yongren

Dongchuan

Wumeng Shan

Anshun **Longgong**

Huangguoshu Falls

Tengchong

Baoshan

Xiaguan
Nanhua

Dayao

Wuding

Panxian

D e h o n g

Nu Jiang

Chuxiong

Qujing

Xingyi

2

Luxi

Wuliang Shan

Dianchi

Kunming

Yuxi

Shilin (Stone Forest)

Lincang

Y U N

Ailao Shan

Xilin

Tianlin

Ruili

Lancang Jiang

A N

Nanpan Jiang

BUR

Cangyuan

Shiping

Yanshan

Funing Bose

Kaiyuan

Gejiu

Napo

Pu'er

Simao

Yuan Jiang

Lancang

Hekou

Menghai Jinghong

Daluo ✈ **Xishuangbanna**
Damenglong Mengla

Pingxiang

VN

1

| 0 | 100 | 200 | 300 | 400 km |

| 0 | 100 | 200 miles |

LAO

A T B C

232

Quintessential China: karst scenery along the Li River

Far right: a Hani woman, Yunnan province

The Southwest

Fishermen on the Li River at Yangshuo, near Guilin, still use tame cormorants to catch fish

SOUTHERN RESISTANCE
The continuing resistance in the south to Qing rule came to a head between 1857 and 1872, during the Muslim revolt, which occurred at the same times as the Taiping Rebellion. The ensuing slaughter severely reduced the Muslim population. Their leader, Du Wenxiu, declared himself Sultan of Yunnan, and pleaded with Great Britain's Queen Victoria to intervene, a request she declined.

SOUTHWEST CHINA In this guide the Southwest is taken to mean Yunnan and Guizhou provinces along with the Guangxi Zhuang Autonomous Region. It is a region of minority peoples who were assimilated into China only centuries after the first Qin emperor conquered the rest of what was to become China. By the Han dynasty, Chinese vanity was satisfied by bestowing imperial titles on the region's local rulers and more or less paying them to protect the southern borders of the Chinese empire. It was not until the 13th century and the arrival of the Mongols that the region was finally and brutally subsumed within China, although it broke away each time a dynasty collapsed, ensuring that the new rulers would have to go to the trouble of reconquest.

Geographically, much of the area is on the Yunnan–Guizhou plateau, which rises to an average altitude of 1,000m (3,280ft), reaching 2,000m (6,560ft) in the northern part where it meets the border with Burma. The plateau is run through with river valleys (the Red River of Vietnam rises here, as do several major tributaries of the Yangtze) and broken by the occasional towering ridge. The altitude, combined with the region's latitude, means that the climate is the most pleasant in China: warm and mild, it is known as 'spring at all seasons'. There are areas of upland grazing, as well as land devoted to the cultivation of rice, winter wheat, tea, beans, soya, hemp and rape.

At the border with Vietnam and Laos, the plateau falls away and the weather is hotter and wetter, ideal for rubber, bananas and sugar; while Guangxi has a climate typical of southern China, ideal for the intensive farming of rice and tropical fruits and vegetables.

Southwest China, like everywhere else, is the sum of its parts. In some ways, considering its centuries-old resistance to central rule, it is surprising that the region is not more radically dissimilar to the rest of China. Although some of the minority peoples may have different facial features or physiques and, sometimes, different dress, there is no doubt that you are in China. This is the case in the more cosmopolitan parts of the region, and even in the remoter areas, where indigenous customs continue, life has a very Chinese quality.

The greatest difference, other than peculiar attractions like the mountains of Guilin or Kunming's Stone Forest, is the pace of life, which is attractively languid, and the countryside, which is lush and vibrant—Yunnan, in particular, is the home of many plants familiar to Westerners, like camellias and rhododendrons. The other distinctions are perhaps more modern—Kunming, for example, has a surprisingly carefree vitality considering its location. An area that was thought of as a place of exile for centuries, the Southwest has now become very attractive to northerners, who these days are less anxious to return to their staid homeland.

The minority peoples of the area are an important element of the region's strength. Half of China's 55 minorities live in Yunnan, while Guangxi is home to China's most numerous minority people, the Zhuang. Southeast Guizhou is also home to some minority peoples. As modernization hastens the disappearance of their traditional ways of life, interest from abroad has taught the Chinese to treat the minorities with more respect. Not only foreign visitors, but Chinese from other more austere parts of the country delight in the much more relaxed way of life that is the way of the indigenous people of the region.

SORGHUM SPIRIT
Guizhou province is the home of Maotai, China's most famous spirit wine. It is usually served at important banquets and, although for a time unobtainable, is now merely expensive. Its main ingredient is sorghum, which gives it a sharpness that is definitely an acquired taste.

235

SPIRITS AND GHOSTS
In China, spirits or gods (*shen*) were associated with Heaven (which controlled the natural and human world) and the *yang* (male) principle. In folk religion there were *shen* of trees, rivers, rain, thunder, lightning, the household kitchen and the earth, the last particularly important in the agricultural society of ancient China. *Gui*, ghosts or devils, were associated with the Earth and the *yin* (female) principle, and were seen as evil beings. To Buddhists they were human beings who had committed evil acts in a previous life and so had been reborn as 'hungry ghosts'.

Traditional architecture, Lijiang, Yunnan. The 1996 earthquake did much damage, but the town's old houses withstood it better than its modern buildings

*Opposite, lower right:
Jiele Pagoda near Ruili,
in the Dehong area*

▶▶ Anshun
232C2

In Guizhou province, and once a focal point for the opium trade, Anshun is the best transit stop for the **Huangguoshu Falls**▶▶▶ (*Open* daily 8–6. *Admission: expensive*). In this pleasant town of old houses surrounded by pretty country-side, you can visit the Confucian temple or hunt for batik work, for which the area is famous. The falls are outside town (they can also be reached via a 5-hour bus ride from Guiyang). At 73m (240ft) high and 79m (260ft) wide they are the mightiest falls in China. The surrounding country-side is home to the Bouyei tribe, who are related to the Thais. The nearby **Gaotan Falls** are also spectacular, as are the **Longgong underground caves** at Longtan.

▶▶▶ Dali
232B2

Dali is a pretty and lively town in Yunnan, 4–5 hours by bus from Kunming and picturesquely situated on Erhai Lake beneath Cang mountain, which is famous for its mar-ble. The main street is Fuxing Lu, at either end of which are the **Qing gates**▶, part of the old city wall. The **Dali Museum** (*Open* daily 8.30–6. *Admission: inexpensive*) on Fuxing Lu has exhibits on the history of the Bai minority. Almost any road to the east will lead you eventually to the **lake**▶▶, where fishermen still sometimes follow the tradi-tional methods of fishing with tame cor-morants. Dali's most famous landmarks are the **Three Pagodas**▶▶ (*Open* daily 8–12, 2–5. *Admission: inexpensive*), just to the north. The largest of them dates back to AD824, is 64m (210ft) high, and is decor-ated with Buddhas made from the local richly veined marble on each of its 16 floors. On the mountain behind Dali is the **Zhonghe Temple** (*Open* daily 8–7. *Admission: moderate*). Reached by chairlift it sits among gorgeous scenery. North is the **Butterfly Spring (Hudiequan)**, a popu-lar spot surrounded by a marble balustrade and overhung by an ancient tree that produces butterfly-like flowers. **Zhoucheng**, a nearby village, has an old Qing stage on the main square, which was once used by itinerant opera troupes and is now the scene of a bustling market. From here it is possible to take a 3-hour boat trip via a small island with a temple. **Shaping**, north of Dali, is famous for its Monday market, but the daily morning market at the charming Bai town of **Xizhou**▶▶ is also worth a visit.

▶▶ Dehong
232A2

The Dehong Dai-Jingpo Autonomous Prefecture, home to the Dai and Jingpo peoples, is a remote area on the Burmese border that has been open to foreigners only since 1990. Although the Jingpo on the whole are friendly, visits to their vil-lages are not welcome when there has been a recent death. There is also a signifi-cant drug problem in some parts.

*Two of the famous Three
Pagodas, Dali*

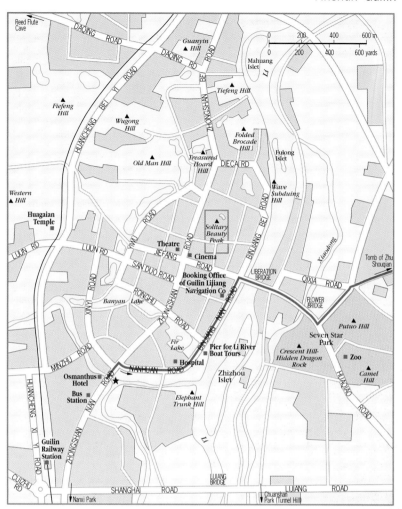

Map of Guilin

▶▶▶ Guilin

233D2

Guilin has become one of the stars of Chinese—indeed, world—tourism. Its fame rests on its magical scenery: vast areas of karst limestone outcrops that shoot up starkly from a flat plain of paddy fields and lush bamboo. The area around Guilin was covered by the sea some 300 million years ago, and its unique landscape is the result of the movement of the earth's crust, which forced up layers of limestone into the distinctive round-topped mountains. Innumerable poems and paintings immortalize the bizarre landscape.

It is alleged that Guilin has been spoiled by 'mass' tourism, but this is a little unfair. True, its attractions have been exploited to draw in large numbers of foreign tourists, hotels have sprung up to accommodate them and petty crime and corruption are on the increase. Indeed Guilin, which by Chinese standards is hardly more than a

Map not to scale

River cruise

Down the Li River from Guilin to Yangshuo

This worthwhile, but rather expensive, boat trip begins either in Guilin itself, from the pier on Binjiang Nan Road, or—if the water level is too low, which it frequently is—at a point about 40 minutes' drive downstream. The cruise lasts between four and five hours and ends at the town of Yangshuo. From Yangshuo, passengers take a two-hour bus ride back to Guilin.

The river passes an endless procession of peaks, each of which has a descriptive soubriquet—Paint Brush Hill, Cock-fighting Hill, Oxen Gorge, Embroidery Hill and so on. Even in the rain (and this is an all too regular occurrence), the scenery is breathtaking.

Purists will be dismayed at the level of organization demonstrated on the cruise—flotillas of double-decker boats crammed with tourists leave one after the other. However, all this is forgotten as soon as the journey begins, and the boats dwindle into insignificance as they are dwarfed by the grandeur of the surroundings.

The shallow river runs clear, past overhanging bamboo fronds and simple villages, and fishermen using trained cormorants to catch the fish (see panel, page 239) drift placidly by on bamboo rafts. Less expensive cruises can be arranged locally at Yangshuo.

village, feels like a gold-rush town, such is the frenzy to make money, but the chief attraction, the scenery, has remained untainted.

The towering sugar-loaf mountains are apparent as you fly in. Guilin itself is attractive, but the highlight of a visit here is a trip on the **Li River▶▶▶**, which threads its way through the heart of the mountains (see above).

Guilin started as a garrison town during the Qin dynasty and became a trading hub when the Lingqu Canal linking the Pearl and Yangtze rivers was built. It was the capital of Guangxi from the Ming until 1914, when it was replaced by Nanning. During the Sino-Japanese War in the 1930s, its population swelled with refugees from the north and the town was heavily bombed, which explains the almost complete absence of ancient buildings. Guilin's name means 'Forest of Cassia Trees' and in the last few years some million specimens have been planted in and around the town. The trees are in full bloom in autumn, when they give off a lovely perfume, scenting the air all over the city.

Having seen so many peaks in the vicinity, you may also wish to climb some. There are, among others, **Duxiufeng (Solitary Beauty Peak)**, **Fuboshan (Wave Subduing Hill)** with caves containing ancient statues, and **Diecaishan (Folded Brocade Hill)**, also with inscriptions and statues. All have superb views from their summits.

A short way outside the town is **Reed Flute Cave**►► (*Open* daily 7.30–5.20. *Admission: expensive*), an underground cavern of exotic rock formations, its fantastical shapes lit by gaudy lights. A path will lead you along a circuit that takes about 45 minutes.

Since the land between the peaks is flat, Guilin is an ideal place for riding bicycles, which can be hired easily and cheaply at many places throughout the town. See below for a suggested cycle ride.

Reed Flute Cave, Guilin, gaudy but entertaining

CORMORANT FISHING
Although a great draw for tourists, who like to be photographed with them, the cormorants of Guilin are not just a pretty sight. The Li River fishermen still use them to catch fish, controlling them by means of a leash tied around their throats that prevents them from swallowing the fish they catch, but does not asphyxiate them. When fully trained the birds are valuable helpers.

Cycle ride

From Guilin to Zhu Shouqian's tomb

See highlighted map, page 237.
This cycle ride takes about 45 minutes one way, leaving from the Osmanthus Hotel. Cross the bridge (Zhongshan Nanlu) over a tributary and turn immediately right (Nanhuan Road) to the Li River. Follow the road as it bears left by the river, with Elephant Trunk Hill to your right, until you come to Liberation Bridge. Turn right to cross the bridge, and take the first left on the other side. Follow the road as it curves right, staying with it for some time as it crosses a major road and gradually enters the countryside, passing fields and brick kilns. Out of the town, not long after passing the first peak, you will come to a track on the left that leads to a graveyard and the statues belonging to the sacred way of the tomb of **Zhu Shouqian**►►, nephew of the first Ming emperor, who established a principality here.

These guides at Stone Forest, near Kunming, are members of the Sani

TRANSPORT
Despite, or because of, their comparative remoteness, both Lijiang and Dali have opened airports that make arrival easier and which have opened them to mass tourism. From Kunming, a railway line has been built to Dali and is being extended to Lijiang, which will provide an extremely scenic way of reaching these towns in some comfort.

Celestial temple guardian, Huatingsi, Kunming

Three of the 500 clay figures (luohans) at the Bamboo Temple, Kunming

▶ Guiyang
232C2

The capital of Guizhou province, Guiyang is an industrial city with attractive scenery outside town. It is a possible departure point for the **Huangguoshu Falls**▶▶▶ (see page 236); otherwise there is **Huaxi Park** (16km/10 miles southwest), the **Hongfu Monastery** and **Kanzhu Pavilion**, the graceful **Jiaxiu Pavilion**, or scenic **Qianling Park**. The **Regional Museum** (*Open Tue–Sun 9–5. Admission: inexpensive*) on Beijing Lu, concentrates on the past and present ways of life of the minority peoples of the province.

▶▶▶ Kunming
232B2

The capital of Yunnan province has as its main attraction the Stone Forest but, with its pleasant climate and bustling streets, it is of interest on its own account. It has played an important historical role since 100BC when it became the capital of the Dian, a slave-owning society perhaps related to the peoples of Southeast Asia. In the early 20th century it became an important rail hub when the French built the rail link from Vietnam to China, and during World War II it was one end of the Burma Road built by the Allies as a supply route.

The reopened **Yunnan Provincial Museum**▶▶ (*Open daily 9.30– 5.30. Admission: inexpensive*), at the junction of Dongfeng Lu and Wuyi Lu, has an important collection of bronze artefacts from the Dian kingdom that were excavated in the area. Made by the 'lost wax method', and decorated with scenes of Dian life, the bronzes have a distinctive character quite unlike Chinese examples. There is also a display devoted to the province's minority peoples. The **Yuantong Buddhist Temple**▶▶ (*Open daily 8–5.30. Admission: inexpensive*), on Yuantong Jie and founded in the Tang dynasty, is one of the finest temples in China. A new mosque has been constructed on Zhengyi Lu.

A short distance west of Kunming lies Lake Dian. On its banks is **Daguan Park**▶ with the early Qing-dynasty Grand View Tower (Daguanlou), famous for its inscriptions by the 18th-century poet Sun Ranweng. In Haigeng Park, on

Kunming

the northeast shore of the lake, is the **Yunnan Nationalities Village** (*Open* daily 8.30–5.30. *Admission: inexpensive*), which illustrates the ways of life of Yunnan's minority peoples. Sadly the lake is heavily polluted, but there is a splendid view of it from the heights of the **Western Hills**▶▶, some 16km (10 miles) from Kunming, and the **Dragon Gate**▶▶, a series of winding steps, tunnels and statue-filled grottoes leading to a lookout point also served by a chairlift. The Song-dynasty **Bamboo Temple**▶ (*Open* daily 8–6. *Admission: inexpensive*), northwest of Kunming, thought to be the first Chan Buddhist temple in Yunnan, is known for its hall of 500 clay figures; while the **Golden Temple**▶ (*Open* daily 8–6.30. *Admission: inexpensive*), northeast, has an imitation-timber pavilion in bronze.

The **Stone Forest (Shilin)**▶▶▶ (*Open* daily. *Admission: expensive*), a 270-million-year-old limestone karst formation of tightly bundled grey rocky outcrops, which from a distance resembles a petrified forest, is 130km (80 miles) southeast of Kunming. The journey, through villages built in the traditional local style, lasts about 3 hours.

A walk through this landscape is recommended, for although the tone of the rocks is monotonous, their sharp angles and delineations create strong shadowy contrasts, very good for photography. From the Shilin Hotel, turn left and follow the road until you pass **Lion Pond** on the left, then turn left to the **Lion Pavilion**. From here, continue to a **stone screen**, inscribed with the name of the site. Then take the right-hand path to **Sword Peak Pond**; from here all paths lead back to the starting point.

Shilin, the Stone Forest near Kunming, Yunnan

241

The 'Dongba' characters of the Naxi pictorial language, here depicting the Creation Myth and the Rite of Exorcism

Naxi women in traditional dress meet in a local market

▶▶▶ Lijiang 232B3

The seat of the Naxi minority peoples, Lijiang in the north of Yunnan province lies at 2,500m (8,200ft) in a stupendous mountain setting on the border with Tibet, some 4–5 hours' drive from Kunming and now with its own airport. The route passes through hills covered in red earth and dotted with traditional-style villages, many still with their local temples. The Naxi peoples are a matriarchal society related to the Tibetans. Traditionally couples did not live together, and any children of a union live with the mother, relying on financial support from the father. In Lijiang itself this social structure has broken down, although the old customs are still followed farther north, notably by the Mosuo people of Lugo Lake, a Naxi sub-group.

The earthquake in 1996 badly damaged Lijiang's **Old Town**▶▶▶, and a concerted effort is being made to rebuild in the old style. Despite this, the Old Town, now a UNESCO World Heritage Site, is utterly charming. It has a network of narrow streets lined with small restaurants, which are intersected by canals, and a lively market square—take any ascending path for superb views across the rooftops and to visit the Wanggu Lou Pagoda (*Open daily 6am–7pm. Admission: inexpensive*). On the northern edge of town is the very pretty **Black Dragon Pool Park** with the Ming-dynasty **Wufenglou Temple**. In the evenings, there are concerts of Naxi music in the Old Town, including recitals of Taoist Temple music lost elsewhere in China. The orchestra director, Xuan Ke, has opened a museum about Naxi culture in his house at Dong Dajie, Gucheng Qu (*Open* daily 8am–9.30pm. *Admission: expensive*).

Outside Lijiang you can visit the **Yufengsi Monastery**, on a slope overlooking a plain. The surrounding countryside beneath the 5,596m (18,360ft) Yulong Xueshan (Jade Dragon Snow Mountain, or Mount Satseto) is excellent for cycling and walking. The highest chairlift in Asia can be found here. Some 90km (60 miles) from Lijiang is **Tiger Leaping Gorge (Hutiaoxia)**▶▶▶ on the Yangtze, 16km (10 miles) long and up to 3,000m (9,840ft) deep. You can walk its length along a path high above the river.

▶ Nanning

233D1

The capital of Guangxi province since 1914, Nanning is a heavily industrialized city made important by the railway line from Beijing to Vietnam, linking Nanning with Guilin and Kunming to the north. It is possible to obtain a visa for Vietnam from here. The **Guangxi Provincial Museum**▶▶ (*Open* daily 8.30–12, 2.30–5.30. *Admission: inexpensive*), has a good collection of tribal and historical items. Xinling Lu, near the river, or the exotic open market off the main street, Chaoyang Lu, are pleasant places to wander through. The **Nanning Arts Institute**▶▶ exhibits arts and crafts of the minority peoples. The **Dragon-boat races** are held on the fifth day of the fifth lunar month (around mid-June).

243

Naxi musicians, Lijiang, perhaps the last place where you can hear true Taoist music from the Tang dynasty

In China, rice is the staple food. Although you are frequently told that rice is the staple of the south and wheat that of the north, in fact almost everyone in China eats rice, and anyone deprived of his or her daily portion feels uncomfortable and at a loss.

RICE RESEARCH
In the 11th and 12th centuries, Chinese farmers succeeded in producing strains of rice that matured in only 60 days, allowing a double, sometimes triple, harvest. Eventually, 30-day varieties were developed, reducing the risk of flood damage at a crucial moment in the crop's cycle and thus invaluable in obviating the worst effects of the chronic flooding that afflicts China to this day.

244

History Rice's distinguishing feature is its immersion in water for part of the year, a characteristic that conjures up for the foreigner an image that is almost inseparable from the picture of China as a land of straw-hatted farmers toiling under a torrid sky.

During the first century, the most densely populated part of China was the area around the Yellow River in the north, where rice cultivation was uncommon, but where millet was grown, and pigs and sheep reared. Southern China was populated then by Tai-speaking peoples who used a primitive form of wet-rice farming, and the Chinese of the frontier regions of the Yangtze valley also had a tradition of wet-rice cultivation. Organized irrigation techniques on any scale only began to be introduced in the third and fourth centuries BC. The Chinese of the north were familiar with intensive farming methods, and the use of fertilizer, both animal and human, was known even if not yet widely used. In the fourth century, when many northerners were driven south as a result of political upheaval, they left their sheep but brought their pigs and their farming techniques. They applied these techniques to the wet-rice cultivation methods of the southerners, whose use of water buffalo and fondness for poultry they also adopted. By the 14th century, with the shift of Chinese civilization from the Yellow River to the Yangtze, irrigated cultivation of rice was well established. Fast-growing rice was imported from India, making crop rotation possible. Strains were developed that required less water and could be grown on hillside terraces. Following the shift in population there was also a demand for more food variety, so sorghum, groundnuts, and later sweet potatoes (from the New World) were introduced.

*Top: flooded rice fields in Guangxi province
Below: paddy terraces, Yunnan*

Cultivation Rice is not a particularly demanding cereal—it tolerates a wide range of soils and gives a high yield in a comparatively small area. Certain conditions must be met, however. Rice needs an average temperature of at least 20°C (68°F) over a period of three to four months and at least 180cm (70in) of rain during the growing season. Wet rice, as opposed to upland rice (which can be sustained on rain or spring water), must be submerged beneath water to an average depth of between 10cm and 15cm (4–6in) during three quarters of the growing period; the water has to be of equal depth to ensure even growth. For this reason cultivation takes place in small level fields (paddies, from the Malay word *padi* meaning 'rice in the husk'), surrounded by low earthen *bunds* (walls) that keep the water in and are quickly breached to let it out. Hillside terracing is often associated with rice cultivation, but most rice crops are grown in deltas or in the lower reaches of rivers where it is inexpensive to level fields. Here, water is near at hand, and the soil tends to be heavy and fine-grained, which prevents excessive drainage.

At the beginning of the season, the dykes, bunds and irrigation canals must be repaired and the soil ploughed to reduce it to a muddy consistency. Ten per cent of the fields are set aside as nurseries. After four or five weeks the seedlings are transplanted to the paddies and arranged in rows. As harvest approaches, the fields are drained and reaping begins. Finally, the stalks are ploughed back into the field, which is then fertilized for the next crop, which may be wheat or, in the deep south, another of rice. Paddy fields do not need to lie fallow, possibly because the water acts as a protection against damage by sun, wind and rain, so the same fields are used year after year.

To Chinese children, a bowl of rice is what a slice of bread is to a Western child

STAPLE FOODS
Although rice is the mainstay of agriculture in China, the Chinese have also imported foreign crops into their agriculture, several from the Americas. Maize and the sweet potato arrived through the Philippines via the Spanish in the 17th century, while the potato itself came via the Dutch from Indonesia, as did the mange-tout pea, which is still called 'Dutch bean' by the Chinese.

The Southwest

THE DAI

Linguistically and ethno-logically, the Dai people are closely related to the Tai peoples who are scattered over the very wide area that takes in Thailand, Burma, north Vietnam and Laos, and who once lived in much of southern China. Although the Dai are subdivided into four, all speak Dai, which is broadly similar to Thai, although the Dai script differs considerably from Thai writing.

246

Manfeilong White Pagoda—the Baita, Damenglong, Xishuangbanna

▶▶▶ Xishuangbanna 232B1

Xishuangbanna Dai Autonomous Prefecture, in south Yunnan near the Burmese and Laotian borders, is the home of the Buddhist Dai people, who are related to the Thais. The Dai state was taken by the Mongols in the 13th century and subsequently by the Chinese, but although evidence of colonization remains, the area retains enough indigenous character from its many minority peoples to warrant a visit, particularly between mid-September and mid-May when the weather is warm but not stifling.

The capital and main port of entry is **Jinghong**, a pleasant town on the Mekong River and a good base. The town is modern, but on the southern edge is the village of **Manjing ▶**, where traditional Dai houses stand opposite more recent constructions. Every evening. performances of the famed Dai Peacock dance take place in several restaurants and hotels. There are good cafés, one of the best being Mei Mei, a popular meeting place for backpackers.

In the heart of town is the **Tropical Plant Research Institute** (Redai Zhiwu Yanjiusuo)▶ (*Open* daily. *Admission: moderate*), with a charming display of palms, fruit trees and cascading flowers. But the main items of interest, **the minority villages▶▶▶**, lie outside the town.

Journeying west from Jinghong soon brings you to the Dai villages of **Manjing Dai** and **Manluan Dian**, where the tradition of weaving bags, rugs and richly hued cloth still thrives. Beyond is a succession of villages belonging either to the Dai or to the Aini. Continuing west brings you to **Menghai**, a modern town known for its Sunday market, although those at **Menghun** and at **Xiding** are just as interesting. After Menghai the road passes the Qing-dynasty **Octagonal Pavilion**, next to a Buddhist school, and continues to **Mengzhe** with its Tang-dynasty **Wat Gau Temple**,

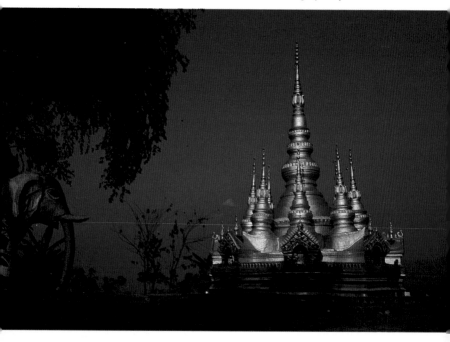

rebuilt in 1985. In the far west, **Daluo** has a Sunday market that attracts Burmese traders.

South of the western road is **Nannuoshan**, famous for the King of Tea Trees, planted by the Hani 55 generations ago. Farther south from Jinghong is the **Manfeilong White Pagoda** at **Damenglong**, built in 1204 to commemorate a footprint left behind by the Buddha. In late October or early November, the pagoda is the focal point of the Tan Ta festival, drawing hordes of local people who come to dance and set off amulet-filled rockets.

East of Jinghong, the **Botanical Garden** in the Dai village of **Menglun** is open to visitors. South of Menglun the road takes you to the Dai and Yao area of **Mengla**. On the route to the frontier with Laos, Mengla's rain forest, as well as its villages, have a fresh novelty and interest.

Menghan (**Ganlanba**), on the Mekong south of Jinghong, has a morning market. The nearby Dai village of **Manting** boasts a temple with the tallest Buddha in the area; just southwest of Menghan is the **Wat Ban Suan Men** (**Manchunman**), a fine example of Dai architecture.

Wild Elephant Valley ► ► is a nature reserve 50km (30 miles) north of Jinghong. You are unlikely to see the wild elephants unless you stay in the reserve's tree-house lodge, although there is a touristy show with tame elephants. The highlights are a cable-car ride above the rain forest canopy and forest walks.

There are more delightful forest walks among the hills outside Jinghong. The easier walks and a waterfall are at **Mandian**, while those at the Tropical Primeval Rain Forest Park, 8km (5 miles) from Jinghong, are more demanding walks for the fit and energetic.

Xishuangbanna's famous Water Splashing Festival takes place on 12–15 April, over the Dai New Year.

247

Dai people at Menghan Market, Xishuangbanna

'The very concept of completion is utterly alien to the Chinese way of thinking. The Chinese painter deliberately avoids a complete statement because he knows that we can never know everything.' Michael Sullivan, A Short History of Chinese Art, 1967.

PAINTING *QI*
As in so many other aspects of traditional life in China, the vital force known as *qi* plays an essential role in painting. For the Chinese painter, each living creature, every plant and the oldest, stillest rock possesses *qi* that reacts with the *qi* of the painter. One must imagine, therefore, how it is to look and then put brush to paper at a moment that is both absolute concentration and absolute release.

Top: calligraphy brushes
Below: papier-mâché
New Year's masks

248

Painting One of the delights of a visit to China is the opportunity to admire, and buy, Chinese art. A Chinese painting is a distinctive object, based, like so many things in China, on centuries-old traditions. Modern painters in China have found it difficult to escape age-old conventions (and political pressures have not encouraged experimentation), but the traditional styles, when executed with real skill, remain enormously attractive.

Traditional Chinese painting is carried out using a brush on paper or silk, often with black ink alone, resulting in a monochrome style similar to calligraphy. The ink is made from soot scented with musk or camphor and solidified with animal glue into the form of small inksticks, often intricately decorated. Highly regarded as one of the 'four treasures of the study' (*wenshusibao*, the others being brush, paper and inkstone), the inksticks' vibrant, faintly mysterious presence makes a visit to a traditional Chinese stationery shop a delight.

Traditional brushes are made of animal hair glued into bamboo. The inkstone, usually black or grey, is a heavy ovoid block made of slate with a shallow bowl often surrounded by carved designs. A little water is placed in the bowl and the inkstick ground into it, with more water added until the correct consistency is reached. Intensely black in its original state, the ink can be diluted to the palest grey.

Painting styles The Song dynasty is considered to have been the greatest period of Chinese painting. Although few earlier examples survive, it is clear that painting in China was already a sophisticated art by the Han dynasty. Painters were either gentlemanly amateurs or professional craftsmen hired for particular occasions. Two styles of painting developed—academic painting, with its naturalistic approach to artistic excellence in which birds and flowers were reproduced in perfect detail; and a more scholarly style that specialized in grandiose representations of nature, concentrating on mountains in particular, where reality is stylized to expose its essence. The art of painting was to grasp reality, not merely the illusion of reality. Unlike in Western art, perspective is not from a fixed point, but moves between several different viewpoints. Man plays an insignificant role—a tiny figure diminished by mountains might help to direct the onlooker to the correct viewpoint, but it also shows how finite is man and how great and timeless is nature.

During the Cultural Revolution painters, like writers, suffered terrible hardships and ridiculous indignities. The painter Huang Yongyu was sent to work in the countryside; then, after his return, he was accused by Mao Zedong's wife and Gang of Four member of insulting her by painting an owl with one eye closed. When his accuser was arrested, Huang celebrated by painting a similar owl every day.

249

Left: a Song-dynasty painting, Willows and Distant Mountains, *by Ma Yuan*
Below: the dramatic puppets of Fujian

Paintings were presented in two ways—the hand scroll or the hanging scroll. The former is read like a book, by unrolling one end as quickly or as slowly as one desires. The hanging scroll is designed to be appreciated all at once. Neither was intended to be out on show all the time—mounted on silk with clasps of jade, scrolls were wrapped in damask and concealed in boxes to be opened and pored over on certain occasions.

Lacquerware Distinctively Chinese, lacquer is produced from the sap of the *Rhus verniciflua*, or lac tree, native to China; it was originally used as a timber preservative. By the Han dynasty lacquer dishes were used as food containers, and it was soon discovered that the addition of minerals produced fine shades. The typical features of Chinese art, such as mountains and animals, began to appear on lacquer vessels with a wood or cloth base. Lacquer is carved by cutting through the thick coats built up in layers on a wooden or metal base. It is still produced but only rarely with authentic materials.

Continued on page 250

CHINESE CARPETS

One of the crafts most often associated with China is that of carpet-making. Traditional Chinese carpets are now made in factories in Wuhan, Tianjin and Shanghai, while other nationalities produce carpets on a smaller scale in Tibet and Xinjiang. Chinese carpets are distinguished by the fact that the pattern is in relief, usually produced by means of a combination of electric scissors and a sure eye.

Right: an example of the painting style of Huxian county, Shaanxi

At work in a cloisonné *factory*

Continued from page 249
Cloisonné A craft that excites disdain as much as admiration is *cloisonné* (from the French, meaning 'cloistered'; *jingtailan* in Chinese).

The technique for this gaudy enamelware, made mainly in Beijing and Xi'an, was probably first introduced into China during the Yuan dynasty. The process of production is painstaking. First, a base is made of bronze or copper, such as a vase, and then thin copper wires are glued over the surface to produce a network of tiny cells. Into each, by means of a dropper, mineral paints of different hues are added. When dry, the article is fired in an oven, polished with a metal brush, topped up with more enamel, fired again and burnished. The final touch is the gilding of the exposed wires. When the paints are carefully chosen the effect can be very pleasing, although all too often the result is somewhat tacky. Antique *cloisonné* is usually more satisfying because the tones are richer but less brash.

Crafts unlimited The range of Chinese crafts is almost limitless. Many are ingenious fun (paper cut-outs, or dough-figurine models), but all demonstrate intricacy and dexterity. Some cities—Shanghai, for example—boast Arts and Crafts Research Institutes, which are worth a visit.

250

Chinese dynasties and historical events

CHINA	REST OF THE WORLD

600,000BC–400,000BC

First hominids (Lantian Man and Peking Man) — Homo sapiens *in Africa*

5000BC

Yangshao culture (red earthenware pots) and Longshan culture (black burnished wares) — *Egyptians invent the calendar of 12 months, each of 30 days*

Xia (2100–1600BC)

Earliest recorded dynasty Earliest bronzeware and carved jade objects — *Pyramids, the Great Sphinx, first great libraries in Egypt Minoan culture in Crete*

Shang (1600–1027BC)

Earliest Chinese characters— 15,000 pictographs carved on oracle bones used in harvest rituals and medical diagnosis Sophisticated bronze vessels — *Trojan War (1193BC) Moses leads the Israelites to Canaan Burial of Tutankhamun*

Western Zhou (1027–771BC)

Bronze working reaches its technical and artistic peak Chinese script fully developed First mathematical textbooks — *King David rules Israel (1000–960BC) Carthage founded (814BC)*

Eastern Zhou (770–256BC) Spring and Autumn period (722–476BC)

Iron replaces bronze for tools and weapons Confucius (ca551–479BC) Laozi, founder of Taoism (c570–549 BC) — *Rome founded (753BC) Homer (700BC) Buddha in India (560–483BC) Roman Republic founded (530BC)*

Warring States period (475–221BC)

Metal coinage The Legalists Invention of crossbow, calligraphy brushes, chopsticks — *Socrates condemned to death (399BC) Plato (428–347BC) Alexander the Great (356–323BC) Mexican sun temple at Teotihuacan (300BC)*

Chronological chart

Qin (221–206BC)

Qin Shihuang: first emperor
  to rule all China
Great Wall completed
Standardization of weights,
  measures and coinage
Suppression of Confucianism,
  rise of Legalist ideas
The Terracotta Army at Xi'an

Hannibal crosses the Alps
  to invade Italy (218BC)
Cato, the Roman politician
  (234–149BC)
Death of Archimedes, Greek
  mathematician (212BC)

Han (206BC–AD220): Western Han (206BC–AD24)

Revival of Confucianism
First civil service examination
Silk Road opened

First clock (159BC)
Venus de Milo carved (140BC)
Virgil, Roman poet (70–19BC)
Modern calendar introduced (46BC)

Eastern Han (AD24–220)

Buddhism brought to
  China via the Silk Road
Seismograph invented
Value of pi (π) calculated
  to the first five decimal places
First treatises on acupuncture
  and moxibustion

Christ crucified (AD30)
First Christian church in Corinth (AD40)
London founded (AD43)
St. Paul's missionary travels
  begin (AD45)
Gospels written (AD85)
First Mayan monuments (AD164)

Disunity and partition (220–581)

Three clans (Wu, Wei and Shu)
  fighting for supremacy
  (221–265)
'Barbarians' (non-Chinese
  nomadic peoples) conquer
  parts of China and adopt
  Chinese customs
Chinese population shifts south
  to Yangtze valley

Constantinople becomes
  capital of the Roman Empire (331)
The Roman Empire splits into
  Eastern and Western empires
  with two emperors (340)
Alaric the Goth sacks Athens
  (398) and Rome (410)
Death of British King Arthur (537)
Rats spread plague throughout
  Europe (542–547)

Sui (581–618)

The Grand Canal built
  from Beijing to Hangzhou

Petroleum ('burning water')
  first discovered in Japan (615)

Tang (618–907)

China's Golden Age:
  flourishing trade with central
  Asia
China's only empress
  (Wu Zetian, 690–705)
The poetry of Du Fu (712–770)
First printed books
Arabs defeat the Chinese
  in the Battle of the River Talas
  (751)

Muhammad (570–632)
Greek fire (sulphur, petrol, resin
  and salt) first used in warfare
  during the siege of
  Constantinople (678)
Charlemagne crowned first
  Holy Roman Emperor (800)
Doge's Palace, Venice (814)
  and St. Mark's (828)
Vikings discover Iceland (861)

Five Dynasties and Ten Kingdoms (907–960)

Paper money (910)
Gunpowder (919)

Fatamid dynasty in North Africa
Cordoba in Spain is a flourishing
* city of Arabic learning and*
* commerce*

Song (960–1279): Northern Song (960–1127)

First movable type printing
Landscape painting reaches
* a peak of excellence*
Neo-Confucianism

Arabic numerals first used in
* Europe (975)*
Leif Ericson sails to America (1000)
First Crusade (1096)

Southern Song (1127–1279)

Mongols capture Beijing (1215)
Marco Polo's journeys in
* China (1271–92)*
Celadon porcelain

Earliest European windmills (1180)
First tea imports (1191)
Leprosy imported to Europe
* by Crusaders (1230)*
Paris University founded (1250)
* followed by Oxford (1263)*

253

Yuan (1279–1368)

Mongol rule in China
Kublai Khan (1214–94)
Drama flourished

Dante (1265–1321)
Black Death in Europe
* (1347–51)*

Ming (1368–1644)

Admiral Zheng He (1371–1433)
* makes extensive voyages of*
* exploration to Arabia*
First Dalai Lama (1447)
First Portuguese explorers
* reach Guangdong (1514)*
First British trade with
* Hangzhou (1637)*

Protecting the Wall for posterity

Gutenberg prints the first book
* in Europe (1450)*
Columbus sails to the
* Americas (1492)*
Vasco da Gama sails around the
* Cape of Good Hope to India (1498)*
Luther's 59 Theses spark
* the Reformation (1517)*
Cortes enters Mexico (1519)
Galileo's trial by the Inquisition (1633)

Chronological chart

Qing (1644–1912)

Opium Wars (1839–42) open
  ports to Western powers
Hong Kong ceded to
  Britain 'in perpetuity' (1842)
Taiping Rebellion (1850–64)
Boxer Rebellion (1900)
1st Sino-Japanese War (1904–05)
Boy emperor Puyi abdicates
  (February 1912) ending 2,000
  years of imperial rule in China

American Declaration of Independence
  (1776)
French Revolution (1789)
Marx (1818–83)
Communist Manifesto issued
  by Marx and Engels (1848)
Industrial Revolution begins in
  Britain (late 18th century)

The Republic of China (1911–49)

Sun Yatsen first president (1911)
Communist Party founded (1921)
With the death of Sun Yatsen
  (1925), Chiang Kaishek becomes
  nationalist leader
Massacre of communists in
  Shanghai (1927). Chiang Kaishek
  tries to drive communists
  from China by means of
  'Encirclement Campaigns' (1930)
Japan occupies Manchuria (1931)
Mao gathers the surviving
  communists to begin
  the Long March (1934–35)
War with Japan (1937–45)
Civil War (1946–49)
Chiang Kaishek and nationalists
  flee to Taiwan (1949)

World War I (1914–18)
Russian Revolution (1917)
Hitler becomes Chancellor
  of Germany (1933)
Wall Street Crash (1937)
Chamberlain's Munich Pact
  with Hitler (1938)
World War II (1939–45)
Yalta Agreement (1945)
Atom bombs dropped on Hiroshima
  and Nagasaki; Japan surrenders
  (August 1945)
United Nations created out of the
  old League of Nations with
  New York as its permanent
  headquarters (1945)
Indian independence and creation of
  Pakistan (1947)

People's Republic of China (1949 to the present)

First Five-Year Plan (1953–57)
Great Leap Forward (1958)
Tibetan uprising (1959)
Sino-Indian Border War (1962)
Cultural Revolution launched (1966)
Mao dies. Gang of Four
  arrested (1976)
Democracy movement (1978–79)
Open-door policy launched (1982)
Sino-British agreement on the
  future of Hong Kong (1984)
Hu Yaobang forced to resign in
  aftermath of student
  demonstrations (1987)
Fourteenth Party Congress endorses
  concept of a socialist market economy
Tiananmen Square massacre (1989)
Death of Deng Xiaoping (1997)
Hong Kong reverts to China (1997)
President Jiang Zemin visits USA
  (1997)
Macau reverts to China (1999)
Beijing to host Olympics Games (2008)

Korean War (1950–53)
Death of Stalin (1953)
Kennedy assassinated (1963)
Vietnam War (1964–75)
Martin Luther King assassinated
  (1968)
Student riots in Paris, and Prague
  Spring ends in the invasion of
  Czechoslovakia by Russian tanks
  (1968)
First Moon landing (1969)
President Nixon visits China
  and establishes diplomatic
  relations (1972)
Mikhail Gorbachev becomes Soviet
  head of state (1988), introduces
  glasnost (openness) and presides
  over the collapse of communism
  in Europe (1989–91)
Chinese embassy in Belgrade accidentally
  bombed by US (1999)
New York's World Trade Center attacked
  (2001)

Travel Facts

Passengers getting organized outside Shanghai railway station

Arriving and departing

By air Most visitors begin their trip to China in either Beijing or Hong Kong. There are direct flights from all over the world both on Air China and other major national carriers to Beijing. All China's major cities are served by direct flights from Hong Kong either on Air China or via the Hong Kong carriers Dragonair and Cathay Pacific. Some cities, for example Shanghai, Guangzhou, Kunming, Xiamen, Dalian and Ürümqi, are served by direct flights from other countries.

By train You can enter by train either via Siberia and Mongolia, or through Hong Kong. The former is time-consuming (about six days from Moscow to Beijing) but fascinating; the journey from Hong Kong to Guangzhou takes under three hours.

Commuters on the Beijing subway

There is also a train link between Alma Ata (Kazakhstan) and Ürümqi, in Xinjiang. There is also a service from Vietnam, and one linking Hong Kong with Beijing. A new train service links Golmud in Qinghai with Tibet.

By boat The growth of China's aviation industry has sounded the death knell for virtually all long-distance passenger ship services in China. Ferry links still operate on short routes. Catamaran, ferry and hovercraft services link Hong Kong and Guangzhou.

Customs
Four hundred cigarettes and 2L of liquor are permitted, plus limitless cash or securities. Pornographic items are forbidden. Visitors are recommended to take no more than one Bible into China. You will be required to fill in a customs declaration form that must be retained until departure.

The import of wildlife souvenirs sourced from rare or endangered species may be either illegal or require a special permit. Before purchase you should check regulations.

Departing
A departure tax is now included in the flight ticket price. X-ray machines are widespread and are advertised as film-safe.

Entry requirements

Entering the country is straight-forward provided visas are obtained in advance. Upon arrival in China, a simple health form and a landing card (unnecessary for people on group visas) will have to be completed. Currency declaration forms are no longer required. In most ports of entry there will be a red and green customs channel, but usually only a few luggage carts. Taxis are freely available, but there are few tourist information facilities except at Beijing airport.

Travel insurance

You are strongly advised to obtain travel insurance sufficiently comprehensive to cover repatriation in the event of serious illness and, ideally, to cover delays.

Visas

If you are a member of a group, you will probably travel on a group visa organized on your behalf by the tour company and held by the group leader. An individual visa is easily obtained and usually valid for 30 days' travel in China, but easily extended at Public Security Bureau offices in China. To obtain a Chinese visa, contact the consular section of your nearest Chinese embassy; the procedure requires completion of a simple form, a full passport (which must have at least two blank pages and six months' validity) and one recent passport-size photograph. Three working days to process the visa are usually required, although visas can be rushed through for an extra fee and on the presentation of airline tickets.

Hong Kong does not require a Chinese visa. Visas for the mainland, including 90-day or 6-month visas, can be easily obtained either from **CITS** (6/F Tower 2, South Seas Centre, 75 Mody Road, Tsimshatsui, Kowloon) or directly from the visa office of the Hong Kong Immigration Department of the People's Republic of China at 7 Gloucester Road, Wanchai.

Visitors often ask if they can have their passports stamped upon entering or leaving China, but the immigration officers will exhibit a marked reluctance to do so unless the passport contains an individual visa.

Individual tourists wishing to visit Tibet must possess a Tibet Tourism Bureau (TTB) Permit. Travel agents in Chengdu and Beijing can arrange these. A specific itinerary is required for a permit to be issued. Allow at least 5–7 days for the permit to be issued. Check before setting off, or with Tibet Tourism Bureau offices (10 Renmin Beilu, Chengdu; tel: 028 8555 1719 and Room MO21 Poly Plaza, 14 Dongzhimennanjie, Beijing; tel: 8447 7899).

A typical hallway in an apartment block, Shanghai

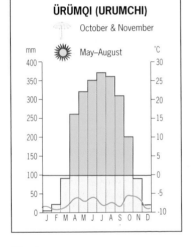

Essential facts

When to go

China is a vast country with wide-ranging climatic conditions, so decide about when to go based on the regions your trip will cover.

Standard tours usually take in a little of everywhere, so the most comfortable seasons are late spring (May) or early autumn (September to early October). There are other considerations, however: blossom in the north appears in April, orchids in the south bloom in February.

Some national holidays (see opposite) may be attractions or deterrents. Bear in mind that hotels at these times can be heavily booked.

Climate

Broadly speaking, summers (late May to August) are extremely hot everywhere (except at high altitude, as in Tibet) and very humid in the south. Winters vary from one part of China to another. Central China, along the Yangtze, has a short, cold winter (late November to mid-March) while the regions to the north are very cold and, in Beijing and the north, well below freezing. South of the Yangtze temperatures rarely fall below freezing, but vary from cool to warm; in the lowland southwest, winters are very warm. The rainy season runs from May to August. In April, sandstorms sometimes occur in Beijing and Inner Mongolia.

National holidays

China has nine national holidays: New Year's Day (1 January); Chinese New Year or Spring Festival (the first day of the lunar calendar, usually February), which lasts between three days and a week, when everything closes (an added irritation is the popular pastime of exploding terrifyingly loud firecrackers; this has been banned in major cities but the ban is widely ignored); International Working Women's Day (8 March); International Labour Day (1 May); Youth Day (4 May); Children's Day (1 June); Communist Party Anniversary Day (1 July); People's Liberation Army Day (1 August); National Day (1 October, with an etxra day).

Other festivals include the Lantern Festival on the 15th day of the first lunar month; the Dragon Boat Festival on the 5th day of the 5th lunar month; and the Mid-Autumn Festival on the 15th day of the 8th lunar month.

Time differences

China is 8 hours ahead of GMT, 13 hours ahead of New York, and 2 hours behind Melbourne. China briefly observed daylight saving time between 1986 and 1991 but maintains the same time throughout the year now.

Clocks throughout China are set according to Beijing time, which means, given the size of the country, that sunrise and sunset can occur at peculiar hours.

Roads like this (in Beijing) remain an essentially urban phenomenon

Money matters

Previously, there were two types of money—one for locals, called Renminbi (RMB), and another for foreigners which came in the form of Foreign Exchange Certificates or FECs. Thankfully this system no longer exists and everybody now uses the national currency, the *yuan* or RMB, divided into 100 *fen*. Ten *fen* are called a *mao* or *jiao*. Exchange rates vary from day to day but little, if at all, from place to place. When you buy *yuan*, keep the receipts in case you need to re-exchange when you leave China (although you are allowed to return no more than 50 per cent of what you have bought). Traveller's cheques and all major currencies are acceptable, and many larger shops are happy to accept US dollars directly. Credit cards can be used in all major hotels and in some shops.

Foreigners may sometimes pay more than locals for hospital care, hotels and museums.

China's police, ever present

Emergencies

Crime and the police

China used to be one of the safest places in the world for foreign visitors. It remains very safe compared to almost everywhere else, but you are advised to take sensible precautions:

• keep valuables in safe boxes where available;
• do not leave valuables in hotel rooms;
• conceal money and valuables when out on the streets;
• lock your suitcases.

Violent crime against foreigners is rare, but reports of muggings may indicate that this is changing.

Unless the crime is serious enough to reflect badly on China, swift action is unlikely. None the less, report cases of theft to the police or the nearest Foreign Affairs branch of the Public Security Bureau for insurance purposes.

If you feel a serious crime is being ignored, you should contact your embassy or consulate.

Emergency telephone numbers

The emergency travel assistance number of CITS is Beijing (010) 8511 8522 or 8522 8888.
Other emergency numbers are:
  Police 110;
  Fire 119;
  Ambulance 120

Embassies and consulates

In Beijing

Australia: 21 Dongzhimenwai Dajie
  (tel: 010 5140 4111)
Canada: 19 Dongzhimenwai Dajie
  (tel: 010 6532 3536)
Ireland: 3 Ritan Donglu
  (tel: 010 6532 2691)
New Zealand: 1 Ritan Donger Jie
  (tel: 010 6532 2731)
United Kingdom: 11 Guanghua Lu,
  Jianguomenwai (tel: 010 5192 4000)
United States: 3 Xiushui Beijie,
  Jianguomenwai (tel: 010 6532 3431)

In Guangzhou (Canton)

Australia: Main Building, GITIC Plaza,
  339 Huanshi Donglu (tel: 020 8335 0909)
Canada: Room 801, China Hotel
  (tel: 8666 0569)
France: Room 810, GITIC Plaza,
  339 Huanshi Donglu (tel: 8330 3405)
Japan: Garden Hotel Tower,
  368 Huanshi Donglu (tel: 8334 3090)
Thailand: 2/F, Garden Hotel,
  368 Huanshi Donglu (tel: 8385 8988)
United States: White Swan Hotel,
  1 Shamian Nanjie, Shamian Island
  (tel: 8121 8000)
Vietnam: 2/F, Landmark Hotel,
  Haizhu Square, 8 Qiao Guang Road
  (tel: 8330 5910)

In Shanghai

Australia: Rm 401, Shanghai Centre,
  1376 Nanjing Xilu (tel: 021 6279 8098)
Canada: West Tower, Shanghai Centre,

1376 Nanjing Xilu (tel: 6279 8400)
France: 21–23 Floor, Qihua Tower,
1375 Huaihai Zhonglu
(tel: 6437 7414)
United Kingdom: Rm 301, Shanghai
Centre, 1376 Nanjing Xilu
(tel: 6279 7650)
United States: 1469 Huaihai Zhonglu
(tel: 6433 6880)

Lost property (*shiwu zhaolingchu*)

If you lose anything, inform your
hotel—there is every chance that it will
have been handed in to Reception.

If credit cards or traveller's cheques
have been stolen, inform the issuer as
soon as possible. If in doubt contact
your embassy.

Health, vaccinations and pharmacies

Health Considering its comparative
poverty and its climatic extremes,
China is a remarkably healthy country.
In the main tourist areas, the Chinese
are punctilious about hygiene, particularly where food and drink are served.

Tap water is not safe, but any water
you are offered to drink will almost
certainly have been boiled, and mineral
water is widely available. Food ingredients are always fresh and cooked or
cleaned thoroughly. But stomach
upsets are possible, so take a
proprietary medicine with you.

More common ailments are sore
throats and chest colds. A steady supply of liquids is essential to prevent
dehydration in the summer heat.

Hospital care is, on the whole,
reasonable, and in major cities
foreigners receive special attention
(for special prices). Usually payment
is made after treatment, but some
hospitals may ask for payment in
advance; check the cost beforehand.

Traditional Chinese medicine can be
efficacious, but requires patience. For
minor ailments, hotels often have
their own clinics. For information on
Beijing, see page 79.

Vaccinations Currently no
vaccinations are required, but you
should check with your doctor for up-
to-date information. Tetanus and
typhoid injections are essential for
travel anywhere, and it is advisable to
consider vaccinations against rabies
and hepatitis. There is a risk of malaria
in south China in the remoter areas;
check on the situation before you go.

Pharmacies Pharmacies in the big
cities are well stocked with both
Western and Chinese drugs. Without
a prescription, however, it will be
difficult to explain what you want, so if
you are already taking a course of pre-
scribed drugs, bring your own supply.

Women are advised to stock up on
personal hygiene items if visiting
remoter areas.

*The British Embassy, Beijing. Most of
the embassies are grouped together in an
area close to the Friendship Store*

261

Getting around

Car rental

It is possible to rent cars in Hong Kong, Macau and several mainland cities including Beijing and Shanghai. However, to rent a car on the mainland requires a temporary Chinese driver's licence, obtainable from the local Public Security Bureau if you have a residency permit valid for at least three months. You also need to pass an exam and take a medical. Driving conditions are bad and self-drive can't really be recommended. Cars with drivers may be hired by the day or week in major cities—details can be obtained through CITS, your hotel or rental companies such as Avis, which now operate in China.

Traffic tips

Roads and traffic regulations generally aid pedestrians and bicycles, but this becomes less the case as traffic increases. Urban traffic moves very slowly, and learning to negotiate it needs special skills. Patience is vital

Maglev train at Pudong, Shanghai— part of China's modern rail network

and so is the ability to thread your way through streams of bicycles, handcarts, cars, trucks and donkey- and horse-drawn carts.

On the whole people are law-abiding road-users. Stiff on-the-spot fines are dishes out to those caught speeding by police radar traps. Chinese roads are very noisy, as horns are honked all the time for seemingly any reason.

Night drivers often dispense with headlights, merely using full-beam from time to time to warn on-coming vehicles, a rather unnerving habit.

Drive on the right-hand side of the road. Most cities allow right turns on red lights.

Public transport

Domestic flights China's size means that the principal methods of getting from place to place are train and plane, although its expressway road network is growing fast. Chinese airlines did not enjoy a good reputation in the past, thanks to delays, old aircraft and a poor safety record. That has changed. After being broken up into a series of regional carriers, supposedly to increase efficiency, they have now consolidated into three main airline groups—Air China, China Eastern and China Southern.

Delays are much less frequent, fleets comprise the latest Boeing and Airbus planes and airports across China have been modernized, incorporating the latest facilities and check-in security procedures. Flying in China is now as painless an experience as anywhere in the West or other developed parts of Asia. If anything, Chinese airlines are more efficient, and delays are rare unless caused by bad weather.

Domestic air travel is growing by about 15 per cent a year. Flight tickets are reasonably priced, but prices are rising. Main routes are very busy, especially at holiday times, and need to be reserved well in advance through agencies such as CITS or direct from airlines. Airport tax is payable for all flights and is now included in the ticket price. All flights are non-smoking. Hand luggage is limited to one small item but passengers often ignore this and take

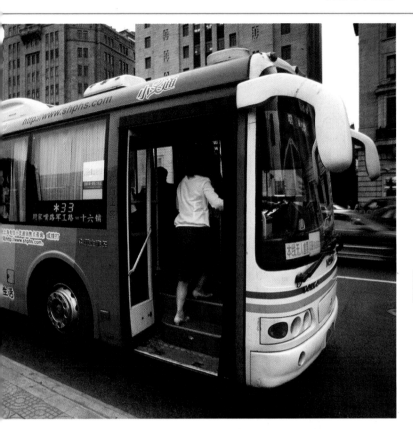

impossibly large bags on board with them. Flights are announced in English as well as Chinese.

Trains The train system in China is very good, and is being improved and extended. Tickets, obtainable through CITS and other agents or directly from stations, are reasonably priced and the trains generally dependable. There are two classes, so-called 'soft' and 'hard', both of which are staffed by attendants. Pullman cars exist (wooden benches in hard class, upholstered seats in soft) but, because of the distances involved, most rolling stock is made up of sleeping-cars.

A hard-class sleeping-car (*yingwoche*) has a series of alcoves filled with triple-tiered, wooden-slat bunks with thin mattresses and no bedding. There will be a basic bathroom at one end.

A soft-class sleeping-car

City bus on the Bund, Shanghai

(*ruanwoche*) is divided into compartments, each containing four bunks with bedding and flasks filled with hot water. There will be a bathroom at each end of the car, one Western, one Eastern. Very few cars are air-conditioned; most have fans. Long-distance trains have dining cars, often serving meals of surprisingly high quality.

Trains are graded according to speed at which they travel: *tekuai* is very fast, *zhikuai* is fast and *kuaike* reasonably fast.

Buses Buses are the life-blood of towns and cities. The cheapest form of travel, they are also the least comfortable. Urban buses are frequently impossibly crowded and rarely air-conditioned; long-distance buses are rather old-fashioned, although newer buses operate non-stop on some routes. Some cities have brought in new buses, and Beijing has pledged all its inner-city buses will run on natural gas by the 2008 Olympics. Buy tickets for urban buses on board; for long-distance buses, buy in advance from the bus station. There is little room for luggage inside—it will frequently go on the roof.

Above: pedicab driver
Below: transport, Chengdu-style

Taxis Taxis are easy to hire in most cities and can generally be hailed on the street. Most drivers use the meter; if a reminder to use it is greeted with disdain, agree to a price before you start. There are several categories of taxi, both state-owned and private. Basically, the smaller the taxi the cheaper the fare. (See also page 79).

Bicycles
Bicycles (*zixingche*) are widely used and can be hired at little cost in most cities from hotels or from specialist outlets. Check the condition of the bicycle and observe how the traffic functions—joining it unprepared can be an unnerving experience. Wayside repairs can often easily be effected by mechanics who ply their trade on the pavements.

Student and youth travel
The China Youth Travel Service (23-B Dongjiaominxiang, Beijing 100006; tel: 6513 0333) is the branch of CITS that deals in travel arrangements for students. Tour operators that specialize in travel to China can often make arrangements for younger people, especially for groups of children or students, and it is often possible to make arrangements to visit institutions that may be of particular interest. Few concessions are made to youth, though, particularly when it comes to money.

Other information

Camping
There are no opportunities for camping in the casual way that is taken for granted in many other countries. Even if the authorities permitted it, bedding down at the side of the road with a small tent would prove difficult because there is precious little land that is not cultivated, except in the wide empty provinces in the fringe areas of China. Camping is possible only when organized through CITS or one of its branches, and there are no organized campsites.

There are no opportunities for renting a house, unless you happen to know a foreign resident who is vacating his or her home.

Visitors with disabilities
Despite a general improvement in many services and facilities, China's provision for dealing with visitors with disabilities is almost non-existent. In general, public transport, institutions and Chinese towns lack facilities for visitors with disabilities, and although modern hotels are well equipped, most towns have crowded streets and steps to negotiate. Airlines and airports have made some efforts to improve their facilities, and wheelchairs can be found when necessary.

Opening times
Banks, offices, government departments and public security bureaus Monday to Friday, usually 8–5. Most close for at least one hour at lunchtime, usually from noon. Banks open Saturdays, 8–11.30am.

Shops Usually remain open seven days a week, generally 9–7.

Monuments and museums Aside from the larger ones, like the Forbidden City, most often close for lunch and shut finally at 5pm. Many are open seven days a week; those that are not usually close on a Monday.

Restaurants and bars These are beginning to stay open later at night, and although at one time it was impossible to eat after 8pm, now you can find a meal at most times of the day. Small open-air restaurant kiosks often stay open until after midnight and many bars open until 1 or 2am.

Places of worship
Buddhists will have no trouble finding places of worship since temples reopened all over China after the Cultural Revolution. They are open all day, every day.

For Muslims, there is usually at least one mosque in every major city.

There are currently no synagogues in China. In theory Christian worship, still subject to persecution, is feasible in most large cities (and in some smaller ones), but churches often open only for services, usually at difficult hours.

Lavatories (*cesuo*)
Where they exist, public lavatories in China are usually dreadful, even in large cities. You are advised to do your utmost to avoid them, but when desperate enter armed with

your own toilet paper at the very least. Be prepared for a hole in the ground, no privacy, and a lack of accuracy by other users. Do not expect any washing facilities (except in a few cases where there is an attendant, to whom you will be required to pay a small fee). In restaurants or places that cater for foreigners, the standard is higher, though toilet paper may be absent here, too.

Photography
In many ways China is a photographer's dream. Despite the general absence of brilliant hues, the country is immensely photogenic because so much happens on the streets or in the fields and because the countryside is uniquely beautiful. Furthermore, people are oblivious to cameras on the whole,

Computing in the 21st century: the abacus is still widely used

although you should make sure that the privacy of those who do object is respected.

Photography is forbidden in most museums and archaeological sites (notably the main pit of the Terracotta Warriors), but some institutions permit it on payment of a fee, in advance, with a stiff fine for those who do not comply.

Print film is widely available, black and white or slide film much less so. Digital camera memory cards can be found everywhere but can be expensive. Video film can be found but not always readily. Security X-ray machines on mainland China and at Hong Kong airport are film-safe.

As the atmosphere in China is often hazy, filters are advisable.

Electricity
Electricity is 220 volts, 50 cycles AC. Plugs are usually two-prong, set at an angle to each other, and adaptors can come in handy.

Etiquette and local customs

Getting along with the Chinese One of the purposes of a visit to China is to see and try to understand a culture that is, at least superficially, contrary to everything taken for granted at home. The Chinese people are a vital, fascinating part of the experience. The word often used to describe the Chinese is 'inscrutable', and while it is certainly true that the Chinese give few emotional messages, this is not to say that they are unfathomable or that foreigners cannot empathize with them.

The Chinese do not display emotion and feelings in public and find plain-speaking unnerving. Often, therefore, decisions that would be made instantly elsewhere are accompanied by long preambles and detailed, if futile, consultations. This demands patience and politeness from those on the outside, for anger is seen as weakness.

Many Chinese are quick to appreciate humorous situations, but usually not sexual or political subjects. Skimpy clothing, while sometimes worn by the more daring among the nation's youth, is frowned upon on the whole.

The lack of information or the omission of relevant facts that may be obvious to the Chinese host but not to his visitor can be particularly irritating to the foreigner. It is important, therefore, to check all arrangements as unobtrusively as possible.

Foreign visitors may attract attention, especially in the country, which can be unsettling but is nothing more than harmless curiosity. Privacy, it must be remembered, is an alien notion to the Chinese.

Tipping Despite official disapproval, tipping is no longer an offence; indeed it is now expected by tourist guides, who prefer money—preferably American dollars—to any well-intentioned gift. Hotel porters will usually happily accept a tip, and so will taxi drivers although it is not necessarily expected. Tips are not usually expected in restaurants, except in some of the top establishments.

267

CONVERSION CHARTS

FROM	TO	MULTIPLY BY
Inches	Centimetres	2.54
Centimetres	Inches	0.3937
Feet	Metres	0.3048
Metres	Feet	3.2810
Yards	Metres	0.9144
Metres	Yards	1.0940
Miles	Kilometres	1.6090
Kilometres	Miles	0.6214
Acres	Hectares	0.4047
Hectares	Acres	2.4710
Gallons	Litres	4.5460
Litres	Gallons	0.2200
Ounces	Grams	28.35
Grams	Ounces	0.0353
Pounds	Grams	453.6
Grams	Pounds	0.0022
Pounds	Kilograms	0.4536
Kilograms	Pounds	2.205
Tons	Tonnes	1.0160
Tonnes	Tons	0.9842

MEN'S SUITS							
UK	36	38	40	42	44	46	48
Rest of Europe	46	48	50	52	54	56	58
US	36	38	40	42	44	46	48

DRESS SIZES						
UK	8	10	12	14	16	18
France	36	38	40	42	44	46
Italy	38	40	42	44	46	48
Rest of Europe	34	36	38	40	42	44
US	6	8	10	12	14	16

MEN'S SHIRTS							
UK	14	14.5	15	15.5	16	16.5	17
Rest of Europe	36	37	38	39/40	41	42	43
US	14	14.5	15	15.5	16	16.5	17

MEN'S SHOES						
UK	7	7.5	8.5	9.5	10.5	11
Rest of Europe	41	42	43	44	45	46
US	8	8.5	9.5	10.5	11.5	12

WOMEN'S SHOES						
UK	4.5	5	5.5	6	6.5	7
Rest of Europe	38	38	39	39	40	41
US	6	6.5	7	7.5	8	8.5

Tourism is now highly developed in some areas

Tourist Offices

China has very few tourist information offices, as most people travel in tour groups. The China International Travel Service (CITS, the state-run travel service) will often help even when you are not organizing your trip through them; otherwise, try an independent agent.

CITS main offices and other travel services

Beijing: Beijing Tourism Group, 28 Jianguomenwai Dajie (tel: 010 6515 8562; fax: 010 6515 86063); China Travel Service (CTS), 2, Belsanhuan Dong Lu, Beijing 100028 (tel: 6462 2288; fax: 6461 2576)
Changchun: CITS, 14 Xinmin Dajie (tel: 0431 690 9011)
Changsha: 9 Wuyi Dadao (tel: 0731 228 0439)
Chengdu: 65 Renmin Nan Lu (tel: 023 6363 3805)
Chongqing: 120 Zaozilanya Street, Yu Zhong District (tel: 023 6363 3805)
Dalian: 1 Chantong Jie (tel: 0411 8368 7843)
Fuzhou: 6th Floor, Yifada Plaza, 298 Hudong Road (tel: 0591 8787 7778)
Guangzhou (Canton): Guangdong CITS 618 Jiefang Beilu (tel: 020 2201 3401; fax: 020 8666 8048)

Guangdong CTS, 10 Qiaoguang Lu, Guangzhou 6510115, Guangdong (tel: 020 8333 6888; fax: 020 8333 6625)
Guilin: 11 Binjiang Lu, Guilin (tel: 282 7254)
Haikou: Qiongyuan Hotel, 38 Bailong Nanlu (tel: 0898 6538 1526)
Hangzhou: 1 Beishan Lu (tel: 0571 8515 2888)
Harbin: 95–1 Zhongshan Lu (tel: 230 2476)
Jinan: CITS, 20-1 Jiefang Lu, 6th Floor, Guohua Plaza (tel: 0531 8296 0760)
Kunming: 218 Huancheng Nan Lu (tel: 0871 356 6726)
Lanzhou: Luyou Bldg, 11th Floor, 2 Nongmin Street (tel: 0931 883 5566)
Lhasa: Beijing Zhonglu (tel: 0891 683 2980)
Nanchang: 368 Bayi Dadao (tel: 0791 627 9415)
Nanjing: 202–1 Zhongshan Beilu (tel: 025 8353 8660)
Nanning: 40 Xinmin Lu (tel: 0771 2835 8546)
Shanghai: 1277 Beijing Xilu (tel: 021 6289 8899); Shanghai Jinjiang Tours Ltd, 191 Changle Lu (tel: 021 6466 2828)
Tourist Information (tel: 021 6439 0630)
Hongqiao Airport (tel: 6268 8899)
Shenyang: 113 South Huanghe Nan Dajie, Huangu District (tel: 024 8612 1870)
Suzhou: 94 Siqian Jie (tel: 0512 6520 7581)

Taiyuan: 38 Pingyuan Lu (tel: 0351 723 8509)
Tianjin: 22 Youyi Lu (tel: 022 2810 9988)
Ürümqi: 38 Xinhua Nanlu (tel: 0991 282 1428)
Wuhan: 909 Zhongshan Dadao (tel: 027 8578 4125)
Wuxi: 18 Zhongshan Lu (tel: 0510 8270 5369)
Xiamen: 708 Liangian Xilu (tel: 0592 223 1259)
Xi'an: 48 Changan Bei Lu, Xi'an (tel: 029 8522 7331; fax: 8526 1454)
Xining: 156 Huanghe Lu (tel: 0971 614 3950)
Yinchuan: 375 Beijing Donglu (tel: 0951 671 9792)
Zhengzhou: 16th Floor, Yubo Bldg, West Tower, No 1 Nongye Road (tel: 0371 6585 2339)

The China National Tourism Administration has 15 overseas tourist offices:
China National Tourist Office
Australia: 19th Floor, 44 Market Street, Sydney, NSW 2000 (tel: 61 2 9299 4057; fax: 61 2 9290 1958)
Canada: 480 University Avenue, Suite 806, Toronto, Ontario M5G 1V2 (tel: 1 416 499 6636; fax: 1 416 599 6382)

Chinese people travel around China in greater numbers today

France: 15 Rue De Berri, 75008, Paris (tel: 33 1 56591010; fax: 33 1 53753288)
Germany: Ilkenhansstrasse 6, 60433 Frankfurt (tel: 49 69 520135; fax 49 69 528490)
Japan: 4F OCAT Building, 1-4-1 Minatomachi, Nanwa-ku, Osaka 556, (tel: 81 6 6635 3280; fax: 81 6 6635 3288)
Air China Building, 2–5–2 Toranomon Minato-Ku, Tokyo 105 (tel: 81 3 3591 8686; fax: 81 3 3591 6886)
Nepal: PO Box 3639, Heritage Plaza II, Kamaladi, Kathmandu (tel: 977 1 255936; fax: 977 1 267695)
Singapore: 7 Temasek Boulevard, No. 12–02, Suntec Tower One, Singapore 038987 (tel: 65 337 2220; fax: 65 338 0777)
South Korea: (100 706) 15F Daeyongak Bldg, 25 5, 1-Ka, Chungmu-ro, Chung-ku, Seoul (tel: 82 2 773 0393; fax: 82 2 757 3210)
Spain: Gran Via 88, Grupo 2, Planta 16, 28013 Madrid (tel: 34 91 548 0011; fax: 34 91 548 0597)
Switzerland: Genfer Strasse 21, CH-8002 Zurich (tel: 41 1 201 8877; fax: 41 1 201 8878)
UK: 4 Glentworth Street, London NW1 5PG (tel: 44 20 7935 9787; fax: 44 20 7487 5842)
USA: 550 North Brand Boulevard, Suite 910, Glendale, CA 91203 (tel: 1 818 545 7507; fax: 1 818 545 7506)
Suite 6413, Empire State Building,

Newspapers for sale at a newsstand in Shanghai

350 Fifth Avenue, New York, NY 10118 (tel: 1 212 760 8218; fax: 1 212 760 8809)
Asia Tourism Exchange Centre Ltd Hong Kong: 13th Floor, Tower A, 14 Xinwenhua Centre, Science Museum Road, Hong Kong (tel: 852 2732 5801; fax: 852 2721 7154)

Communications

The media
Freedom of the press does not yet exist in China. Foreign observers trying to establish political trends, notoriously difficult in China, have learned to read the newspapers for clues, since they tend to act as subtle mouthpieces for the government.

However, the English-language newspaper, the *China Daily*, reads quite well and is not overtly biased, and international magazines such as the *Economist* are easily available in the major cities, although there is still a tendency to cut out articles considered offensive to the Chinese Government.

Although national television is similarly restricted, the CNN and BBC world services are received uncensored in hotels across China. The same is also true of radio services.

The internet is accessible but can be slow and is subject to censorship.

Post offices
China's postal service is extremely efficient. It is easiest to buy stamps for letters and postcards from your hotel. The airmail rate for postcards is slightly less than for letters.

For insured postage, express mail and other services, you will usually have to go to public post offices, which are open from 8 to 7.

Telephone (*dianhua*)
The international telephone system is surprisingly good, and the national service is improving as the system is gradually updated. Local calls are usually free, although hotels often levy a charge. Some public phones take coins, but most payphones now use cards. An IC card allows you to call within the city where you bought the card. For long-distance calls, you need an IP card. Both come in different denominations and are widely available. Small shops often have phones you can use, especially in popular tourist areas. There is often a minimum charge for international calls and faxes, even when there is no answer. Many hotels now boast business centres with fax machines, internet and other office services.

The Chinese language

The national language is Mandarin (*putonghua*), based on the Beijing dialect. Although there are a vast number of other dialects, most people understand *putonghua,* and all Chinese speakers share the same written language. A surprisingly large number of people know a smattering of English. However, knowledge of some basic spoken Chinese is useful as well as courteous.

Each Chinese character represents a single-syllable sound, which in turn is converted into the Latin alphabet by the process of 'romanization'. The official romanization system is *pinyin*, used throughout China. In addition, syllables are given 'tone' values in order to differentiate between several characters that have the same romanization but radically different meanings—thus the syllable *ma* can mean 'mother', 'horse', 'hemp' or 'scold' depending on which tone is used.

Putonghua has four tones, indicated by the following symbols:

- ˉ 1st tone: high, level
- ´ 2nd tone: starting lowish and rising
- ˇ 3rd tone: starting low, falling then rising
- ` 4th tone: starting high and falling.

Pinyin pronunciation guide

a as in car
b as in back
c when an initial consonant is a 'ts' sound as in bits
d as in doll
e as in her
f as in fat
g as in go
h as in house
i is an 'ee' sound as in feet unless preceded by c, ch, r, s, sh, z, zh, when it becomes 'e' as in her
j is like the g in gin
k as in kit
l as in lot
m as in man
n as in ran
o as in ford
p as in pin
q is 'ch' as in chin
r as in rum
s as in simple; sh as in shut
t as in time
u is 'oo' as in cool
w as in wade
x is like the 'sh' in sheep but with more emphasis on the s
y as in yoyo
z is a 'ds' sound as in lids; zh is a 'j' sound as in jam.

Geographic legend

This list of geographical terms may be useful when reading maps

bandao	peninsula
bei	north
co	lake
da	great, greater
dajie	road, street
dao	island
ding	mountain, peak
dong	east
feng	mount, peak
gang	harbour
gaoyuan	plateau
guan	pass
hai	lake, sea
haixia	strait, channel
he	river
hu	lake
jiang	river
jiao	cape
jie	road, street
kou	estuary, river mouth
la	pass (in Tibetan)
ling	mountain, range
lu	road, street
nan	south
nur	lake, salt lake (in Mongolian)
pao	lake
pendi	basin
qu	canal
qundao	archipelago, islands
ringco	lake
shamo	desert
shan	mountain, range
shan kou	pass
shi	municipality
tagh	mountains
wan	gulf, bay
xi	west
xiao	lesser, little
yanchi	salt lake
yumco	lake
yunhe	canal
zangbo	river (in Tibetan)

271

Numerals

English	Pinyin	Chinese
1	yī	一
2	èr	二
3	sān	三
4	sì	四
5	wŭ	五
6	liù	六
7	qī	七
8	bā	八
9	jiŭ	九
10	shí	十
11	shí yī (10+1)	十一
12	shí èr	十二
13	shí sān	十三
20	èr shí	二十
21	èr shí yī (2x10+1)	二十一
100	(yī) băi	一百
101	yī băi yī	一百一
1000	(yī) qīan	(一) 千
10,000	(yī) wàn	(一) 万

Useful words and phrases

English Pinyin	Chinese
hello/how are you? ní hăo/ní hăo ma?	你好?/你好吗?
goodbye zài jiàn	再见
thank you xiè xiè	谢谢
good/OK hăo	好
very good hén hăo	很好
not good/bad bù hăo	不好
cheers/to your health gān bēi	干杯
please qĭng	请
yes/have/ there is/are yŏu	有
no/have not/ there isn't/aren't (any) méi yŏu	没有
I wŏ	我
you (you, plural) nĭ/nĭmen	你/你们
he/she tā	他
we wŏmen	我们
be/is/yes shi	是
when? shĕn me shí hòu?	什么时候?
today jīn tiān	今天
tomorrow míng tiān	明天
yesterday zuó tiān	昨天
morning shàng wŭ/ or zăo shàng	上午/早上
evening wăn shàng	晚上
afternoon xià wŭ	下午
where?/ where is? zài ná lĭ / zài năr	哪里/在哪儿?

Calligrapher at work

At the post office/bank/stores

post office *yóu jú*	邮局
stamps *yóu piào*	邮票
postcards *míng xìn piàn*	明信片
airmail *háng kōng*	航空
phone call/ telephone *diàn huà*	电话
long-distance phone call *cháng tú diàn huà*	长途电话
bank/ Bank of China *yín háng/ zhōng guó yín háng*	银行/中国银行
money exchange *huàn qián*	换钱处

Travelling around

CITS (China International Travel Service) *zhōng guó lǚ xíng shè*	中国旅行社
can you take me to.....? *nǐ ké bù ké yǐ dài wǒ qù.....?*	你可不可 以带我去 ......?
(to) buy *mǎi*	买
ticket *piào*	票
taxi *chū zū qì chē*	出租汽车
airport/CAAC *fēi jī chǎng/ zhōng guó mín háng*	飞机场/ 中国民航
train/train station *huǒ chē/ huǒ chē zhàn*	火车/火车站

---

wait a minute *děng yī xià*	等一下
please give/bring me..... *qǐng géi wǒ......*	请给我
I would like..... *wó xiǎng yào.....*	我想要 ......
is there anyone who speaks English? *yǒu méi yǒu rén huì shuō yīng wén?*	有没有人 会说英文?
may I take a photograph? *wǒ ké yǐ zhào xiàng ma?*	我可以照相吗?
I understand *wǒ dǒng*	我懂
I don't understand *wǒ bù dǒng*	我不懂
please write (it down) *qíng xiě*	请写

At the hotel

hotel/guest house *fàndiàn/bīnguǎn*	饭店/宾馆
room *fáng jiān*	房间
how much is it? *duō shǎo qián?*	多少钱?
cheap/cheaper *pián yí/pián yí de*	便宜/便宜的
expensive/ too expensive *guì/tài guì*	贵/太贵

bus: public bus 公共汽车
gōng gòng qì chē

long-distance bus 长途汽车
cháng tú qì chē

bus station 汽车站
qì chē zhàn

boat 船
chuán

bicycle 自行车
zì xíng chē

In a restaurant

restaurant:
fàn guǎn 饭馆

fàn diàn 饭店

cān tīng 餐厅

do you have an 有没有英
English menu? 文菜单?
*yǒu méi yǒu
yīng wén cài dān?*

I am a vegetarian 我是素食者
wǒ shì sù shí zhě

May I have the bill? 请给我帐单
qǐng gěi wǒ zhàng dān

water/boiled water 水/开水
shuǐ/kāi shuǐ

coffee 咖啡
kā fēi

black tea 红茶
hei chá

jasmine tea 茉莉花茶
mò lì huā chá

beer 啤酒
pí jiǔ

soft drink 汽水
qì shuǐ

rice 饭
fàn

glass/cup 玻璃杯/杯子
bō lí bēi/bēi zi

274

table knife 餐刀
cān dāo

fork 叉子
chā zi

spoon 勺子
sháo zi

Medical emergencies

I feel ill 我不舒服
wǒ bù shū fú

doctor 医生
yī shēng

pharmacy 药店
yào diàn

Signs you will see in public places

entrance 入口
rén kǒu

exit 出口
chū kǒu

lavatory 厕所
cè suǒ

embassy 大使馆
dà shí guǎn

Countries

USA 美国
měi guó

Canada 加拿大
jiā ná dà

Australia 澳大利亚
ào dà lì yà

Great Britain 英国
yīng guó

France 法国
fǎ guó

Germany 德国
dé guó

Japan 日本
rì běn

China 中国
zhōng guó

Hotels & Restaurants

Hotels and Restaurants

HOTELS

Most significant tourist destinations in China have a wide range of hotels, from budget to five-star, international standard hotels. You will be spoiled for choice in large cities, but more rural choices have far more limited options. Service standards are reflected in the price, English skills vary enormously; restaurant options are generally good. Push for discounts in the low season.

It should be noted that the telephone system in China is undergoing constant modernization and this may result in changes in telephone and fax numbers.

Hotels have been graded as follows:
- Inexpensive hotels with private facilities (£)
- Good, comfortable hotels in medium range (££)
- The best hotels available (£££)

Beijing

Bamboo Garden Hotel (££)
24 Xiaoshiqiao Hutong tel: 5852 0088 fax: 5852 0066 www.bgh.com.ch
Attractively set mid-range hotel to the northwest of the Drum and Bell Towers and within reach of Beijing's more historic lanes and alleys.

Beijing Hotel (£££)
33 Raffles Avenue tel: 6513 7766 fax: 6513 7307 www.raffles.com
Century-old historic hotel left somewhat behind by the recent explosion in five-star hotels. Excellent location with additional wing.

China World Hotel (£££)
1 Jianguomenwai Dajie tel: 6505 2266 fax: 6505 3167 www.shangri-la.com
Large, modern business hotel in the China World Trade Centre with a wide choice of restaurants, east of the city's central districts.

Crowne Plaza (£££)
48 Wangfujing Dajie tel: 6513 3388 fax: 6513 2513 www.crowneplaza.com
A good-value hotel in a very central location. The hotel has a pool and several restaurants. A baby-sitting service is also available.

Far East Hotel (£)
90 Tieshuxie Jie tel: 5195 8811 fax: 6301 8233
Nicely located budget hotel in Beijing's *hutongs* near the antique shopping district of Liulichang.

Friendship Hotel (££)
1 Zhongguancun Nan Da Jie tel: 6849 8888 fax: 6849 8866
Old, sprawling Mao-era hotel with a certain sense of history; decent value and an excellent outdoor pool.

Grand Hotel Beijing (£££)
35 Dong Chang'an Avenue tel: 6513 0057 fax: 6513 0050 www.grandhotelbeijing.com
Superbly located, top-notch hotel just up the road from Tiananmen Square and the premier shopping district of Wangfujing, with rooms overlooking the Forbidden City.

Grand Hyatt Beijing (£££)
1 Dong Chang An Jie tel: 8518 1234 fax: 8518 0000 www.beijing.grand.hyatt.com
A blend of West and East in the city centre with more than 850 rooms, five restaurants, a fitness centre and China's largest hotel swimming pool.

Great Wall Sheraton (£££)
10 Dongsanhuan Beilu tel: 6590 5566 fax: 6590 5398
One of Beijing's first luxury hotels, reasonably near to the diplomatic zone. There are restaurants, adjacent Hard Rock Café, nightclub, health club, pool, auditorium and tennis courts.

Haoyuan Hotel (££)
53 Shijia Hutong tel: 6512 5557 fax: 6525 3179
Clean, restful hotel hidden away down a *hutong* (alley) to the east of Wangfujing. Very good value rooms for those on a budget.

Holiday Inn Lido (££/£££)
6 Jiangtai Lu tel: 6437 6688 fax: 6437 6237 www.beijin-lido.holidayinn.com
Massive and excellently equipped Holiday Inn—absolutely first rate. Not central, but handy for the airport. Great value for money. Tennis courts, indoor pools, decent nightclub.

Jianguo Hotel (££/£££)
5 Jianguomenwai Dajie tel: 6500 2233 fax: 6500 2871 www.hoteljianguo.com
Good-value and popular four-star hotel—one of Beijing's first joint-venture efforts. Business suite, pool and airport shuttle bus.

Jinghua Youth Hostel (£)
Xiluoyuan Nanli, Yongdingmenwai tel: 8781 2211 fax: 6721 1455
Very popular non-central backpacker haunt, and an excellent place to plan a trip around China. Bicycle hire, travel info, internet, trips to the Great Wall.

Kempinski Hotel (£££)
Lufthansa Centre, 50 Liangmaqiao Lu tel: 6465 3388 fax: 6465 3366 www.kempinski-beijing.com
Luxury hotel. Shoppers will find the adjacent Lufthansa shopping mall a marvel, and it's near the wining and dining Sanlitun district.

Leo Hostel (£)
Guang Ju Yuan, 52 Dazhalan Xi Jie tel: 6303 3318 www.leohostel.com
Great location on Beijing's famous market street, a short walk from Tiananmen Square. Its accommodation ranges from double rooms to dorms.

Lusongyuan Hotel (££)
22 Banchang Lane, Kuanjie tel: 6404 0436 fax: 6403 0418 www.the-silk-road.com
Picturesque, albeit a bit tatty, traditional walled courtyard hotel in Beijing's historic *hutong* district. Inexpensive, centrally located; bicycle hire.

Novotel Peace Hotel (££/£££)
3 Goldfish Lane (Jinyu Hutong), Wangfujing tel: 6512 8833 fax: 6512 6863 www.accorhotels-asia.com
Excellently positioned and inexpensive four-star hotel, just off the Wangfujing shopping district.

The Palace Peninsula (£££)
8 Goldfish Lane (Jinyu Hutong), Wangfujing tel: 8516 2888 fax: 6510 6311 www.beijing.peninsula.com
The Palace is a splendid hotel, centrally positioned just off Wangfujing and not far from the Forbidden City. Fine spread of restaurants, indoor pool, Rolls Royce limousine service.

Qianmen Jianguo Hotel (££/£££)
175 Yongan Lu tel: 6301 6688 fax: 6301 3883

Older 1950s hotel within striking distance of Liulichang and Tiananmen Square, with modernized and inexpensive rooms.

Qiaoyuan Hotel (£)
6 Kaiyang, Youanmenwai, Fentai
tel: 6301 2244 fax: 6303 0119
Long-running budget option to the southeast of Tiantan (Temple of Heaven) Park. Gets mixed reviews.

Shangri-La Hotel (£££)
29 Zizhuyuan Lu tel: 6841 2211 fax: 6841 8006 www.shangri-la.com
A superb link in the glittering chain of first rate Shangri-La hotels that cover China. Situated in northwest Beijing, this hotel has a pool, delicatessen and several fine restaurants.

Sino-Swiss Hotel (££/£££)
Capital Airport, Xiaotianzhu Nan Lu, Shunyi County tel: 6456 5588 fax: 6456 5678 www.sino-swisshotel.com
Four-star hotel at the airport, with tennis courts, swimming pool and business facilities.

Trader's Hotel (££/£££)
1 Jianguomenwai Dajie tel: 6505 2277 fax: 6505 0818 www.shangri-la.com
Decent, four-star business hotel in the east of town with a large spread of restaurants.

Youhao Hotel (£)
7 Houyuansi, Jiaodaokou tel: 6403 1114 fax: 6401 4603
Pleasantly located courtyard (*siheyuan*) hotel in the engaging *hutong* district southeast of the Drum and Bell Towers. Former residence of Chiang Kaishek.

Canton: see Guangzhou

Chengdu
Crowne Plaza Chengdu (£££)
31 Zongfu Lu tel: 028 8678 6666 fax: 8678 9789
Chengdu's premier hotel, this five-star extravaganza of a hotel is equipped with a dazzling lobby and a plethora of restaurants. Facilities include an indoor pool and health club.

Jinjiang Hotel (£££)
80 Renmin Nanlu er Duan tel: 8558 2222 fax: 8558 1849 www.jjhotel.com
The Jinjiang (by the Jinjiang River) is still one of Chengdu's best hotels. Bristling with first-rate facilities, including a medical clinic, an outdoor pool, tennis courts and a bowling alley.

Sheraton Chengdu (£££)
No. 15, Section 1, Renmin Zhong Lu tel: 8676 8999 fax: 8676 8888 www.sheraton.com
Set in the heart of Chengdu's central business district, this classy hotel has a four-floor lobby and one of Chengdu's best restaurants for Sichuan and Cantonese food—Celestial Court.

Chongqing
Huixian Hotel (£)
186 Minzu Lu tel: 023 6384 5101 fax: 6384 4234
Slap-bang in the middle of town, a presentable budget option with decent ticketing service. Very good value for money, not far from the Luohan Temple.

Yangtze Chongqing Holiday Inn (£££)
87 Nanping Xinjie tel: 62803380 fax: 62800884 www.ichotelsgroup.com

Competent four-star hotel with spacious rooms and decent restaurants. Not in an excellent location out of it all south of the Yangzi River, but equipped with the usual Holiday Inn reliability. Outdoor pool and health club.

Dali
Jinhua Hotel (£)
306 Fuxing Lu tel: 0872 267 3343/267 3845 fax: 267 3846
The hotel doesn't fit in with the overall character of Dali, but offers maybe marginally more in terms of comfort than most of the other outfits in town.

Dalian
Shangri-La Hotel (£££)
66 Renmin Lu tel: 0411 8252 5000 fax: 8252 5050 www.shangri-la.com
Well-placed on Renmin Lu not far from picturesque Zhongshan Square, the Shangri-La is a sophisticated and reliably excellent hotel. Tennis courts.

Dunhuang
The Silk Road Dunhuang Hotel (££/£££)
Dunyue Lu tel: 0937 888 2088 fax: 888 2086 www.the-silk-road.com
South of town in the sand dunes and well placed for excursions to Crescent Moon Lake, the palatial exterior is attractive and the setting fabulous. Not cheap, but worth the outlay. Camel riding tours.

Fuzhou
Hot Spring Hotel (££/£££)
218 Wusi Lu tel: 0591 8785 1818 fax: 8783 5150
Decent facilities, a pool and piped-in hot spring water in the bathrooms. In the north of town.

Guangzhou (Canton)
China Hotel (£££)
Liuhua Lu tel: 020 8666 6888 fax: 8667 7288
Magnificent hotel just west of Yuexiu Park. Built in the 1980s and well equipped. Outdoor pool, bowling alley, tennis courts. Restaurant options include a Four Seasons with dim sum breakfasts to die for.

Garden Hotel (£££)
368 Huanshi Donglu tel: 8333 8989 fax: 8335 0467 www.thegardenhotel.com.cn
Well located for the Friendship Store, airport and railway station. Magnificent five-star achievement, with first-rate facilities. Revolving restaurant.

Shamian Hotel (£)
52 Shamian Nanjie, Shamian Island tel: 8121 8822 fax: 8121 8628
This is a good budget option on the south of Shamian Island. Quite rudimentary and no credit cards, but clean and dependable.

White Swan Hotel (£££)
1 Shamian Nanjie, Shamian Island tel: 8188 6968 fax: 8186 1188 www.white-swanhotel.com
Excellent amenities and services. Sits resplendently on the attractive Shamian Island. Wide range of restaurants. Pearl River night cruises. Outdoor pools, tennis courts, squash courts.

Guilin
Dadi Hotel (£)
84 Zhongshan Nanlu tel: 0773 383 4943

Hotels and Restaurants

fax: 0773 383 4282
Usefully placed just by the railway station, popular budget option albeit rather crowded. Bicycle hire.
Guilin Bravo Hotel (££/£££)
14 Ronghu Nanlu tel: 282 3950 fax: 282 2101
Comfortable, good value hotel, but very busy during the peak months. Discounts offered during quieter periods. Outdoor swimming pool, tennis courts.
Guilin Fubo Hotel (£)
27 Binjiang Lu tel: 0773 256 9898
fax: 282 2328
Clean, well-managed three-star hotel, just by one of Guilin's famous peaks and the Li River. Experienced at dealing with foreign tourists.
Sheraton Guilin (££/£££)
15 Binjiang Nanlu tel: 282 5588
fax: 282 5598 www.sheraton.com
Superb location near the Li River and close to the city centre. Outdoor swimming pool, health club, billiard room.

Hangzhou
Huagang Hotel (£)
1 Yanggongdi tel: 0571 8799 8899
fax: 0571 8796 2481
Located in attractive surroundings on the southwest of West Lake, the hotel is well situated for visits to Huagang Park. Good value rooms.
Shangri-La Hotel Hangzhou (£££)
78 Beishan Lu tel: 87977951 fax: 87073545
Spectacularly positioned above the north shore of West Lake, set in picturesque, forested grounds, this is Hangzhou's best hotel. Indoor swimming pool, snooker/billiards hall. Bicycle hire.
Wanghu Hotel (££)
2 Huangcheng Xilu tel: 8707 1024
fax: 8707 1350 www.wangchuhotel.com
Large and affordable, with a wide range of rooms, on the northeastern shore. Bicycle hire.

Harbin
Shangri-La Hotel, Harbin (£££)
555 You Yi Lu, Dao Liqu tel: 0451 8485 8888
fax: 0451 8462 1666 www.shangri-la.com
Harbin's top hotel, on the banks of the Songhua River, gives guests a grandstand view of Sun Island and its fairytale Ice and Snow World park, especially at night. Near the city's shopping and commercial district, it has a health club, indoor pool, outdoor tennis and China's only ice restaurant in winter.

Hong Kong Island
Island Shangri-La (£££)
Pacific Place, Supreme Court Road, Central
tel: 0852 2877 3838 fax: 0852 2521 8742
www.shangri-la.com
Staying at the stylish Shangri-La, set above the fantastic shopping mall of Pacific Place, is a splendid experience. Chinese, Japanese and French restaurants. Outdoor swimming pool.
Jockey Club Mount Davis Youth Hostel (£)
Mount Davis Path tel: 2817 5715
www.yha.org.hk
Not a central location at all (Kennedy Town area), but the most popular backpacker site in Hong Kong. A midnight curfew is imposed.
Mandarin Oriental (£££)
5 Connaught Road, Central tel: 2522 0111

fax: 2810 6190 www.mandarinoriental.com
Famous hotel in the heart of Central. Great reputation, top-grade service and rooms. Undergoing a £78 billion ($140 billion) makeover.
Ritz-Carlton (£££)
3 Connaught Road, Central tel: 2877 6666
fax: 2877 6778
Hong Kong's smallest five-star establishment, but a real gem, with an attentive, personable staff; small-scale, unrushed and welcoming. Excellent spread of restaurants, including the fine Toscana (Italian).
YWCA Garden View International (££)
1 MacDonnell Road, Central tel: 2877 3737
fax: 2845 6263 www.ywca.org.hk
Good location uphill off Garden Road for the Zoological and Botanical Gardens, with Hong Kong Park farther downhill. Well placed for the Peak Tram.

Hong Kong Kowloon
Kowloon Hotel (££)
19–21 Nathan Road tel: 2929 2888
fax: 2739 9811 www.harbourplaza.com
Found on Nathan Road and owned by the Peninsula group, the Kowloon Hotel is a cheaper alternative to staying at the group's flagship hotel nearby. Modern facilities; very near Tsimshatsui underground.
The Peninsula (£££)
Salisbury Road tel: 2920 2888 fax: 2722 4170
www.peninsula.com
Splendid and remarkably styled hotel with spectacular nocturnal views over to Central. At hand among all the marble are some of Hong Kong's finest restaurants. Indoor pool. Excellent shopping arcade.
Sheraton Hong Kong Hotel + Tower (£££)
20 Nathan Road tel: 2369 1111
fax: 2739 8707 www.sheraton.com
Renovated and impressive luxury hotel at the foot of Nathan Road and a stone's throw from the Star Ferry. Near Tsimshatsui underground.
YMCA of Hong Kong (££)
41 Salisbury Road tel: 2268 7000
fax: 2739 9315 www.ymcahk.org.hk
Again, excellently located in Tsimshatsui. Inexpensive rooms and certainly one of the most appealing mid-range hotels in Hong Kong. Indoor pool.

Jinghong
Tai Garden Hotel (££)
6 Minghanglu tel: 0691 212 3888
fax: 212 6060 www.xsbn-taigardenhotel.com
Smart hotel set in peaceful surrounds in the south of town that tries hard to be a cut above the rest.

Jiuzhaigou
Sheraton Jiuzhaigou Resort (£££)
Jiuzhaigou Scenic Spot tel: 0837 773 9988
fax: 0837 773 9666 www.sheraton.com
Five-star resort hotel next to the entrance of Sichuan's mountainous Jiuzhaigou National Park, a UNESCO World Heritage Site. Its decor echoes strong Tibetan themes and its theatre stages an excellent Tibetan cultural show.

Kunming
Camellia Hotel (£)
96 Dongfeng Donglu tel: 0871 316 3000
fax: 314 7033
This is a reliable budget option. Very good value, with nicer upgraded rooms in the old block. Bicycle

hire, laundry service, ticketing service, garden.

Kunming Hotel (££/£££)
52 Dongfeng Donglu tel: 316 2063/316 2172
fax: 316 3784/313 8220
www.harbour-plaza.com
Clean and smart four-star hotel; well-designed exterior, sparkling interior. Well-located and with good spread of amenities; excellent executive floors. Tennis courts, indoor pool, bicycle hire.

Lanzhou
Lanzhou Hotel (£)
486 Donggang Xilu tel: 0931 841 6321
fax: 841 8608
Large, old but renovated hotel with clean rooms. Good range of prices. Travel service.

Lanzhou Legend Hotel (££)
529 Tianshui Nan Lu tel: 0931 853 2888
fax: 0931 853 2333
Lanzhou's most luxurious hotel. Four stars, good location and facilities. Breakfast included.

Lhasa
Lhasa Hotel (££)
1 Minzu Lu tel: 0891 683 2221 fax: 683 5796
Four-star former Holiday Inn, resembling a prison externally. Needs improving. Five restaurants, business suite, ticketing office. Swimming pool.

Snowlands Hotel (£)
4 Zangyiyuan Lu tel: 632 3687 fax: 632 7145
This accommodating budget outfit near the Jokhang Temple has good amenities. The adjacent Snowlands Restaurant is a must.

Lijiang
Banyan Tree Lijiang (£££)
Shun He Lu, Lijiang tel: 533 1111
fax: 533 2222 www.banyantree.com
Stunning new hotel away from the hustle and bustle of Lijiang, close to She He village. Sumptuous villas all have secluded gardens, private pools and glorious views to Jade Dragon Snow Mountain.

Grand Lijiang Hotel (££)
Xinyi Jie tel: (0888) 5128888 fax: 5127878
Joint venture hotel on the edges of the Old Town, offering the best in terms of service and comfort.

Luoyang
New Friendship Hotel (£/££)
6 Xiyuan Lu tel: 0379 6468 6666
fax: 6468 6667
Tour group hotel out in the west of Luoyang. Comfortable, old-fashioned, with swimming pool.

Peony Hotel (££)
15 Zhongzhou Xilu tel: (0379) 401 3699
fax: 401 3668
Preferred by tour groups, the Peony is a centrally located and inexpensive joint venture hotel.

Macau
East Asia Hotel (£)
1A Rua da Madeira tel: 922433 fax: 922431
www.yp.com.mo
Despite being at the heart of Macau's prostitute industry, this hotel has its colonial charms in the crumbling western district, and is inexpensive.

Holiday Inn (££)
82–86 Rua de Pequim tel: 783333
fax: 782321 www.macau.holiday-inn.com

Good standards as you would expect from a Holiday Inn hotel; indoor pool. Prices are far more reasonable if you book through a Hong Kong travel agent or at the Jetfoil Pier. Shuttle bus from Jetfoil Pier.

Pousada de Sao Tiago (£££)
Avenida de Republica, Fortaleza de Sao Tiago da Barra, tel: 0853 378 111 fax: 552 170
Beautifully located at the tip of the Macau Peninsula with a superb view over the Pearl River Delta. With 23 rooms, the hotel is built into the site of a 17th-century Portuguese fort.

Nanjing
Jinling Hotel (£££)
2 Hanzhong Lu, Xinjiekou tel: 025 8471 1999
fax: 025 471 1666
Well-situated, top-end hotel in the heart of the city; pool, shopping arcade and range of restaurants.

Qingdao
Shangri-La Hotel Qingdao (£££)
9 Xianggang Zhonglu tel: 0532 8388 3838
fax: 8388 6868 www.shangri-la.com
Plush hotel in the east of Qingdao, with superb facilities and restaurants. Indoor pool, tennis court.

Qufu
Queli Hotel (£)
1 Queli Jie tel: 0537 486 6818 fax: 441 2022
Traditional Chinese-style hotel in a good spot near the Confucius Temple and Confucius Mansions.

Shanghai
Garden Hotel (£££)
58 Maoming Nan Lu tel: 021 6415 1111
fax: 6415 8866
Elegant hotel in the old French Concession on the site of the former 'Cercle Sportif Francais'.

Grand Hyatt Hotel (£££)
88 Century Boulevard, Pudong tel: 5049 1234
fax: 5049 1111
www.shanghai.grand.hyatt.com
A hotel in the clouds—the highest in the world, beginning on the 54th floor of the Jinmao Building in Pudong, one of Shanghai's most famous recent constructions. Magnificent views.

Park Hotel (££)
170 Nanjing Xilu tel: 6327 5225
fax: 6327 6958 www.parkhotel.com
Historic hotel excellently located north of People's Square; dating from 1934, the Park has a stunning art-deco interior. Not the most up to date of hotels, but reeking of nostalgia.

Peace Hotel (££)
20 Nanjing Donglu tel: 6321 6888
fax: 6329 0300 www.shanghaipeacehotel.com
Perhaps Shanghai's most famous landmark, the Peace is rather frayed and sitting on its laurels. But the sense of history remains and the Bund is on your doorstep.

Pudong Shangri-La (£££)
Pudong Shangri-La Shanghai, 33 Fucheng Lu, Lujiazui tel: 6882 6888 fax: 6882 0160
www.shangri-la.com
From its waterfront perch in Pudong, you get magnificent views across the Huangpu River to the Bund. Excellent hotel with a large new extension.

Pujiang Hotel (£)
15 Huangpu Lu tel: 6324 6388

Hotels and Restaurants

fax: 6324 3179 www.pujianghotel.com
Excellent value and superbly located 19th-century hotel with a great sense of ages past. Period photos line the walls. Superb wooden floorboards and huge rooms, with the Bund just down the road.

Ruijin Guesthouse (£/££)
118 Ruijin Erlu tel: 6472 5222 fax: 6473 2277
Splendid rooms in an historic building in the old French Concession; variety of room prices to suit your budget. Attractive gardens.

Sofitel Hyland Hotel (£££)
505 Nanjing Donglu tel: 6351 5888
fax: 6351 4088 www.accorhotels-asia.com
Excellent position on Nanjing Donglu, and very near the Bund. One of Shanghai's best hotels.

The Portman Ritz-Carlton (£££)
Shanghai Centre, 1376 Nanjing Xilu
tel: 6279 8888 fax: 6279 8800
www.ritzcarlton.com
One of Shanghai's finest hotels, the Portman is set in the prestigious Shanghai Centre. Impressive range of Oriental and Western restaurants. Pool, tennis courts.

Shenyang

Liaoning Hotel (£)
97 Zhongshan Lu tel: 024 2383 9166
fax: 2383 9103
Looking out over the square with its bizarre Mao statue, the Liaoning is a historic and atmospheric hotel built in the early 20th century.

Traders Hotel (£££)
68 Zhonghua Lu tel: 2341 2288
fax: 2341 1988 www.shangri-la.com
Shenyang's best hotel, full of amenities and next to the excellent Traders Shopping Centre.

Suzhou

Bamboo Grove Hotel (££)
168 Zhuhui Lu tel: 0512 6520 5601
fax: 6520 8778 www.bghotel.com
Well located in the south of town, the Bamboo Grove is attractively set with a central rock pool. A bit frayed, but not overly expensive either.

Suzhou Hotel (£)
345 Shiquan Jie tel: 6520 4646 fax: 6520 4015 www.suzhou-hotel.com
This hotel has good amenities and caters mainly to tour groups. Well located, comfortable and with a branch of CITS next door.

Tianjin

Astor Hotel (££)
33 Taierzhuang Lu tel: 022 2331 1688
fax: 2331 6282 www.astorhotel.com
Famous and grand hotel built in the mid-19th century, still oozing history via period pieces. The Last Emperor stayed here.

Hyatt Regency Hotel Tianjin (££/£££)
219 Jiefang Beilu tel: 2330 1234
fax: 2331 1234 www.tianjin.regencyhyatt.com
Fabulous, grand four-star hotel, ideally located and boasting some first-rate restaurants. Top-notch service. Much recommended.

Ürümqi

Xijian Grand Hotel (££/£££)
168 Xinhua Beilu tel: 0991 281 8788
fax: 281 7422

Ürümqi's best hotel (but there's not much competition). Decent western and Uyghur restaurants and delicatessen. Limousine hire.

Wuhan

Jianghan Hotel (££)
245 Shengli Jie tel: 027 6882 5888 fax: 027 8281 4342
Smart, early 19th-century French hotel with an impressive colonial feel in old concession quarter of Hankou. Post office, fine Chinese restaurant.

Shangri-La Hotel Wuhan (££/£££)
700 Jianshe Dadao tel: 027 8580 6868
fax: 8577 6868 www.shangri-la.com
Expect the usual high standards of Shangri-La attentiveness and excellence. Entertaining sports bar (BATS) and decent restaurants.

Wuxi

Sheraton Hotel (££)
403 Zhongshan Lu tel: 272 1888
fax: 275 2781 www.sheraton.com
Welcome addition to the Wuxi hotel scene, offering high standards of service and facilities. Complimentary breakfast.

Xiamen

Crowne Plaza Harbour View (£££)
12-8 Zhenhai Lu tel: 202 3333 fax: 203 6666
www.hi592.com
First rate hotel with great range of facilities and some excellent restaurants. Views over to Gulangyu Island. Outdoor swimming pool.

Xi'an

Bell Tower Hotel (££)
Southwest corner of Bell Tower tel: 029 8760 0000 fax: 8721 8767 www.belltowerhtl.com
Finest location of any hotel in Xi'an and very good value rooms; one of Xi'an's first hotels to be built since the explosion in tourism.

City Hotel (£)
70 Nan Dajie tel: 8721 9988
fax: 8721 6688 www.cityhotel.xian.com
Comfortable hotel south of the Bell Tower in Central Xi'an. Clean rooms and efficient service.

Hyatt Regency Xi'an (£££)
158 Dong Dajie tel: 8769 1234
fax: 8769 6799 www.xian.regency.hyatt.com
Five-star hotel with fabulous location within Xi'an's city walls. The hotel has a stunning interior, high standards of service and excellent facilities. Indoor pool, tennis court.

Shangri-La Golden Flower Xi'an (£££)
8 Changle Xilu tel: 8323 2981
fax: 8323 5477 www.shangri-la.com
Not an ideal location outside the city walls, but the Shangri-La is still a magnificent hotel, with some fine dining options. Indoor pool, shopping arcade.

Yangshuo

Yangshuo Resort Hotel (££)
116 Xi Jie tel: 0773 882 2109 fax: 882 2106
Most hotels in Yangshuo are the abundant budget choices; this hotel has a relaxed atmosphere in an attractive landscaped setting and offers a certain degree of luxury.

Zhongdian

Banyan Tree Ringha (£££)

Hong Po Village, Jiang Tang Town tel: 828 8822 fax: 828 8911 www.banyantree.com
The tortuous journey on unmade roads is soon forgotten as you arrive at this luxurious new hideaway eco-resort, adjoining a Tibetan village and using traditional local houses reconstructed on site for the accommodation.

Gyalthang Dzong Hotel (££)

Zhongdian tel: 0887 822 3646 fax: 0887 822 3620 www.coloursofangsana.com/gyalthang
Beautifully appointed boutique hotel on the outskirts of old Zhongdian. Built in the style of a Tibetan lamasery, it has 45 Tibetan-style rooms, a central courtyard and an intimate spa.

RESTAURANTS

It is invidious to give a list of recommended restaurants in China when the country is still in a state of flux—eateries come and go like the seasons—and little that is new seems to have much sense of permanence. As prices are very often governed more by what you eat than by the standard of the restaurants, no price grading for restaurants is given.

However, it is possible to make some generalizations about eating in China. Firstly, you can be reasonably sure of eating well in the restaurants of major hotels, but you will pay a premium for the privilege. Secondly, there are certain restaurants that are used by CITS for tourist groups, and in the smaller, poorer cities, where there appears to be less choice, this can be quite reassuring. Thirdly, it is fair to say that you run little risk of eating really badly in a country where good food is so highly appreciated. Fourthly, aside from the CITS-recommended establishments, there is no way of knowing what is exceptionally good and what is not. Sticking to expensive hotels and CITS-approved restaurants will ensure quality at a price. Otherwise, you must trust your instincts.

Price and hygiene are the two things you must scrutinize. Foreigners are sometimes seen as fair game for higher prices and, in the simpler restaurants, you may need to judge the cleanliness. The Chinese themselves will often check chopsticks and bowls, often rinsing them in tea.

It is easy to eat cheaply in China. Most streets have kiosks selling plates of noodles or bowls of dumplings for next to nothing, where the quality is often high and the food is generally safe to eat. Small restaurants, selling beer and soft drinks, have more variety and are a little more expensive. They often have another, costlier section offering more sophisticated food and surroundings.

How to order Eating in China is a group activity. In most of the restaurants listed below, tables can be booked in advance.

A Chinese meal is normally served in sequence according to local delicacies. Different dishes are placed in the middle of the table, and diners are expected to serve themselves (except at banquets and in Cantonese restaurants, where it is customary to be served) either with chopsticks or with serving spoons if provided. Cold dishes are served first, then hot dishes, which will arrive singly or in clusters. Rice usually arrives late in the meal, and soup usually appears at the end.

Chopsticks Chopsticks (*kuaizi*) are provided as a matter of course, but forks (*chazi*) are usually available or can be requested.

Beijing

Donglaishun

44 Dongjiaomin Lane tel: 6524 1042 or 198 Wangfujing Dajie tel: 6513 9661 www.donglaishun.com
Well-known restaurant serving up hotpot (*huoguo*)—a very fun and sociable way to eat. Slide the lamb sliver, vegetables and *doufu* into the boiling soup, and try the local beer.

Fangshan

1 Wenjin Jie, Beihai Park tel: 6401 1879/ 6401 1889 www.fangshan.com
Imperial-style recipes from the regal kitchens of the Forbidden City, Perhaps rather over priced, but a chance to sample good quality cooking in an unusual atmosphere. Situated in Beihai Park.

Gongdelin Vegetarian Restaurant

158 Qianmen Nandajie tel: 6702 0867/6511 2542
Very inexpensive and wholesome Buddhist vegetarian delights at this very famous eatery south of Qianmen. Magnificent food arranged artfully to resemble meat—sometimes tasting more like meat than the real thing. Highly recommended. English menu at hand.

Nengrenju

49 Xinei Dajie, Nancaochang tel: 6656 1268
Near the White Pagoda Temple, this is Beijing's most popular hot spot for Mongolian hot pot. Best eaten during winter.

Qianmen Quanjude Roast Duck Restaurant

32 Qianmen Dajie tel: 6511 2418
The best roast duck on the planet, at a highly affordable price and a very convenient location. Choose from the different sections according to your budget and then walk off your meal at adjacent Tiananmen Square or the Forbidden City.

The Sichuan

14 Liuyin Jie tel: 6615 6924/6615 6925
Ensconced in the historic residence of Prince Gong, this well-known hotel is famous for spicy Sichuan cooking. The restaurant is attractively located in one of the few older sections of the city.

TGI Friday's

1 Nan Dajie, Zhonggwancun tel: 6849 8738 19 Jianguomenwai Dajie tel: 8526 3388 www.fridays.com
A shameless slice of home cooking peeking out amid the mounds of rice and noodles. Very American and with that rarity in China—a no-smoking section.

Canton: see Guangzhou

Chengdu

Baguobuyi

20 Renmin Nanlu Siduan tel: 028 8557 3839/8553 1688 www.baguobuyi.com

281

Hotels and Restaurants

Chengdu is the heartland of fiery Sichuan food, and this respectable restaurant serves this up in spades. Sichuan food in the rest of China is a pale imitation of what is served here. This is not a tourist restaurant, so there's no English menu.

Qin Shan Zhai Restaurant
247 Wuhouchi Dajie tel: 8505 3333
Popular Sichuan cuisine restaurant which uses many different herbs in its dishes not only to spice up the food, but also as a tonic to build up strength. Dishes include hotpot flavoured with more than 10 different herbs.

Fuzhou
Shanghai Restaurant
155 Bayiqi Lu tel: 0591 755 3620
This highly popular chain serves great *dim sum* and *xiaolongbao*—Shanghai pastry dumplings stuffed with pork. Bakery on premises.

Guangzhou (Canton)
Light sauces and the freshest ingredients are the main characteristics. *Dim sum* are the snacks sold at the tables from trays.
Foyouyuan Vegetarian Restaurant
1 Fuer Lu, Xingfuxincun tel: 8125 0428

As the saying goes, the Cantonese will eat anything on four legs unless it's a table. If you don't want to join them, come to this Buddhist vegetarian option.
Dongbeiren
2nd floor, 1 Taojin Beilu tel: 8357 6277
Excellent chain of restaurants serving up a huge and tasty range of dumplings (*jiaozi*)—very popular and fun. Come here to snack or for a fully fledged meal. English menu. Also at 36 Garden Building, Tianhe Nanerlu, tel: 87501711.
Guangzhou
2 Wenchang Nan Lu tel: 8138 9840
Famous Cantonese restaurant, built around a central garden courtyard. Quite expensive.
Panxi
151 Longjin Xilu tel: 020 8181 5955
Very famous restaurant noted for its Cantonese *dim sum* (including shark's fin dumplings and monkey brains) and other regional dishes.
Taotaoju
20 Dishipu Lu tel: 8139 6111
Very popular central restaurant with a long history, noted for its *dim sum*.

Guilin
Ju Fu Lin
10 Zhengyang Lu tel: 0773 282 9542
Basic but good-value restaurant on Guilin's main pedestrian street, with outdoor seating for people-watching as you tuck into local dishes.

Hangzhou
Louwailou
30 Gushan Lu tel: 0571 8796 9023
Hanghzou's most famous restaurants serving up local delicacies alongside sweeping views over West Lake.
Tianwaitian Restaurant
2 Tianzhu Lu tel: 87965450
Situated by the Lingyin Temple, this is the place for excellent seafood dishes.

Hong Kong
Felix
The Peninsula, Tsimshatsui
tel: 0852 2315 3188
Imaginatively designed restaurant in an unbeatable location on the 28th floor of the Peninsula. International/Pan-Asian cuisine. Pricey, but impressive, and there are some splendid views.
Hunan Garden
3rd Floor, The Forum, Exchange Square, Central
tel: 2868 2880
If you want dishes with more bite than Cantonese cuisine, come here for spicy, hot Hunan food. Fine menu, elegant environment and excellent wine list.
Jimmy's Kitchen
South China Building, 1 Wyndham Street, Central tel: 2526 5293
and 1st floor, Kowloon Centre, 29 Ashley Road, Kowloon tel: 2376 0327
Long-standing European restaurant that constantly garners enthusiastic reviews. Reasonably priced food in a relaxing environment.
Luk Yu Teahouse & Restaurant
24-26 Stanley Street tel: 25235464
Famous central old Hong Kong tea-house, serving up decent *dim sum* daily from 7am to 6pm.

Sai Kung Town
Sampan Seafood Restaurant
16 Main Street, Yung Shue Wan, Lamma Island
tel: 29822388
Cantonese seafood-specializing restaurant with a fine view out to sea from Lamma Island's main community; not far from the ferry pier. Satisfyingly rounds off a trip to the island.
Toscana
Ritz-Carlton Hotel, 3 Connaught Rd, Central
tel: 25322062
Excellent, very civilized Italian restaurant in the fine Ritz-Carlton Hotel. Closed on Sundays.

Kunming
Wei's Pizzeria
78 Tuodong Lu tel: 0871 316 6189
For southwest China, these pizzas are excellent and a welcome diversion. No credit cards.

Lhasa
Dunya Restaurant & Bar
100 Beijing Dong Lu tel: 0891 633 0482
www.dunyarestaurant.com
Very popular Dutch-run watering hole and restaurant near the centre of old Lhasa with excellent Asian fusion food and great yak burgers—and they can arrange travel in Tibet.
Snowlands Restaurant
4 Zangyiyuan Lu tel (0891) 6337323
Very popular restaurant offering a range of dishes including Tibetan, Nepalese and Indian. Near the Jokhang Temple.

Lijiang
Sakura Café
123 Cuiwen Lane, Xinhua Street tel: 0888 518 7619 www.sakura.yn.cn
Lively restaurant on Lijiang's famous bar street, lining one of its canals. The Western food is superb and good value, and there is also a choice of Korean, Japanese and local cuisine.

Macau
A Lorcha
289 Rua do Almirante Sergio
tel: 0853 313 193
Famous Portuguese restaurant near the southern tip of the Macau Peninsula. Try the African chicken, pork knuckles or the raw codfish. Closed Tue.
Fernando's
9 Hac Sa Beach, Coloane Island tel: 882 531
Probably Macau's most celebrated restaurant, tucked away on Hac Sa Beach on Coloane Island. It's well worth the small adventure coming out here, for the Portuguese dishes are divine. Fine wine list; weekend reservations necessary.
Mezzaluna
Mandarin Oriental Hotel, 956 Avenida da Amizade tel: 567 888
Refined Italian restaurant noted for its excellent pasta dishes and some fantastic pizza. Not cheap, but stylish.

Nanjing
Wuzhou Treehouse Restaurant
22 Xiaofenqiao tel: 025 906 6066
Good value, central Chinese eatery used to dealing with foreigners.

Shanghai
Gongdelin Vegetarian Restaurant
445 Nanjing Xilu tel: 6327 0218
Like its Beijing counterpart, the Buddhist Gongdelin excels at preparing vegetable food to look and taste like meat.
Huxinting Teahouse
257 Yuyuan Lu tel: 6373 6950
In the middle of the pond in the Old Chinese City, the Huxinting (lake heart pavilion) is a traditional Chinese tea-house.
Jade on 36
Pudong Shangri-La, 33 Fucheng Lu
tel: 021 6882 3636 www.shangri-la.com
Rooftop restaurant of the new tower at one of Shanghai's top hotels, and already an icon. Bold architecture features a striking entrance through a giant deconstructed rice bowl, while the avant-garde cuisine is a voyage of surprises.
M on the Bund
20 Guangdong Lu tel: 6350 9988
A relative of a famous Hong Kong restaurant, serving up fantastic international dishes by the historic Bund. Welcome symptom of a new international presence in Shanghai.
Nanxiang Steamed Bread Shop
85 Yuyuan Lu tel: 6355 4206
Excellent restaurant for sampling Shanghai's most famous snack—*xiaolongbao*—little steamed scalding dumplings of meat. Takeaway also available.
Quanjude
786 Huaihai Zhonglu tel: 5404 5799
Heaving at the weekends, this Shanghai sibling of the famous Beijing restaurant is the place for *kaoya* (Peking duck). On one of Shanghai's premier shopping streets.

Suzhou
Authentic Chinese Dumpling House
420 Shiquan Jie tel: 0512 6519 2728
The place to come for delicious and inexpensive dumplings (*jiaozi*)—simple, but filling food.

Songhelou
18 Taijian Nong, 141 Guanqian Jie
tel: 6770 0688
Restaurant with a long history and Imperial connections (Emperor Qianlong apparently feasted here). Near the Xuanmiao Taoist Temple.

Tianjin
Xiang Wei Zhai
Hyatt Hotel Tianjin, 219 Jiefang Beilu
tel: 022 2331 8888
Traditionally designed dumpling restaurant in this fabulous hotel. The emphasis is on pastoral tastes and the dumplings (*jiaozi*) are superb.

Ürümqi
Kashgari's
Xinjiang Hotel, 168 Xinhua Beilu
tel: 0991 281 8788
Uighur cuisine in a comfortable setting. Emphasis on heavily seasoned lamb dishes set to occasional Uighur entertainment nights.

Xiamen
A Feng Seafood Restaurant
Haishan Bldg, 1 Jiayuanli, Jiahe Lu
tel: 0592 559 6959
This Siming District seafood restaurant has lobster, crab, grouper and scallops among its dishes, diners picking their meal straight from the tanks.
Shuyou (Binbei) Seafood Restaurant
Zhonghang Bldg, Hubin Beilu
tel: 0592 509 8888 www.shuyou.com
This large, upmarket restaurant in Xiamen's financial district is part of a chain. Specials include Fujian dish *fotiaoqiang*, or 'Buddha jumps over the wall', which uses a mix of ingredients including sea cucumber, abalone and shark's fin.

283

Xi'an
Shang Palace Shangri-La Golden Flower
8 Changle Xilu tel: 8323 2981
This civilized restaurant known for its Cantonese dishes can be found in one of the best hotels in town.
Xi'an Restaurant
298 Dong Dajie tel: 029 8768 0618
Simple but decent dishes in this popular restaurant that goes to town on dumplings, noodles and other filling recipes.

Wuhan
Laotongcheng
1 Dazhi Lu, Hankou tel: 8281 0616
Busy Chinese restaurant famous for its dumplings and word has it a haunt of Mao Zedong during his sojourns in Wuhan.

Wuxi
Wuxi specializes in Wuxi spare ribs and whitebait from Lake Tai.
Jinxi Revolving Restaurant
218 Zhongshan Lu tel: 0510 275 1688
Chinese and Western food set to a revolving panorama. Good value and quality.
Zhongguo Hotel
90 Hanchang Lu tel: 0510 272 0041
Near the railway station, the hotel has a popular restaurant serving up dumplings (*jiaozi*).

Index

Index

Index/Acknowledgements/Contributors

Publisher's Acknowledgements

The Automobile Association wishes to thank the following photographers and libraries for their assistance in the preparation of this book.

INGRID MOREJOHN/BILDBRUKET PICTURE WORKS was commissioned to take all the pictures in this book with the exception of:
ALAMY 105 (© Dennis Cox); AA WORLD TRAVEL LIBRARY 3 (A. Kouprianoff), 8 (A. Kouprianoff), 42/43 (G. Clements), 50 (A Mockford & N Bonetti), 77b (G. Clements), 79 (A Mockford & N Bonetti), 222a (M. Trelawny), 222b (R. Holmes), 223a (R. Victor), 256a (A Mockford & N Bonetti), 256b (A Mockford & N Bonetti), 262 (A Mockford & N Bonetti), 263 (A Mockford & N Bonetti), 270 (A Mockford & N Bonetti); AXIOM PHOTOGRAPHIC LIBRARY 14b; BRIDGEMAN ART LIBRARY 249a *Willows and Distant Mountains* by Ma Yuan (*fl.*1190–1225) Song Dynasty (ink and colours on silk) Zhang Shui Cheng/Bridgeman Art Library, London; MARY EVANS PIC-TURE LIBRARY 42b Sun Yatsen, 43b Shanghai, The Club 1926; FEI CHONG XIAN 118b Shanghai Peace Hotel; RONALD GRANT ARCHIVES 78a *Raise the Red Lantern*, 118/119 *The Last Emperor*; HULTON DEUTSCH COLLECTION LTD 119b Pu yi Henry; MAGNUM PHOTOS 44a Chiang Kaishek, Madam Chiang & General Stilwell, 46/47 People's Army arriving at Yan'an (Rene Burri); NATURE PHOTOGRAPHERS LTD 158a Père David's deer (E.A. Janes), 158b Giant Panda (R. Tidman), 159 Tiger (B. Burbridge); THE MANSELL COLLECTION 42/3 Port of Shanghai; PUDONG SHANGRI-LA HOTEL, SHANGHAI 16c Rolls Royce Phantom; SPECTRUM COLOUR LIBRARY 116/117 Dalian Harbour; WORLD PICTURES 11 Beijing skyline.

Contributors

Original copy editor: Susan Whimster
Revision verifier: Peter Ellegard **Revision editor:** Stephanie Smith